McDougal Littell Science

The Changing Earth

LAVA

hot spot

geosphere

EARTH SCIENCE

A ▶ Earth's Surface
B ▶ The Changing Earth
C ▶ Earth's Waters
D ▶ Earth's Atmosphere
E ▶ Space Science

PHYSICAL SCIENCE

A ▶ Matter and Energy
B ▶ Chemical Interactions
C ▶ Motion and Forces
D ▶ Waves, Sound, and Light
E ▶ Electricity and Magnetism

LIFE SCIENCE

A ▶ Cells and Heredity
B ▶ Life Over Time
C ▶ Diversity of Living Things
D ▶ Ecology
E ▶ Human Biology

Acknowledgments: Excerpts and adaptations from *National Science Education Standards* by the National Academy of Sciences. Copyright © 1996 by the National Academy of Sciences. Reprinted with permission from the National Academies Press, Washington, D.C.

Excerpts and adaptations from *Benchmarks for Science Literacy: Project 2061*. Copyright © 1993 by the American Association for the Advancement of Science. Reprinted with permission.

ISBN: 0-618-33424-6   5 6 7 8 VJM 08 07 06 05

Internet Web Site: http://www.mcdougallittell.com

Science Consultants

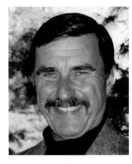

Chief Science Consultant

James Trefil, Ph.D. is the Clarence J. Robinson Professor of Physics at George Mason University. He is the author or co-author of more than 25 books, including *Science Matters* and *The Nature of Science.* Dr. Trefil is a member of the American Association for the Advancement of Science's Committee on the Public Understanding of Science and Technology. He is also a fellow of the World Economic Forum and a frequent contributor to *Smithsonian* magazine.

Rita Ann Calvo, Ph.D. is Senior Lecturer in Molecular Biology and Genetics at Cornell University, where for 12 years she also directed the Cornell Institute for Biology Teachers. Dr. Calvo is the 1999 recipient of the College and University Teaching Award from the National Association of Biology Teachers.

Kenneth Cutler, M.S. is the Education Coordinator for the Julius L. Chambers Biomedical Biotechnology Research Institute at North Carolina Central University. A former middle school and high school science teacher, he received a 1999 Presidential Award for Excellence in Science Teaching.

Instructional Design Consultants

Douglas Carnine, Ph.D. is Professor of Education and Director of the National Center for Improving the Tools of Educators at the University of Oregon. He is the author of seven books and over 100 other scholarly publications, primarily in the areas of instructional design and effective instructional strategies and tools for diverse learners. Dr. Carnine also serves as a member of the National Institute for Literacy Advisory Board.

Linda Carnine, Ph.D. consults with school districts on curriculum development and effective instruction for students struggling academically. A former teacher and school administrator, Dr. Carnine also co-authored a popular remedial reading program.

Donald Steely, Ph.D. serves as principal investigator at the Oregon Center for Applied Science (ORCAS) on federal grants for science and language arts programs. His background also includes teaching and authoring of print and multimedia programs in science, mathematics, history, and spelling.

Sam Miller, Ph.D. is a middle school science teacher and the Teacher Development Liaison for the Eugene, Oregon, Public Schools. He is the author of curricula for teaching science, mathematics, computer skills, and language arts.

Vicky Vachon, Ph.D. consults with school districts throughout the United States and Canada on improving overall academic achievement with a focus on literacy. She is also co-author of a widely used program for remedial readers.

Content Reviewers

John Beaver, Ph.D.
Ecology
Professor, Director of Science Education Center
College of Education and Human Services
Western Illinois University
Macomb, IL

Donald J. DeCoste, Ph.D.
Matter and Energy, Chemical Interactions
Chemistry Instructor
University of Illinois
Urbana-Champaign, IL

Dorothy Ann Fallows, Ph.D., MSc
Diversity of Living Things, Microbiology
Partners in Health
Boston, MA

Michael Foote, Ph.D.
The Changing Earth, Life Over Time
Associate Professor
Department of the Geophysical Sciences
The University of Chicago
Chicago, IL

Lucy Fortson, Ph.D.
Space Science
Director of Astronomy
Adler Planetarium and Astronomy Museum
Chicago, IL

Elizabeth Godrick, Ph.D.
Human Biology
Professor, CAS Biology
Boston University
Boston, MA

Isabelle Sacramento Grilo, M.S.
The Changing Earth
Lecturer, Department of the Geological Sciences
San Diego State University
San Diego, CA

David Harbster, MSc
Diversity of Living Things
Professor of Biology
Paradise Valley Community College
Phoenix, AZ

Richard D. Norris, Ph.D.
Earth's Waters
Professor of Paleobiology
Scripps Institution of Oceanography
University of California, San Diego
La Jolla, CA

Donald B. Peck, M.S.
*Motion and Forces; Waves, Sound, and Light;
  Electricity and Magnetism*
Director of the Center for Science Education (retired)
Fairleigh Dickinson University
Madison, NJ

Javier Penalosa, Ph.D.
Diversity of Living Things, Plants
Associate Professor, Biology Department
Buffalo State College
Buffalo, NY

Raymond T. Pierrehumbert, Ph.D.
Earth's Atmosphere
Professor in Geophysical Sciences (Atmospheric Science)
The University of Chicago
Chicago, IL

Brian J. Skinner, Ph.D.
Earth's Surface
Eugene Higgins Professor of Geology and Geophysics
Yale University
New Haven, CT

Nancy E. Spaulding, M.S.
Earth's Surface, The Changing Earth, Earth's Waters
Earth Science Teacher (retired)
Elmira Free Academy
Elmira, NY

Steven S. Zumdahl, Ph.D.
Matter and Energy, Chemical Interactions
Professor Emeritus of Chemistry
University of Illinois
Urbana-Champaign, IL

Susan L. Zumdahl, M.S.
Matter and Energy, Chemical Interactions
Chemistry Education Specialist
University of Illinois
Urbana-Champaign, IL

Safety Consultant

Juliana Texley, Ph.D.
Former K–12 Science Teacher and School Superintendent
Boca Raton, FL

English Language Advisor

Judy Lewis, M.A.
Director, State and Federal Programs for reading proficiency
and high risk populations
Rancho Cordova, CA

Teacher Panel Members

Carol Arbour
Tallmadge Middle School,
Tallmadge, OH

Patty Belcher
Goodrich Middle School,
Akron, OH

Gwen Broestl
Luis Munoz Marin Middle School,
Cleveland, OH

Al Brofman
Tehipite Middle School,
Fresno, CA

John Cockrell
Clinton Middle School,
Columbus, OH

Jenifer Cox
Sylvan Middle School,
Citrus Heights, CA

Linda Culpepper
Martin Middle School,
Charlotte, NC

Kathleen Ann DeMatteo
Margate Middle School,
Margate, FL

Melvin Figueroa
New River Middle School,
Ft. Lauderdale, FL

Doretha Grier
Kannapolis Middle School,
Kannapolis, NC

Robert Hood
Alexander Hamilton Middle School,
Cleveland, OH

Scott Hudson
Covedale Elementary School,
Cincinnati, OH

Loretta Langdon
Princeton Middle School,
Princeton, NC

Carlyn Little
Glades Middle School,
Miami, FL

Ann Marie Lynn
Amelia Earhart Middle School,
Riverside, CA

James Minogue
Lowe's Grove Middle School,
Durham, NC

Joann Myers
Buchanan Middle School,
Tampa, FL

Barbara Newell
Charles Evans Hughes Middle School,
Long Beach, CA

Anita Parker
Kannapolis Middle School,
Kannapolis, NC

Greg Pirolo
Golden Valley Middle School,
San Bernardino, CA

Laura Pottmyer
Apex Middle School,
Apex, NC

Lynn Prichard
Booker T. Washington Middle Magnet
School, Tampa, FL

Jacque Quick
Walter Williams High School,
Burlington, NC

Robert Glenn Reynolds
Hillman Middle School,
Youngstown, OH

Stacy Rinehart
Lufkin Road Middle School,
Apex, NC

Theresa Short
Abbott Middle School,
Fayetteville, NC

Rita Slivka
Alexander Hamilton Middle School,
Cleveland, OH

Marie Sofsak
B F Stanton Middle School,
Alliance, OH

Nancy Stubbs
Sweetwater Union Unified School District,
Chula Vista, CA

Sharon Stull
Quail Hollow Middle School,
Charlotte, NC

Donna Taylor
Okeeheelee Middle School,
West Palm Beach, FL

Sandi Thompson
Harding Middle School,
Lakewood, OH

Lori Walker
Audubon Middle School & Magnet Center,
Los Angeles, CA

Teacher Lab Evaluators

Andrew Boy
W.E.B. DuBois Academy,
Cincinnati, OH

Jill Brimm-Byrne
Albany Park Academy,
Chicago, IL

Gwen Broestl
Luis Munoz Marin Middle School,
Cleveland, OH

Al Brofman
Tehipite Middle School,
Fresno, CA

Michael A. Burstein
The Rashi School,
Newton, MA

Trudi Coutts
Madison Middle School,
Naperville, IL

Jenifer Cox
Sylvan Middle School,
Citrus Heights, CA

Larry Cwik
Madison Middle School,
Naperville, IL

Jennifer Donatelli
Kennedy Junior High School,
Lisle, IL

Melissa Dupree
Lakeside Middle School,
Evans, GA

Carl Fechko
Luis Munoz Marin Middle School,
Cleveland, OH

Paige Fullhart
Highland Middle School,
Libertyville, IL

Sue Hood
Glen Crest Middle School,
Glen Ellyn, IL

William Luzader
Plymouth Community Intermediate School,
Plymouth, MA

Ann Min
Beardsley Middle School,
Crystal Lake, IL

Aileen Mueller
Kennedy Junior High School,
Lisle, IL

Nancy Nega
Churchville Middle School,
Elmhurst, IL

Oscar Newman
Sumner Math and Science Academy,
Chicago, IL

Lynn Prichard
Booker T. Washington Middle Magnet
School, Tampa, FL

Jacque Quick
Walter Williams High School,
Burlington, NC

Stacy Rinehart
Lufkin Road Middle School,
Apex, NC

Seth Robey
Gwendolyn Brooks Middle School,
Oak Park, IL

Kevin Steele
Grissom Middle School,
Tinley Park, IL

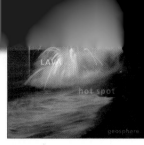

eEdition

Unit Features

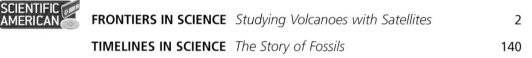

1 Plate Tectonics   6

the BIG idea

The movement of tectonic plates causes geologic changes on Earth.

2 Earthquakes   42

the BIG idea

Earthquakes release stress that has built up in rocks.

What caused these rails to bend, and how long did it take?
page 42

How does new land form from molten rock? page 74

3 Mountains and Volcanoes   74

Mountains and volcanoes form as tectonic plates move.

3.1 Movement of rock builds mountains.   77
MATH IN SCIENCE *Calculating the Mean of a Data Set*   85

3.2 Volcanoes form as molten rock erupts.   86
CHAPTER INVESTIGATION *Make Your Own Volcanoes*   94

3.3 Volcanoes affect Earth's land, air, and water.   96
SCIENCE ON THE JOB *Rangers at Yellowstone*   103

4 Views of Earth's Past   108

Rocks, fossils, and other types of natural evidence tell Earth's story.

4.1 Earth's past is revealed in rocks and fossils.   111
CONNECTING SCIENCES *Could T. Rex Win a Race?*   118

4.2 Rocks provide a timeline for Earth.   119
MATH IN SCIENCE *Interpreting Graphs*   126

4.3 The geologic time scale shows Earth's past.   127
CHAPTER INVESTIGATION *Geologic Time*   134

5 Natural Resources   144

Society depends on natural resources for energy and materials.

5.1 Natural resources support human activity.   147
CONNECTING SCIENCES *Got Oil Spills?*   155

5.2 Resources can be conserved and recycled.   156
MATH IN SCIENCE *Comparing Decimals*   160

5.3 Energy comes from other natural resources.   161
CHAPTER INVESTIGATION *Wind Power*   170

Handbooks and Resources   R1

Scientific Thinking Handbook   R2
Lab Handbook   R10
Math Handbook   R36
Note-Taking Handbook   R45

Appendix   R52
Glossary   R58
Index   R66
Acknowledgments   R75

Table of Contents **vii**

Features

Visual Highlights

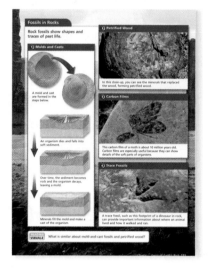

Internet Resources @ ClassZone.com

INVESTIGATIONS AND ACTIVITIES

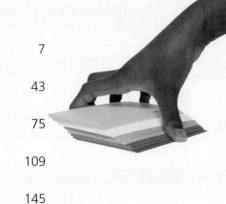

Each chapter in **The Changing Earth** covers some of the learning goals that are described in the *National Science Education Standards* (NSES) and the Project 2061 Benchmarks for Science Literacy. Selected content and skill standards are shown below in shortened form. The following National Science Education Standards are covered on pages xii-xxvii, in Frontiers in Science, and in Timelines in Science, as well as in chapter features and laboratory investigations: Understandings About Scientific Inquiry (A.9), Understandings About Science and Technology (E.6), Science and Technology in Society (F.5), Science as a Human Endeavor (G.1), Nature of Science (G.2), and History of Science (G.3).

Content Standards

1 Plate Tectonics

National Science Education Standards

D.1.a	Earth's layers include a hot, dense, metallic core; hot, convecting mantle; and a lithosphere.
D.1.b	Lithospheric plates move around Earth, carrying continents and ocean basins with them. Plate movements can build mountain ranges and often produce earthquakes and volcanoes.
D.1.c	Movements in Earth's crust help build the planet's landforms.

Project 2061 Benchmarks

4.C.1	Heat flow and material within Earth create mountains and ocean basins.
4.C.2	Some changes in Earth's surface take place gradually over very long times.

2 Earthquakes

National Science Education Standards

D.1.b	Earthquakes result from movement of lithospheric plates.
F.3.a	Internal and external processes in the Earth system cause natural hazards such as earthquakes.
F.4.a	Earthquakes present serious dangers to human and wildlife habitats.

Project 2061 Benchmarks

4.C.2	Some changes in Earth's surface, such as earthquakes, can happen suddenly.
4.F.4	Earthquake waves spread away from the source and move at different speeds through different materials.

3 Mountains and Volcanoes

National Science Education Standards

D.1.b	Tectonic plate movements can build mountain ranges.
D.1.c	Landforms can be built by volcanic eruptions.
F.3.a	Internal and external processes in the Earth system cause natural hazards such as volcanic eruptions.
F.4.a	Volcanic explosions can present serious risks to human and wildlife habitats.

Project 2061 Benchmarks

4.C.1	Gas and dust from large volcanoes can change the atmosphere.
4.C.2	Some changes in Earth's surface happen very slowly, such as the uplift and wear- ... ntains. Other changes are sudden, such as volcanic eruptions.

4 Views of Earth's Past

National Science Education Standards

D.2.a | The processes that shape Earth today, including erosion, plate movements, and climate changes, are similar to those in Earth's past. Earth's history is also influenced by sudden catastrophes, such as the impact of an asteroid.

F.3.a | The impacts of asteroids can cause great damage to Earth's surface and life forms.

Project 2061 Benchmarks

4.C.5 | Thousands of layers of sedimentary rock and their fossils confirm the long history of Earth's changing surface and life forms.

5 Natural Resources

National Science Education Standards

B.3.f | The Sun is a major source of energy that produces phenomena and changes on Earth's surface.

E.6.f | All technological solutions have benefits and consequences.

F.3.b | Human activities, such as urban growth and waste disposal, can introduce pollution and other hazards into the environment.

F.4.b | The risks of using different types of energy include air, water, and soil pollution.

Project 2061 Benchmarks

4.B.10 | Recycling and developing synthetic materials can extend natural resources but may also be costly.

4.B.11 | Earth's resources can be reduced by using them wastefully or by destroying them. Cleaning up polluted air and water, and restoring the environment can be difficult and costly.

8.C.2 | Different ways of obtaining and using energy have different consequences on the environment.

8.C.5 | Energy from the Sun, wind, and water is unlimited, but requires large collection systems to make use of it. Other types of energy are not renewable or are replaced very slowly.

Process and Skill Standards

National Science Education Standards

A.1 | Identify questions that can be answered using scientific methods.

A.2 | Design and conduct a scientific investigation.

A.3 | Use appropriate tools and techniques to gather and analyze data.

A.4 | Use evidence to describe, predict, explain, and model.

A.5 | Use critical thinking to find relationships between results and interpretations.

A.7 | Communicate procedures, results, and conclusions.

A.8 | Use mathematics in scientific investigations.

E.2 | Design a solution or product.

E.3 | Implement the proposed solution.

E.4 | Evaluate the solution or design.

Project 2061 Benchmarks

9.A.3 | Write numbers in different forms.

9.B.2 | Use mathematics to describe change.

9.B.3 | Use graphs to show relationships.

11.B.1 | Use models to think about processes.

11.C.4 | Use equations to summarize change.

11.D.2 | With complex systems, use summaries, averages, ranges, and examples.

12.B.3 | Calculate volumes of rectangular solids.

12.B.5 | Estimate distances and travel times from maps.

12.B.7 | Determine, use, and convert units.

12.C.3 | Use and read measurement instruments.

12.D.3 | Read, interpret, and describe tables and graphs.

12.D.4 | Understand graphs and charts.

12.D.5 | Use coordinates to find locations on maps.

Introducing Earth Science

Scientists are curious. Since ancient times, they have been asking and answering questions about the world around them. Scientists are also very suspicious of the answers they get. They carefully collect evidence and test their answers many times before accepting an idea as correct.

In this book you will see how scientific knowledge keeps growing and changing as scientists ask new questions and rethink what was known before. The following sections will help get you started.

What Is Earth Science?

Earth science is the study of Earth's interior, its rocks and soil, its atmosphere, its oceans, and outer space. For many years, scientists studied each of these topics separately. They learned many important things. More recently, however, scientists have looked more and more at the connections among the different parts of Earth—its oceans, atmosphere, living things, and rocks and soil. Scientists have also been learning more about other planets in our solar system, as well as stars and galaxies far away. Through these studies they have learned much about Earth and its place in the universe.

The text and pictures in this book will help you learn key concepts and important facts about earth science. A variety of activities will help you investigate these concepts. As you learn, it helps to have a big picture of earth science as a framework for this new information. The four unifying principles listed below will give you this big picture. Read the next few pages to get an overview of each of these principles and a sense of why they are so important.

- **Heat energy inside Earth and radiation from the Sun provide energy for Earth's processes.**

- **Physical forces, such as gravity, affect the movement of all matter on Earth and throughout the universe.**

- **Matter and energy move among Earth's rocks and soil, atmosphere, waters, and living things.**

- **Earth has changed over time and continues to change.**

the **BIG** idea

Each chapter begins with a big idea. Keep in mind that each big idea relates to one or more of the unifying principles.

Heat energy inside Earth and radiation from the Sun provide energy for Earth's processes.

The lava pouring out of this volcano in Hawaii is liquid rock that was melted by heat energy under Earth's surface. Another, much more powerful energy source constantly bombards Earth's surface with energy, heating the air around you, and keeping the oceans from freezing over. This energy source is the Sun. Everything that moves or changes on Earth gets its energy either from the Sun or from the inside of our planet.

What It Means

You are always surrounded by different forms of energy, such as heat energy or light. **Energy** is the ability to cause change. All of Earth's processes need energy to occur. A process is a set of changes that leads to a particular result. For example, **evaporation** is the process by which liquid changes into gas. A puddle on a sidewalk dries up through the process of evaporation. The energy needed for the puddle to dry up comes from the Sun.

Heat Energy Inside Earth

Underneath the cool surface layer of rock, Earth's interior is so hot that the solid rock there is able to flow very slowly—a few centimeters each year. In a process called **convection,** hot material rises, cools, then sinks until it is heated enough to rise again. Convection of hot rock carries heat energy up to Earth's surface, where it provides the energy to build mountains, cause earthquakes, and make volcanoes erupt.

Radiation from the Sun

Earth receives energy from the Sun as **radiation**—energy that travels across distances in the form of certain types of waves. Visible light is one type of radiation. Radiation from the Sun heats Earth's surface, making bright summer days hot. Different parts of Earth receive different amounts of radiation at different times of the year, causing seasons. Energy from the Sun also causes winds to blow, ocean currents to flow, and water to move from the ground to the atmosphere and back again.

Why It's Important

Understanding Earth's processes makes it possible to

- know what types of crops to plant and when to plant them
- know when to watch for dangerous weather, such as tornadoes and hurricanes
- predict a volcano's eruption in time for people to leave the area

Physical forces, such as gravity, affect the movement of all matter on Earth and throughout the universe.

The universe is everything that exists, and everything in the universe is governed by the same physical laws. The same laws govern the stars shown in this picture and the page on which the picture is printed.

What It Means

What do the stars in a galaxy, the planet Earth, and your body have in common? For one thing, they are all made of matter. **Matter** is anything that has mass and takes up space. Rocks are matter. You are matter. Even the air around you is matter. Matter is made of tiny particles called **atoms** that are too small to see through an ordinary microscope.

Everything in the universe is also affected by the same physical forces. A **force** is a push or a pull. Forces affect how matter moves everywhere in the universe.

- One force you experience every moment is **gravity,** which is the attraction, or pull, between two objects. Gravity is pulling you to Earth and Earth to you. Gravity is the force that causes objects to fall downward toward the center of Earth. Gravity is also the force that keeps objects in orbit around planets and stars.

- **Friction** is the force that resists motion between two surfaces that are pressed together. Friction can keep a rock on a hillside from sliding down to the bottom of the hill. If you lightly rub your finger across a smooth page in a book and then across a piece of sandpaper, you can feel how the different surfaces produce different frictional forces. Which is easier to do?

- There are many other forces at work on Earth and throughout the universe. For example, Earth has a magnetic field. A compass needle responds to the force exerted by Earth's magnetic field. Another example is the contact force between a rock and the ground beneath it. A contact force occurs when one object pushes or pulls on another object by touching it.

Why It's Important

Physical forces influence the movement of all matter, from the tiniest particle to you to the largest galaxy. Understanding forces allows people to

- predict how objects and materials move on Earth
- send spacecraft and equipment into space
- explain and predict the movements of Earth, the Moon, planets, and stars

Matter and energy move among Earth's rocks and soil, atmosphere, waters, and living things.

When a wolf eats a rabbit, matter and energy move from one living thing into another. When a wolf drinks water warmed by the Sun, matter and energy move from Earth's waters into one of its living things. These are just two examples of how energy and matter move among different parts of the Earth system.

What It Means

Think of Earth as a huge system, or an organized group of parts that work together. Within this system, matter and energy move among the different parts. The four major parts of Earth's system are the

- **atmosphere,** which includes all the air surrounding the solid planet
- **geosphere,** which includes all of Earth's rocks and minerals, as well as Earth's interior
- **hydrosphere,** which includes oceans, rivers, lakes, and every drop of water on or under Earth's surface
- **biosphere,** which includes all the living things on Earth

Matter in the Earth System

It's easy to see how matter moves within the Earth system. When water in the atmosphere falls as rain, it becomes part of the hydrosphere. When an animal drinks water from a puddle, the water becomes part of the biosphere. When rainwater soaks into the ground, it moves through the geosphere. As the puddle dries up, the water becomes part of the atmosphere again.

Energy in the Earth System

Most of the energy you depend on comes from the Sun and moves among the four major parts of the Earth system. Think again about the puddle that is drying up. Sunlight shines through the water and heats the soil, or geosphere, beneath the puddle. Some of this heat energy goes into the puddle, moving into the hydrosphere. As the water evaporates and becomes part of the atmosphere, it takes the energy that came from the Sun with it. The Sun provides energy for all weather and ocean currents. Without the Sun, life could not exist on Earth's surface.

Why It's Important

Understanding how matter and energy move through the Earth system makes it possible to

- predict how a temperature change in ocean water might affect the weather
- determine how clearing forests might affect rainfall
- explain where organisms on the ocean floor get energy to carry out life processes

Earth has changed over time and continues to change.

You see Earth changing all of the time. Rain turns dirt to mud, and a dry wind turns the mud to dust. Many changes are small and can take hundreds, thousands, or even millions of years to add up to much. Other changes are sudden and can destroy in minutes a house that had stood for many years.

What It Means

Events are always changing Earth's surface. Some events, such as the building or wearing away of mountains, occur over millions of years. Others, such as earthquakes, occur within seconds. A change can affect a small area or even the entire planet.

Records of Change

What was the distant past like? Think about how scientists learn about ancient people. They study what the people left behind and draw conclusions based on the evidence. In a similar way, scientists learn about Earth's past by examining the evidence they find in rock layers and by observing processes now occurring.

By observing that water breaks down rocks and carries the material away to other places, people learned that rivers can slowly carve deep valleys. Evidence from rocks and fossils along the edges of continents shows that all continents were once joined and then moved apart over time. A **fossil** is the trace of a once-living organism. Fossils also show that new types of plants and animals develop, and others, such as dinosaurs, die out.

Change Continues Today

Every year, earthquakes occur, volcanoes erupt, and rivers flood. Continents continue to move slowly. The Himalayan Mountains of Asia push a few millimeters higher. **Climate**—the long-term weather patterns of an area—may also change. Scientists are studying how changes in climates around the world might affect Earth even within this century.

Why It's Important

Understanding the changing Earth makes it possible to

- predict and prepare for events such as volcanic eruptions, landslides, floods, and climate changes
- design buildings to withstand shaking during earthquakes
- protect important environments for plants and animals

You may think of science as a body of knowledge or a collection of facts. More important, however, science is an active process that involves certain ways of looking at the world.

Scientific Habits of Mind

Scientists are curious. They ask questions. A scientist who finds an unusual rock by the side of a river would ask questions such as, "Did this rock form in this area?" or "Did this rock form elsewhere and get moved here?" Questions like these make a scientist want to investigate.

Scientists are observant. They look closely at the world around them. A scientist who studies rocks can learn a lot about a rock just by picking it up, looking at its color, and feeling how heavy it is.

Scientists are creative. They draw on what they know to form possible explanations for a pattern, an event, or an interesting phenomenon that they have observed. Then scientists put together a plan for testing their ideas.

Scientists are skeptical. Scientists don't accept an explanation or answer unless it is based on evidence and logical reasoning. They continually question their own conclusions as well as the conclusions suggested by other scientists. Scientists only trust evidence that can be confirmed by other people or other methods.

Scientists use seismographs to observe and measure vibrations that move through the ground.

This scientist is collecting a sample of melted rock from a hot lava flow in Hawaii.

Science Processes at Work

You can think of science as a continuous cycle of asking and seeking answers to questions about the world. Although there are many processes that scientists use, all scientists typically do the following:

- Observe and ask a question
- Determine what is known
- Investigate
- Interpret results
- Share results

Observe and Ask a Question

It may surprise you that asking questions is an important skill. A scientific investigation may start when a scientist asks a question. Perhaps scientists observe an event or a process that they don't understand, or perhaps answering one question leads to another.

Determine What Is Known

When beginning an inquiry, scientists find out what is already known about a question. They study results from other scientific investigations, read journals, and talk with other scientists. The scientist who is trying to figure out where an unusual rock came from will study maps that show what types of rocks are already known to be in the area where the rock was found.

Ask a question

Determine what is known

Investigate

Interpret results

Share results

Investigate

Investigating is the process of collecting evidence. Two important ways of doing this are experimenting and observing.

A scientist may use photography to study fast events, such as multiple flashes of lightning.

Rocks, such as this one from the Moon, can be subjected to different conditions in a laboratory.

An **experiment** is an organized procedure to study something under controlled conditions. For example, the scientist who found the rock by the river might notice that it is lighter in color where it is chipped. The scientist might design an experiment to determine why the rock is a different color on the inside. The scientist could break off a small piece of the inside of the rock and heat it up to see if it becomes the same color as the outside. The scientist would need to use a piece of the same rock that is being studied. A different rock might react differently to heat.

Observing is the act of noting and recording an event, characteristic, or anything else detected with an instrument or with the senses. A scientist makes observations while performing an experiment. However, some things cannot be studied using experiments. For example, streaks of light called meteors occur when small rocks from outer space hit Earth's atmosphere. A scientist might study meteors by taking pictures of the sky at a time when meteors are likely to occur.

Forming hypotheses and making predictions are two other skills involved in scientific investigations. A **hypothesis** is a tentative explanation for an observation or a scientific problem that can be tested by further investigation. For example, the scientist might make the following hypothesis about the rock from the beach:

The rock is a meteorite, which is a rock that fell to the ground from outer space. The outside of the rock changed color because it was heated up from passing through Earth's atmosphere.

A **prediction** is an expectation of what will be observed or what will happen. To test the hypothesis that the rock's outside is black because it is a meteorite, the scientist might predict that a close examination of the rock will show that it has many characteristics in common with rocks that are already known to be meteorites.

Interpret Results

As scientists investigate, they analyze their evidence, or data, and begin to draw conclusions. **Analyzing data** involves looking at the evidence gathered through observations or experiments and trying to identify any patterns that might exist in the data. Scientists often need to make additional observations or perform more experiments before they are sure of their conclusions. Many times scientists make new predictions or revise their hypotheses.

Scientists use computers to gather and interpret data.

Scientists make images such as this computer drawing of a landscape to help share their results with others.

Share Results

An important part of scientific investigation is sharing results of experiments. Scientists read and publish in journals and attend conferences to communicate with other scientists around the world. Sharing data and procedures gives scientists a way to test each others' results. They also share results with the public through newspapers, television, and other media.

The Nature of Technology

When you think of technology, you may think of cars, computers, and cell phones. Imagine having no refrigerator or radio. It's difficult to think of a world without the products of what we call technology. Technology, however, is more than just devices that make our daily activities easier. Technology is the process of using scientific knowledge to design solutions to real-world problems.

Science and Technology

Science and technology go hand in hand. Each depends upon the other. Even a device as simple as a thermometer is designed using knowledge of the ways different materials respond to changes in temperature. In turn, thermometers have allowed scientists to learn more about the world. Greater knowledge of how materials respond to changes in temperature helped engineers to build items such as refrigerators. They have also built thermometers that could be read automatically by computers. New technologies lead to new scientific knowledge and new scientific knowledge leads to even better technologies.

The Process of Technological Design

The process of technological design involves many choices. What, for example, should be done to protect the residents of an area prone to severe storms such as tornadoes and hurricanes? Build stronger homes that can withstand the winds? Try to develop a way to detect the storms long before they occur? Or learn more about hurricanes in order to find new ways to protect people from the dangers? The steps people take to solve the problem depend a great deal on what they already know about the problem as well as what can reasonably be done. As you learn about the steps in the process of technological design, think about the different choices that could be made at each step.

Identify a Need

To study hurricanes, scientists needed to know what happens inside the most dangerous parts of the storm. However, it was not safe for scientists to go near the centers of hurricanes because the winds were too strong and changed direction too fast. Scientists needed a way to measure conditions deep inside the storm without putting themselves in danger.

Design and Develop

One approach was to design a robotic probe to take the measurements. The probe and instruments needed to be strong enough to withstand the fast winds near the center of a hurricane. The scientists also needed a way to send the probe into the storm and to get the data from the instruments quickly.

Scientists designed a device called a dropsonde, which could be dropped from an airplane flying over the hurricane. A dropsonde takes measurements from deep inside the storm and radios data back to the scientists.

Test and Improve

Even good technology can usually be improved. When scientists first used dropsondes, they learned about hurricanes. They also learned what things about the dropsondes worked well and what did not. For example, the scientists wanted better ways to keep track of where the probe moved. Newer dropsondes make use of the Global Positioning System, which is a way of pinpointing any position on Earth by using satellite signals.

Using McDougal Littell Science

Reading Text and Visuals

This book is organized to help you learn. Use these boxed pointers as a path to help you learn and remember the **Big Ideas** and **Key Concepts**.

Take notes.

Use the strategies on the **Getting Ready to Learn** page.

Read the Big Idea.

As you read **Key Concepts** for the chapter, relate them to **the Big Idea**.

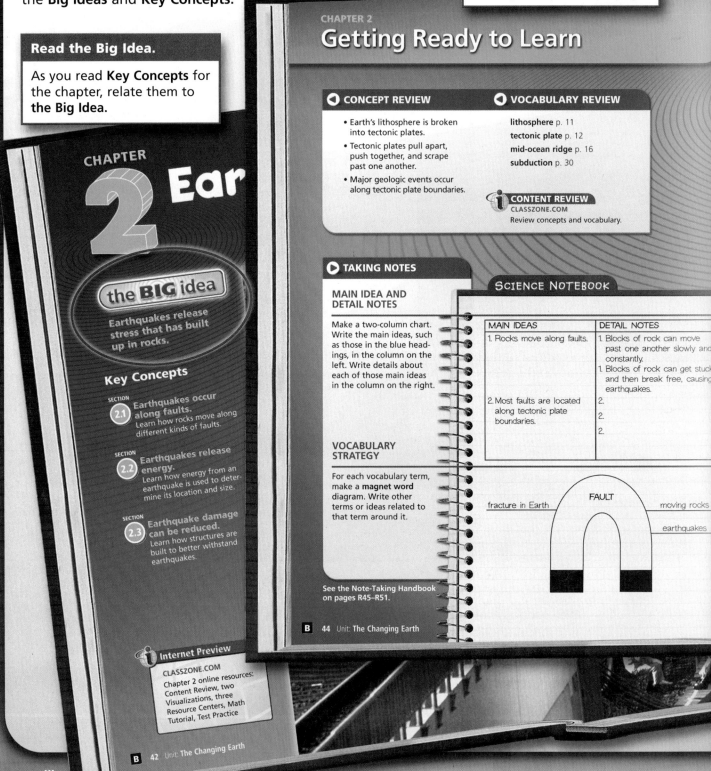

CHAPTER

2 Ear

the **BIG** idea

Earthquakes release stress that has built up in rocks.

Key Concepts

SECTION
2.1 Earthquakes occur along faults.
Learn how rocks move along different kinds of faults.

SECTION
2.2 Earthquakes release energy.
Learn how energy from an earthquake is used to determine its location and size.

SECTION
2.3 Earthquake damage can be reduced.
Learn how structures are built to better withstand earthquakes.

Internet Preview
CLASSZONE.COM
Chapter 2 online resources: Content Review, two Visualizations, three Resource Centers, Math Tutorial, Test Practice

B 42 Unit: The Changing Earth

CHAPTER 2

Getting Ready to Learn

CONCEPT REVIEW

- Earth's lithosphere is broken into tectonic plates.
- Tectonic plates pull apart, push together, and scrape past one another.
- Major geologic events occur along tectonic plate boundaries.

VOCABULARY REVIEW

lithosphere p. 11
tectonic plate p. 12
mid-ocean ridge p. 16
subduction p. 30

CONTENT REVIEW
CLASSZONE.COM
Review concepts and vocabulary.

TAKING NOTES

MAIN IDEA AND DETAIL NOTES

Make a two-column chart. Write the main ideas, such as those in the blue headings, in the column on the left. Write details about each of those main ideas in the column on the right.

VOCABULARY STRATEGY

For each vocabulary term, make a **magnet word** diagram. Write other terms or ideas related to that term around it.

See the Note-Taking Handbook on pages R45–R51.

SCIENCE NOTEBOOK

MAIN IDEAS	DETAIL NOTES
1. Rocks move along faults.	1. Blocks of rock can move past one another slowly and constantly.
	1. Blocks of rock can get stuck and then break free, causing earthquakes.
2. Most faults are located along tectonic plate boundaries.	2.
	2.
	2.

fracture in Earth   FAULT   moving rocks

earthquakes

B 44 Unit: The Changing Earth

Read each heading.

See how it fits into the outline of the chapter.

KEY CONCEPT
2.1 Earthquakes occur along faults.

Remember what you know.

Think about concepts you learned earlier and preview what you'll learn now.

◀ BEFORE, you learned	▶ NOW, you will learn
• The crust and uppermost mantle make up the lithosphere • The lithosphere is cold and rigid • Tectonic plates move over hotter, weaker rock in the asthenosphere	• Why earthquakes occur • Where most earthquakes occur • How rocks move during earthquakes

VOCABULARY

fault p. 45
stress p. 45
earthquake p. 45

Try the activities.

They will introduce you to science concepts.

EXPLORE Pressure

How does pressure affect a solid material?

PROCEDURE

① Hold a wooden craft stick at each end.

② Bend the stick very slowly. Continue to put pressure on the stick until it breaks.

WHAT DO YOU THINK?
• How did the stick change before it broke?
• How might rocks react to pressure?

MATERIALS
wooden craft stick

Rocks move along faults.

Sometimes when you pull on a drawer, it opens smoothly. At other times, the drawer sticks shut. If you pull hard enough, the drawer suddenly flies open. Rocks along faults behave in a similar way. A **fault** is a fracture, or break, in Earth's lithosphere, along which blocks of rock move past each other.

Along some parts of a fault, the rock on either side may slide along slowly and constantly. Along other parts of the fault, the rocks may stick, or lock together. The rocks bend as stress is put on them. **Stress** is the force exerted when an object presses on, pulls on, or pushes against another object. As stress increases, the rocks break free. A sudden release of stress in the lithosphere causes an earthquake. An **earthquake** is a shaking of the ground caused by the sudden movement of large blocks of rock along a fault.

VOCABULARY
Add magnet word diagrams for *fault, stress,* and *earthquake* to your notebook.

Learn the vocabulary.

Take notes on each term.

Chapter 2: Earthquakes 45 **B**

Reading Text and Visuals

Read one paragraph at a time.

Look for a topic sentence that explains the main idea of the paragraph. Figure out how the details relate to that idea. One paragraph might have several important ideas; you may have to reread to understand.

Continental-Continental Collision

A **continental-continental collision** occurs where two plates carrying continental crust push together. Because both crusts are the same density, neither plate can sink beneath the other. If the plates keep moving, their edges crumple and fold, as in the diagram below.

You can see the same effect if you put two blocks of clay on a table and push them together. If you push hard enough, one or both of the blocks will buckle. One cannot sink under the other, so the clay folds under the pressure.

In some cases, the folded crust can be pushed up high enough to form mountains. Some of the world's largest mountains appear along continent-continent boundaries. For instance, the European Alps, shown in the photograph at right, are found where the African and European plates are colliding. The tallest mountains in the world, the Himalayas, first formed when the Indian Plate began colliding with the European Plate.

The Himalayas and the Alps are still forming today. As long as the plates keep moving, these mountains will keep rising higher.

The European Alps began rising nearly 40 million years ago as a section of the African Plate collided with the European Plate.

CHECK YOUR READING Explain how colliding plates form mountain ranges.

Answer the questions.

Check Your Reading questions will help you remember what you read.

Convergent Boundary—Collision

Rocks crumple and fold to form mountains.

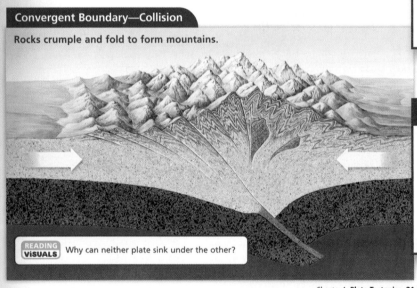

READING VISUALS Why can neither plate sink under the other?

Study the visuals.

- Read the title.
- Read all labels and captions.
- Figure out what the picture is showing. Notice colors, arrows, and lines.

Chapter 1: **Plate Tectonics** 31 **B**

Doing Labs

To understand science, you have to see it in action. Doing labs helps you understand how things really work.

① Read the entire lab first.

② Form a hypothesis.

③ Follow the procedure.

④ Record the data.

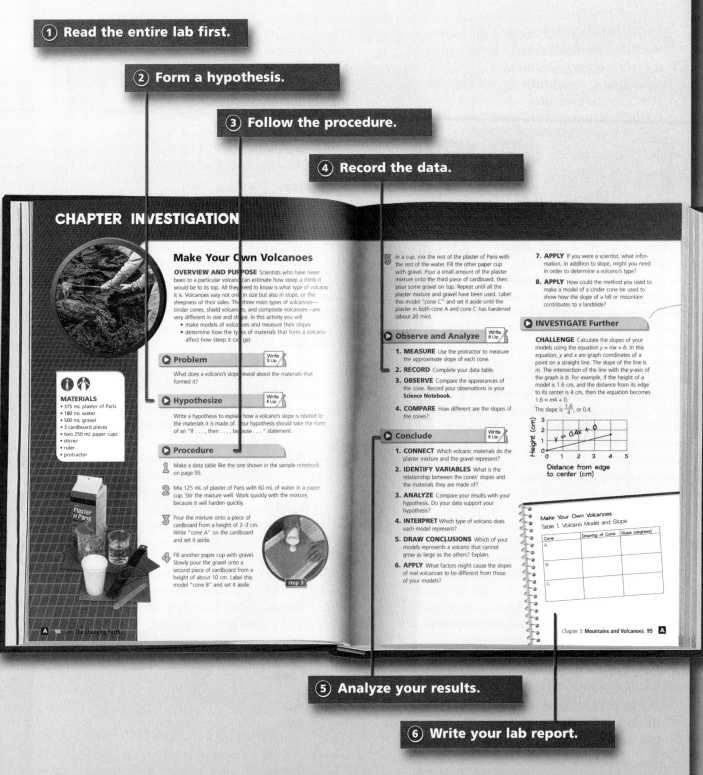

CHAPTER INVESTIGATION

Make Your Own Volcanoes

OVERVIEW AND PURPOSE Scientists who have never been to a particular volcano can estimate how steep a climb it would be to its top. All they need to know is what type of volcano it is. Volcanoes vary not only in size but also in slope, or the steepness of their sides. The three main types of volcanoes—cinder cones, shield volcanoes, and composite volcanoes—are very different in size and shape. In this activity you will
• make models of volcanoes and measure their slopes
• determine how the types of materials that form a volcano affect how steep it can get

▶ Problem   Write It Up

What does a volcano's slope reveal about the materials that formed it?

MATERIALS
• 375 mL plaster of Paris
• 180 mL water
• 500 mL gravel
• 3 cardboard pieces
• two 250 mL paper cups
• stirrer
• ruler
• protractor

▶ Hypothesize   Write It Up

Write a hypothesis to explain how a volcano's slope is related to the materials it is made of. Your hypothesis should take the form of an "If . . . , then . . . , because . . . " statement.

▶ Procedure

1. Make a data table like the one shown in the sample notebook on page 95.

2. Mix 125 mL of plaster of Paris with 60 mL of water in a paper cup. Stir the mixture well. Work quickly with the mixture, because it will harden quickly.

3. Pour the mixture onto a piece of cardboard from a height of 2–3 cm. Write "cone A" on the cardboard and set it aside.

4. Fill another paper cup with gravel. Slowly pour the gravel onto a second piece of cardboard from a height of about 10 cm. Label this model "cone B" and set it aside.

step 3

A 94 Unit: The Changing Earth

5. In a cup, mix the rest of the plaster of Paris with the rest of the water. Fill the other paper cup with gravel. Pour a small amount of the plaster mixture onto the third piece of cardboard, then pour some gravel on top. Repeat until all the plaster mixture and gravel have been used. Label this model "cone C" and set it aside until the plaster in both cone A and cone C has hardened (about 20 min).

▶ Observe and Analyze   Write It Up

1. **MEASURE** Use the protractor to measure the approximate slope of each cone.

2. **RECORD** Complete your data table.

3. **OBSERVE** Compare the appearances of the cone. Record your observations in your **Science Notebook.**

4. **COMPARE** How different are the slopes of the cones?

▶ Conclude   Write It Up

1. **CONNECT** Which volcanic materials do the plaster mixture and the gravel represent?

2. **IDENTIFY VARIABLES** What is the relationship between the cones' slopes and the materials they are made of?

3. **ANALYZE** Compare your results with your hypothesis. Do your data support your hypothesis?

4. **INTERPRET** Which type of volcano does each model represent?

5. **DRAW CONCLUSIONS** Which of your models represents a volcano that cannot grow as large as the others? Explain.

6. **APPLY** What factors might cause the slopes of real volcanoes to be different from those of your models?

7. **APPLY** If you were a scientist, what information, in addition to slope, might you need in order to determine a volcano's type?

8. **APPLY** How could the method you used to make a model of a cinder cone be used to show how the slope of a hill or mountain contributes to a landslide?

▶ INVESTIGATE Further

CHALLENGE Calculate the slopes of your models using the equation $y = mx + b$. In this equation, y and x are graph coordinates of a point on a straight line. The slope of the line is m. The intersection of the line with the y-axis of the graph is b. For example, if the height of a model is 1.6 cm, and the distance from its edge to its center is 4 cm, then the equation becomes $1.6 = m4 + 0$.

The slope is $\frac{1.6}{4}$, or 0.4.

$y = 0.4x + 0$

Height (vertical axis) / Distance from edge to center (cm)

Make Your Own Volcanoes
Table 1. Volcano Model and Slope

Cone	Drawing of Cone	Slope (degrees)
A.		
B.		
C.		

Chapter 3: **Mountains and Volcanoes** 95 A

⑤ Analyze your results.

⑥ Write your lab report.

Using Technology

The Internet is a great source of information about up-to-date science. The ClassZone Website and SciLinks have exciting sites for you to explore. Video clips and simulations can make science come alive.

Look for red banners.

Go to **ClassZone.com** to see simulations, visualizations, resources centers, and content review.

Earth Science: The Changing Earth

Use these exciting animations, visuals, investigations, and links to enhance your knowledge of science.

Watch the videos.

See science at work in the **Scientific American Frontiers video.**

Look up SciLinks.

Go to **scilinks.org** to explore the topic.

NSTA
scilinks.org

SCILINKS

Plates **Code: MDL052**

The Changing Earth
Contents Overview

Unit Features

1 Plate Tectonics 6

the BIG idea

The movement of tectonic plates causes geologic changes on Earth.

2 Earthquakes 42

the BIG idea

Earthquakes release stress that has built up in rocks.

3 Mountains and Volcanoes 74

the BIG idea

Mountains and volcanoes form as tectonic plates move.

4 Views of Earth's Past 108

the BIG idea

Rocks, fossils, and other types of natural evidence tell Earth's story.

5 Natural Resources 144

the BIG idea

Society depends on natural resources for energy and materials.

Studying
VOLCANOES
with Satellites

New ways of viewing Earth are giving
scientists powerful tools for learning
about and predicting volcanic eruptions.

**SCIENTIFIC
AMERICAN
FRONTIERS**

View the video segment
"Paradise Postponed"
to learn how scientists
study volcanoes and
predict eruptions.

During a 1997 eruption of the
Soufrière Hills volcano on
Montserrat, volcanic material
flowed all the way to the ocean.

A plume of volcanic ash and gases rises from Soufrière Hills volcano, Montserrat, in this photograph taken from a satellite on October 29, 2002.

Deadly Eruptions

On the island of Montserrat in the West Indies, small eruptions of the Soufrière Hills volcano began in 1995. These early warnings gave people time to move away several months before the first of the large explosions.

People living in the towns near Nevado del Ruiz volcano in Colombia were not so fortunate. On a night in November 1985, a storm hid the snow-covered volcano. No one could see the start of an eruption. Huge amounts of snow and ice melted and mixed with volcanic ash to form mudflows that killed 25,000 people. The flow that buried much of the town of Armero traveled 74 kilometers in just two and one-half hours.

Throughout history volcanic eruptions have caused some of the world's worst disasters. Warnings might have saved hundreds of thousands of lives. But in most cases people had no idea that a rain of rock, a cloud of toxic gases, or other deadly effects of an erupting volcano would soon engulf their area. By the time people realized that a volcano was erupting, it was too late to get away. Today, scientists monitor volcanoes around the world to help avoid such tragedies.

Alaskan
Peninsula

A 1996 eruption of Alaska's Pavlof volcano was the first to be predicted with the use of data from space. The satellite image recorded during the eruption shows an area of hot ground on the volcano in red.

Predicting Volcanic Eruptions

Scientists who study volcanoes paid close attention when an instrument on a weather satellite unexpectedly "saw" hot ground in 1996. The instrument's usual function is to measure cloud temperatures, but it detected an area of increased heat on Alaska's Pavlof volcano. The scientists predicted that the volcano would soon erupt. Three days later, it did. This eruption was the first to be predicted with information from space. Now computers check satellite data as they receive the data. Any unusually hot areas trigger an automatic e-mail alert to scientists.

In 1999, NASA launched the *Terra* satellite as part of a program to study Earth's surface and atmosphere. Among *Terra's* instruments is one that detects heat given off by the planet's surface. When scientists observe an unusual increase in surface temperature, they determine whether magma is rising underground. In some cases unusual heat has been the first sign that a volcano is building toward an eruption.

After an Eruption

Satellites are also used to monitor eruptions as they happen. Lava flows show up clearly, as you can see in the *Terra* image on page 5. In addition, satellites are used to track the locations of volcanic ash and gas clouds. Airplanes flying into this material can be severely damaged, so pilots need to know where it is. Volcanic material in

View the "Paradise Postponed" segment of your *Scientific American Frontiers* video to learn how scientists monitor volcanic eruptions.

IN THIS SCENE FROM THE VIDEO ▶
Scientist Barry Voigt examines the effects of a powerful eruption that occurred a few days earlier.

STUDYING VOLCANOES Until 1995, the Caribbean island of Montserrat was a peaceful tourist destination. Then, the island's volcano began to erupt. Over the next two years, the volcano erupted dozens of times, spewing out hot ash, rocks, and gases. These eruptions destroyed most of the island's towns and drove away many residents.

Scientists from around the world have come to Montserrat to find out how well they can predict eruptions. Seismic stations buried near the volcano detect earthquakes, which can be a sign that the volcano is about to erupt. Scientists can also predict an eruption by studying changes in the lava dome that has built up on the volcano. When an eruption does occur, scientists visit the site to collect rocks and measure the volcanic ash flow.

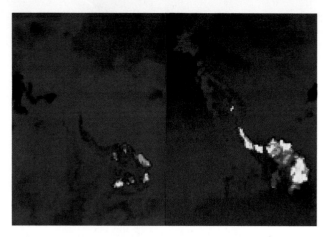

Data collected by the *Terra* satellite show the progress of a Hawaiian lava flow as it enters the ocean on May 13, 2000 (left), and on August 1, 2000 (right).

the air can be difficult to see or to distinguish from normal clouds, especially at night. Satellites are particularly helpful in identifying and tracking eruptions in remote areas where there are few or no observers.

Explosive Neighbors

Satellites such as *Terra* are among the tools scientists use to monitor restless volcanoes near urban areas. Mount Rainier, a volcano in Washington, looms near the large cities of Seattle and Tacoma. In the past, heat from eruptions has melted large amounts of the ice and snow at the top of the volcano, creating mudflows that destroyed everything in their path. Another extremely dangerous volcano is Mount Vesuvius, near Naples, Italy. Timely warnings before eruptions of such volcanoes can allow authorities to safely evacuate the millions of people who live near them.

UNANSWERED Questions

Even when scientists predict that a volcano will erupt soon, many questions still cannot be answered.

- How powerful will the next eruption be?

- On what day (or even during what week) will the volcano erupt?

- How much magma is rising under the volcano, and how fast is it rising? Will it stop?

1

Plate Tectonics

the BIG idea

The movement of tectonic plates causes geologic changes on Earth.

What might have made this huge crack in the Earth?

Key Concepts

SECTION
1.1 Earth has several layers.
Learn about Earth's interior and its rigid surface plates.

SECTION
1.2 Continents change position over time.
Learn how continental drift and plate tectonics changed the way people view Earth.

SECTION
1.3 Plates move apart.
Learn about the three types of plate boundaries and what happens when plates move apart.

SECTION
1.4 Plates converge or scrape past each other.
Learn what geologic events occur at these plate boundaries.

Internet Preview

CLASSZONE.COM

Chapter 1 online resources: Content Review, two Visualizations, one Resource Center, Math Tutorial, and Test Practice

Watching a Pot Boil

Put a medium-sized pot of water on to boil. Place a small wet sponge on the water. Watch the water and sponge as the water heats.

Observe and Think
What happened to the water as it heated? What happened to the sponge as the water became hotter?

Earth's Moving Surface

Place two halves of a peanut butter and jelly sandwich side by side. Very slowly push them together. Then take one half and very slowly tear it into two pieces.

Observe and Think
What happened when you pushed and pulled on the sandwich halves? What might this activity tell you about the movements of Earth's surface?

Internet Activity: Earth's Interior

Go to **ClassZone.com** to explore the makeup of Earth's layers. Find out how scientists learned what the interior of Earth is like.

Observe and Think
Science fiction books and movies show people traveling to the center of Earth. Do you think this can happen any time soon? Why or why not?

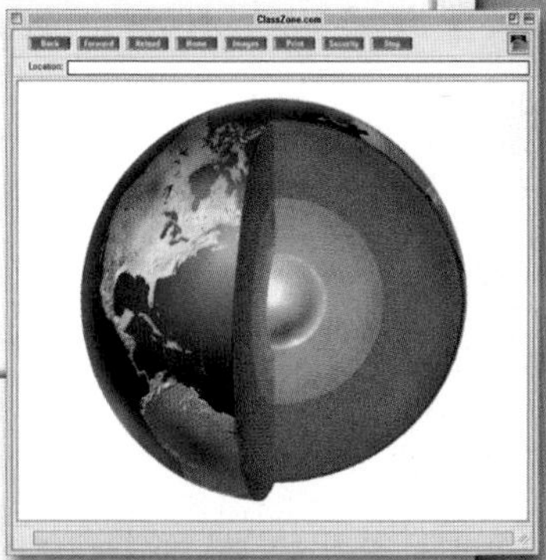

NSTA
scilinks.org
SCI
LINKS

Plates **Code: MDL052**

Getting Ready to Learn

◀ CONCEPT REVIEW

- Most rocks are made of minerals.
- Different types of rocks are formed under different temperatures and pressures.
- Earth's surface has changed over millions of years.

◀ VOCABULARY REVIEW

See Glossary for definitions.

density

mineral

rock

CONTENT REVIEW
CLASSZONE.COM
Review concepts and vocabulary.

▶ TAKING NOTES

SUPPORTING MAIN IDEAS

Make a chart to show main ideas and the information that supports them. Copy each blue heading. Below each heading, add supporting information, such as reasons, explanations, and examples.

VOCABULARY STRATEGY

Place each vocabulary term at the center of a **description wheel** diagram. Write some words describing it on the spokes.

See the Note-Taking Handbook on pages R45–R51.

SCIENCE NOTEBOOK

Earth is made up of materials with different densities.

→ Dense materials—such as iron and nickel—sink toward center

→ Less dense materials rise toward surface

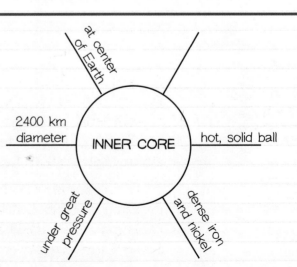

at center of Earth

2400 km diameter

INNER CORE

hot, solid ball

under great pressure

dense iron and nickel

Earth has several layers.

1.1

◀ BEFORE, you learned

- Minerals and rocks are the building blocks of Earth
- Different types of rocks make up Earth's surface

▶ NOW, you will learn

- About the different properties of Earth's layers
- About the plates that make up Earth's outermost layers

VOCABULARY

inner core p. 10
outer core p. 10
mantle p. 11
crust p. 11
lithosphere p. 11
asthenosphere p. 11
tectonic plate p. 12

EXPLORE Density

Will a denser material sink or float?

PROCEDURE

1. Add equal amounts of water to 2 cups. Add 3 spoonfuls of salt to one of the cups and stir until the salt is dissolved.

2. Add 10 drops of food coloring to the same cup in which you dissolved the salt.

3. Gently pour about a third of the colored salt water into the cup of fresh water. Observe what happens.

WHAT DO YOU THINK?

- What did you observe when the two types of water were mixed?
- What does this activity tell you about materials of different density?

MATERIALS

- 2 clear plastic cups
- tap water
- table salt
- plastic spoon
- food coloring

Earth is made up of materials with different densities.

SUPPORTING MAIN IDEAS
Support the main ideas about Earth's layers with details and examples.

Scientists think that about 4.6 billion years ago, Earth formed as bits of material collided and stuck together. The planet grew larger as more and more material was added. These impacts, along with radioactive decay and Earth's gravity, produced intense heat. The young planet became a glowing ball of melted rock.

In time, denser materials, such as iron and nickel, sank toward the center of Earth. Less dense materials moved toward the surface. Other materials settled between the planet's center and its surface. Slowly, Earth's main layers formed—the core, the mantle, and the crust.

Earth's layers have different properties.

VOCABULARY
Draw a description wheel in your notebook for each term. You might want to include the pronunciation of some terms.

How do scientists know what Earth's deep interior is like? After all, no one has seen it. To explore the interior, scientists study the energy from earthquakes or underground explosions they set off. The energy travels through Earth somewhat like ripples move through a pond. The energy moves slower through less dense materials or liquids and faster through denser materials or solids. In this way, scientists infer what each layer is made of and how thick the layers are, as shown in the diagram below.

Core, Mantle, Crust

The core is Earth's densest region and is made up of two parts. The **inner core** is a ball of hot, solid metals. There is enormous pressure at the center of Earth. This squeezes the atoms of the metals so closely together that the core remains solid despite the intense heat.

The **outer core** is a layer of liquid metals that surrounds the inner core. The temperature and pressure in the outer core are lower than in the inner core. The lower pressure allows the metals to remain liquid.

Earth's Layers

Earth's layers formed as denser materials sank toward the center and less dense materials rose toward the surface.

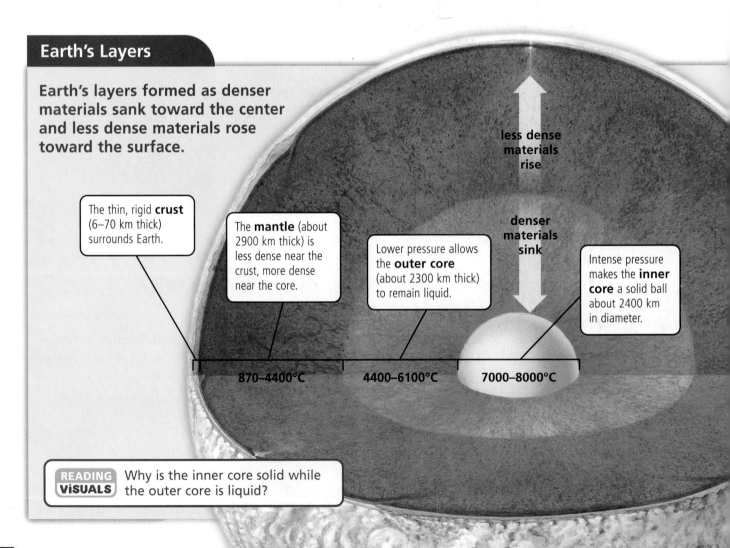

The thin, rigid **crust** (6–70 km thick) surrounds Earth.

The **mantle** (about 2900 km thick) is less dense near the crust, more dense near the core.

Lower pressure allows the **outer core** (about 2300 km thick) to remain liquid.

Intense pressure makes the **inner core** a solid ball about 2400 km in diameter.

less dense materials rise

denser materials sink

870–4400°C   4400–6100°C   7000–8000°C

READING VISUALS Why is the inner core solid while the outer core is liquid?

The **mantle** is Earth's thickest layer, measuring nearly 2900 kilometers (1700 mi). It is made of hot rock that is less dense than the metallic core. The very top part of the mantle is cool and rigid. Just below that, the rock is hot and soft enough to move like a thick paste.

The **crust** is a thin layer of cool rock. It surrounds Earth somewhat like a shell surrounds an egg. There are two basic types of crust. Continental crust includes all continents and some major islands. Oceanic crust includes all the ocean floors. As the diagram below shows, Earth's crust is thinnest under the oceans and thickest under continental mountain ranges. The crust is home to all life on Earth.

Lithosphere and Asthenosphere

Earth's crust and the very top of the mantle together form the **lithosphere** (LIHTH-uh-SFEER). The Greek prefix *litho-* means "stone" or "rock." This layer is the most rigid of all the layers. The lithosphere sits on top of the **asthenosphere** (as-THEHN-uh-SFEER), a layer of hotter, softer rock in the upper mantle. The Greek word *asthenés* means "weak." This layer is not actually weak, but it is soft enough to flow slowly like hot tar. You can imagine the lithosphere as solid pieces of pavement resting on hot tar.

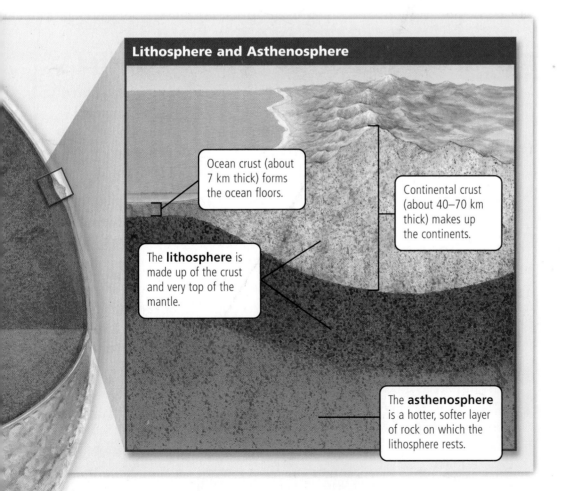

Lithosphere and Asthenosphere

Ocean crust (about 7 km thick) forms the ocean floors.

Continental crust (about 40–70 km thick) makes up the continents.

The **lithosphere** is made up of the crust and very top of the mantle.

The **asthenosphere** is a hotter, softer layer of rock on which the lithosphere rests.

INVESTIGATE Earth's Different Layers

How can you model Earth's layers?

SKILL FOCUS
Modeling

PROCEDURE

1. Put a layer of wooden beads about 1 centimeter thick at the bottom of a clear plastic cup or small jar.

2. Put a layer of gravel about 2 centimeters thick on top of the wooden beads. Stir the beads and gravel until they are well mixed.

3. Put another layer of gravel about 1 centimeter thick on top of the mix. Do NOT mix this layer of gravel.

4. SLOWLY fill the cup about two-thirds full of water. Be sure not to disturb the layers in the cup.

5. Stir the beads and gravel with the stick. Observe what happens.

MATERIALS
- clear plastic cup
- small colored wooden beads
- gravel
- stirring stick
- tap water

TIME
15 minutes

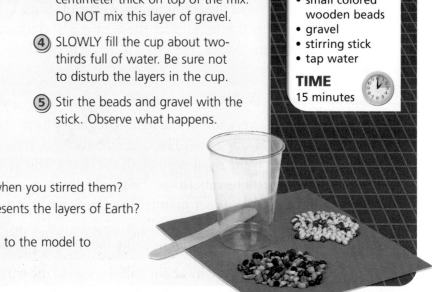

WHAT DO YOU THINK?

- What happened to the materials when you stirred them?
- How do you think this model represents the layers of Earth?

CHALLENGE What could you add to the model to represent Earth's solid core?

The lithosphere is made up of many plates.

READING TiP

The word *tectonic* comes from the Greek *tecktōn,* which means "builder." Tectonic plates are constantly building and changing landforms and oceans around Earth.

As scientists studied Earth's surface, they discovered that the lithosphere does not form a continuous shell around Earth. Instead, they found that the lithosphere is broken into many large and small slabs of rock called **tectonic plates** (tehk-TAHN-ihk). Scientists do not know exactly how or when in Earth's history these giant plates formed.

Tectonic plates fit together like a jigsaw puzzle that makes up the surface of Earth. You could compare the lithosphere to the cracked shell of a hard-boiled egg. The shell may be broken into many pieces, but it still forms a "crust" around the egg itself.

Most large tectonic plates include both continental crust and oceanic crust, as shown in the diagram on page 13. Most of the thicker continental crust rises above the ocean. The rest of the plate is thin oceanic crust, or sea floor, and is underwater. The next time you look at the continents on a world map, remember you are seeing only the part of Earth's crust that rises above the ocean.

CHECK YOUR READING Why do you see only the dry land areas of tectonic plates on a typical world map?

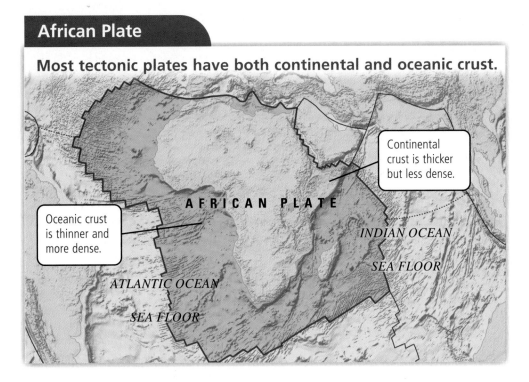

African Plate

Most tectonic plates have both continental and oceanic crust.

Continental crust is thicker but less dense.

Oceanic crust is thinner and more dense.

AFRICAN PLATE

INDIAN OCEAN

SEA FLOOR

ATLANTIC OCEAN

SEA FLOOR

In the diagram above, notice how much of the African Plate, shaded darker blue, lies underwater. The continent of Africa, which looks large on a world map, is actually about half the size of the entire plate. The plate's oceanic crust forms part of the sea floor of the Atlantic and Indian oceans and of the Mediterranean Sea. The ocean crusts of other plates make up the rest of the sea floors.

Earth's layers and tectonic plates are two of the most important discoveries in geology. They helped solve a mystery that had puzzled people for nearly 400 years. The mystery involved two questions. Have the continents always been where they are today? If not, how did they move to their present positions? In Section 1.2, you will find out how scientists are answering these questions.

1.1 Review

KEY CONCEPTS

1. Briefly describe the inner and outer cores, the mantle, and the crust.

2. In what ways is the lithosphere different from the asthenosphere?

3. Describe the structure of most tectonic plates.

CRITICAL THINKING

4. **Draw Conclusions** Suppose you are looking at a scene that has mountains near an ocean. Where do you think the crust would be the thickest? Why?

5. **Hypothesize** What would Earth look like if most of its crust was above sea level?

⬤ CHALLENGE

6. **Predict** You have learned that Earth's lithosphere is made up of many plates. How do you think this fact might help scientists solve the mystery of the moving continents?

1.2 Continents change position over time.

BEFORE, you learned

- Earth's main layers are the core, the mantle, and the crust
- The lithosphere and asthenosphere are the topmost layers of Earth
- The lithosphere is made up of tectonic plates

NOW, you will learn

- How the continental drift hypothesis was developed
- About evidence for plate movement from the sea floor
- How scientists developed the theory of plate tectonics

VOCABULARY

continental drift p. 14
Pangaea p. 16
mid-ocean ridge p. 16
convection p. 17
convection current p. 17
theory of plate tectonics p. 18

EXPLORE Movements of Continents

How do you put together a giant continent?

PROCEDURE

1. Work with a small group. Draw the outline of a large landmass. Fill in mountains, rivers, lakes, and any other features you like.

2. Cut out your landmass, then tear the drawing into several pieces and mix the pieces up. Ask another group to put the puzzle together.

WHAT DO YOU THINK?

- What clues helped you fit the pieces together?
- Do any lands on a world map seem to fit together?

MATERIALS

- sheet of paper
- colored marking pens
- scissors

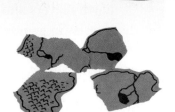

Continents join together and split apart.

VOCABULARY
Draw a description wheel in your notebook for *continental drift*.

The idea that Earth's surface might be moving is not new. As far back as the 1500s, when mapmakers started including North and South America in their world maps, they noticed something curious. The western coast of Africa and the eastern coast of South America seemed to fit together like pieces in a puzzle. Were these continents joined at one time?

In the late 1800s, German scientist Alfred Wegener (VAY-guh-nuhr) began studying this question. In 1912, he proposed a hypothesis known as **continental drift.** According to Wegener's hypothesis, Earth's continents were once joined in a single landmass and gradually moved, or drifted, apart. For many years, people did not accept Wegener's ideas. Not until the mid-1900s did scientists find new evidence that made them consider continental drift more seriously.

Evidence for Continental Drift

Wegener gathered evidence for his hypothesis from fossils, from studies of ancient climate, and from the geology of continents.

Fossils Wegener learned that the fossils of an ancient reptile, *Mesosaurus* (MEHZ-uh-SAWR-uhs), had been discovered in South America and western Africa. This small reptile lived about 270 million years ago. Its fossils were not found anywhere else in the world. Wegener said this fact could easily be explained if South America and Africa were once joined, as shown in the map below.

Climate Evidence of climate change also supported Wegener's hypothesis. For example, Greenland today lies near the Arctic Circle and is mostly covered in ice. Yet fossils of tropical plants can be found on its shores. In contrast, South Africa today has a warm climate. Yet its rocks were deeply scratched by ice sheets that once covered the area.

Wegener suggested that these continents had moved, carrying their fossils and rocks with them. Greenland, for example, had once been near the equator and had slowly moved to the Arctic Circle. South Africa, once closer to the South Pole, had moved slowly north to a warmer region.

Geology Wegener's best evidence for continental drift came from the kinds of rocks that make up the continents. He showed that the type of rock found in Brazil matched the rock found in western Africa. Also, limestone layers in the Appalachian Mountains of North America were exactly like the limestone in Scotland's Highlands.

READING TiP

Climate refers to a pattern of wind, temperature, and rain or snow that occurs in a region over time. Earth's climates have changed many times in the planet's long history.

⬤ **CHECK YOUR READING** Which evidence for continental drift do you think is the most convincing? Explain your answer.

Areas in which *Mesosaurus* fossils have been found

AFRICA

SOUTH AMERICA

The reptile *Mesosaurus* was about 45 cm (18 in.) long. This fossil was found in Brazil, South America.

Pangaea and Continental Drift

Examine continental movement over the past 150 million years.

For Wegener, all the evidence pointed to a single conclusion. The continents had once been joined in a huge supercontinent he called **Pangaea** (pan-JEE-uh). *Pangaea* comes from the Greek word meaning "all lands." This giant continent reached from pole to pole and was centered over the area where Africa lies today.

Pangaea began to split apart some 200 million years ago. In time, the continents moved to where they are today. Yet Wegener could not explain *how* the continents moved. Because of this, his critics called continental drift "a fairy tale" and rejected his hypothesis.

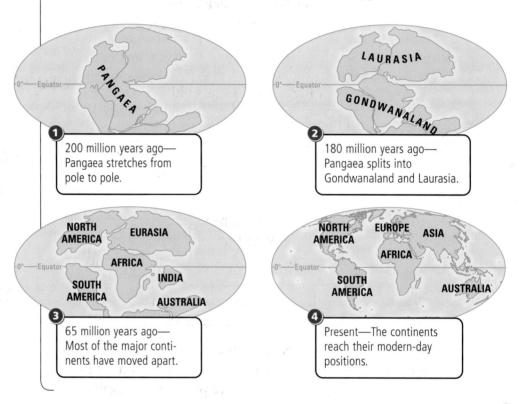

1 200 million years ago—Pangaea stretches from pole to pole.

2 180 million years ago—Pangaea splits into Gondwanaland and Laurasia.

3 65 million years ago—Most of the major continents have moved apart.

4 Present—The continents reach their modern-day positions.

The theory of plate tectonics explains how plates and their continents move.

For many years, Wegener's ideas were pushed aside. Then in the mid-1900s, scientists proved that tectonic plates move. They also offered explanations about how the plates move. Their work eventually led to the theory of plate tectonics, which built on some of Wegener's ideas.

Evidence from the Sea Floor

Scientists began mapping the sea floor in detail in the 1950s. They expected the floor to be smooth and level. Instead, they found huge underwater mountain ranges, called **mid-ocean ridges.** These ridges appeared in every ocean, circling Earth like seams in a baseball.

Sea-Floor Spreading Scientists learned that the ridges form along cracks in the crust. Molten rock rises through these cracks, cools, and forms new oceanic crust. The old crust is pulled away to make room for new material. In this way, the sea floor slowly spreads apart. Scientists call these areas spreading centers. You will read more about spreading centers in Section 1.3.

Age of the Sea Floor Further evidence that the sea floor is spreading apart came from the age of the rocks in the crust. Scientists drilled into the sea floor from a specially equipped vessel called the *Glomar Challenger*. The rock samples revealed that the youngest rock is closest to the ridge, while the oldest rock is farthest away.

The samples also showed that even the oldest ocean floor is young—only 160 to 180 million years old. Continental crust is much older—up to 4 billion years old. These data confirmed that the ocean floor is constantly forming and moving away from the mid-ocean ridges like a conveyor belt. As the sea floor moves, so do the tectonic plates and their continents.

Ocean Trenches Yet, if the sea floor has been spreading for millions of years, why is Earth not getting larger? Scientists discovered the answer when they found huge trenches, like deep canyons, in the sea floor. At these sites, dense oceanic crust is sinking into the asthenosphere. Old crust is being destroyed at the same rate that new crust is forming. Thus, Earth remains the same size.

Scientists now had proof that tectonic plates move. But the same question remained. *How* could the plates move thousands of kilometers around the planet? The asthenosphere provided a possible answer.

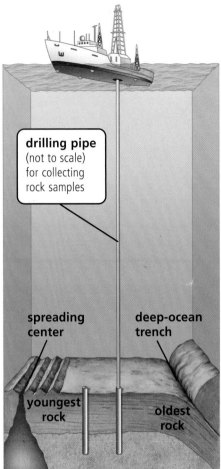

drilling pipe (not to scale) for collecting rock samples

spreading center

deep-ocean trench

youngest rock

oldest rock

Scientists drill into the sea floor to obtain rock samples. The different ages of the rocks prove that plates move.

○ **CHECK YOUR READING** How does the age of the sea floor show that plates move?

Causes of Plate Movement

Tectonic plates rest on the asthenosphere, a layer of soft, hot rock. Rock in this layer and in the mantle just below it moves by convection. **Convection** is energy transfer by the movement of a material. You have seen convection if you have ever boiled a pot of water. The water at the bottom of the pot heats up, becomes less dense, and rises. At the surface, it cools, becomes denser, and sinks, only to be heated and rise again.

The rock in the asthenosphere acts in a similar way. The hot, soft rock rises, cools, and sinks, then is heated and rises again. If this sinking and rising motion continues, it is called a **convection current**—a motion that transfers heat energy in a material.

Convection currents in the mantle are much slower than those in boiling water. The rock creeps only a few centimeters a year. The diagram below shows convection currents circulating. The tectonic plates in the lithosphere are carried on the asthenosphere like long, heavy boxes moved on huge rollers. Over millions of years, convection currents carry the plates thousands of kilometers.

Scientists suspect that two other motions—slab pull and ridge push—help move these huge plates. Slab pull occurs where gravity pulls the edge of a cool, dense plate into the asthenosphere, as shown in the diagram below. Because plates are rigid, the entire plate is dragged along. Ridge push occurs when material from a mid-ocean ridge slides downhill from the ridge. The material pushes the rest of the plate.

Putting the Theory Together

REMINDER

A scientific theory is a well-tested explanation that is consistent with all available evidence.

Geologists combined their knowledge of Earth's plates, the sea floor, and the asthenosphere to develop the **theory of plate tectonics.** The theory states that Earth's lithosphere is made up of huge plates that move over the surface of the Earth.

The map on page 19 shows Earth's major tectonic plates and the directions in which they move. They are the African, the Antarctic, the Australian, the Indian, the Eurasian, the Nazca, the North and South American, and the Pacific plates.

Causes of Plate Movement

Convection currents, slab pull, and ridge push move Earth's huge tectonic plates.

Ridge Push Material from mid-ocean ridges pushes the plates.

Slab Pull Gravity pulls cooler, denser plates into the asthenosphere.

Convection Currents In the asthenosphere, heated rock constantly rises, cools, sinks, and is heated again.

READING VISUALS How do temperature changes create convection currents?

Tectonic Plates

Earth's lithosphere is made up of moving plates.

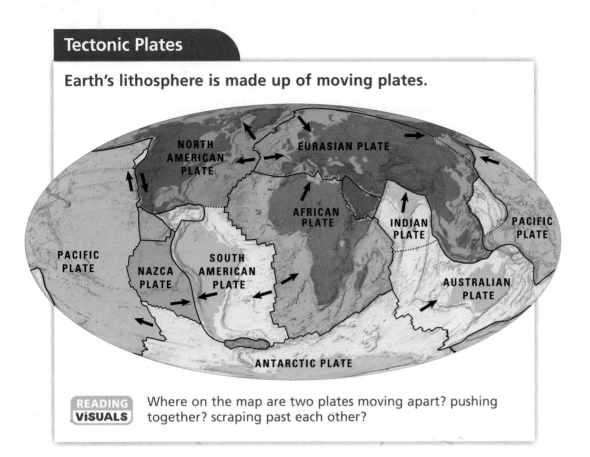

NORTH AMERICAN PLATE

EURASIAN PLATE

AFRICAN PLATE

INDIAN PLATE

PACIFIC PLATE

PACIFIC PLATE

NAZCA PLATE

SOUTH AMERICAN PLATE

AUSTRALIAN PLATE

ANTARCTIC PLATE

READING VISUALS Where on the map are two plates moving apart? pushing together? scraping past each other?

As scientists studied the plates, they realized that one plate could not shift without affecting the others nearby. They found that plates can move apart, push together, or scrape past each other. The arrows on the map above show each type of plate motion.

Plate movements cause great changes in Earth's crust. Most major earthquakes, volcanoes, and mountain ranges appear where tectonic plates meet. You will learn why as you read more about plate movements.

1.2 Review

KEY CONCEPTS

1. What evidence did Wegener gather to support his continental drift hypothesis?

2. Give three types of evidence from the sea floor that prove Earth's tectonic plates move.

3. Explain how motions in the asthenosphere can move tectonic plates around Earth.

CRITICAL THINKING

4. **Apply** A friend tells you he read on a Web site that Earth is getting smaller. What can you tell him that shows Earth's size is not changing?

5. **Evaluate** What other types of scientists, besides geologists, would find the theory of plate tectonics useful in their work?

⚫ CHALLENGE

6. **Infer** Use the arrows on the map above and your knowledge of sea-floor spreading and ocean trenches to answer these questions: What is happening to the size of the Atlantic Ocean? What can you infer is happening to the size of the Pacific Ocean? Explain your answers.

Convection Currents and Plate Movement

OVERVIEW AND PURPOSE South America and Africa are drifting slowly apart. What powerful force could be moving these two plates? In this investigation you will
- observe the movement of convection currents
- determine how convection currents in Earth's mantle could move tectonic plates

▶ Problem

How do convection currents in a fluid affect floating objects on the surface?

▶ Hypothesize

Write a hypothesis to explain how convection currents affect floating objects. Your hypothesis should take the form of an "If . . . , then . . . , because . . ." statement.

▶ Procedure

1. Use two overturned bread pans or two bricks to raise and support the glass lasagna pan. Fill the pan with water to a depth of 4 cm.

2. Hold the food coloring over the middle of the pan. Squeeze several drops into the water. Be careful not to touch or disturb the water with the plastic tip or your hands. Write down your observations.

step 3

3. Light the two candles and place them beneath the center of the pan. Then squeeze several more drops of food coloring into the middle of the pan.

4. Observe what happens for a few minutes, then write down your observations. After you have finished, blow out the candles and wait until the water cools.

5. Moisten the two sponges. Cut one into the shape of South America and the other into the shape of Africa. Insert the pushpins as shown in the photo.

step 5

MATERIALS
- oven-glass lasagna pan
- 2 bread pans or 2 bricks
- water
- liquid food coloring
- 2 small candles
- matches
- 2 sponges
- scissors
- 3–4 pushpins

6 Place the sponges on top of the water in the center of the pan. Fit the two sponges together along their coastlines.

7 Gently hold the sponges together until the water is still, then let go. Observe them for a few minutes and record what you saw.

8 Light the candles again. Place them under the pan and directly beneath the two sponges.

9 Gently hold the sponges together again until the water heats up. Then carefully let go of the sponges, trying not to disturb the water.

10 Observe the sponges for a few minutes, and then record your observations.

▶ Observe and Analyze

1. **RECORD** Draw diagrams to show how the food coloring and the sponges moved in cold water and in heated water. Use arrows to indicate any motion.

2. **ANALYZE** Did the food coloring and the sponges move more with or without the candles? Use what you have learned about convection to explain the role of the candles.

▶ Conclude

1. **EVALUATE** Water is a fluid, but the asthenosphere is not. What properties of the asthenosphere allow it to move like a fluid and form convection currents?

2. **COMPARE AND CONTRAST** In what ways is your setup like Earth's asthenosphere and lithosphere? In what ways is your setup different?

3. **ANALYZE** Compare your results with your hypothesis. Do your observations support your hypothesis? Why or why not?

4. **INTERPRET** Write an answer to your problem statement.

5. **IDENTIFY CONTROLS** Did your experiment include controls? If so, what purpose did they serve here?

6. **APPLY** In your own words, explain how the African continent and the South American continent are drifting apart.

7. **APPLY** Suppose you own an aquarium. You want to make sure your fish are warm whether they swim near the top or near the bottom of the aquarium. The pet store sells two types of heaters. One heater extends 5 cm below the water's surface. The other heater rests on the bottom of the aquarium. Based on what you learned in this activity, which heater would you choose, and why?

▶ INVESTIGATE Further

CHALLENGE Design a new version of this experiment that you think would be a better model of the movements in Earth's asthenosphere and lithosphere. What materials will you need? What changes would you make to the procedure? Sketch your version of the lab, and explain what makes it better.

Convection Currents and Plate Movement

Problem How do convection currents in a fluid affect floating objects on the surface?

Hypothesize

Observe and Analyze

Diagram 1. Sponges on Unheated Water

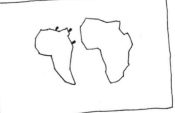

Conclude

1.3 Plates move apart.

◀ BEFORE, you learned	▶ NOW, you will learn
• The continents join and break apart	• About different plate boundaries
• The sea floor provides evidence that tectonic plates move	• What happens when plates move apart
• The theory of plate tectonics helps explain how the plates move	• How the direction and speed of plates can be measured

VOCABULARY

divergent boundary p. 22
convergent boundary p. 22
transform boundary p. 22
rift valley p. 23
magnetic reversal p. 24
hot spot p. 27

EXPLORE Divergent Boundaries

What happens when plates move apart?

PROCEDURE

① Cut the piece of striped paper into two symmetrical pieces slightly less wide than the slit in the oatmeal box.

② Match up the lines of the two pieces and tape the pieces together at one edge. Push the taped edge into the box until only a few centimeters of the free edges show at the top.

③ Grasp each piece of paper, one in each hand. Slowly pull the two pieces horizontally out of the cylinder, pulling them in opposite directions.

WHAT DO YOU THINK?
How is your model similar to the process of sea-floor spreading?

MATERIALS
• scissors
• piece of striped paper
• tape
• small oatmeal box with slit cut in side

Tectonic plates have different boundaries.

A plate boundary is where the edges of two plates meet. After studying the way plates move, geologists identified three types of boundaries.

• A **divergent boundary** (dih-VUR-juhnt) occurs where plates move apart. Most divergent boundaries are found in the ocean.

• A **convergent boundary** (kuhn-VUR-juhnt) occurs where plates push together.

• A **transform boundary** occurs where plates scrape past each other.

In this section, you will discover what happens at divergent boundaries in the ocean and on land. You will read more about convergent and transform boundaries in Section 1.4.

The sea floor spreads apart at divergent boundaries.

In the ocean, divergent boundaries are also called spreading centers. Mid-ocean ridges mark these sites where the ocean floor is spreading apart. As the ridges continue to widen, a gap called a **rift valley** forms. Here molten material rises to build new crust.

Mid-Ocean Ridges and Rift Valleys

Mid-ocean ridges are the longest chain of mountains on Earth. Most of these ridges contain a rift valley along their center, as shown in the diagram below. When molten material rises from the asthenosphere, cold ocean water cools the rock until it becomes solid. As the plates move apart, new cracks open in the solid rock. More molten material rises and hardens. The growing ridge stands high above the sea floor.

The world's longest ridge, the Mid-Atlantic Ridge, runs the length of the Atlantic Ocean. Here the North and South American plates are moving away from the Eurasian and African plates. The ridge extends nearly 11,000 kilometers (6214 mi) from Iceland to near Antarctica. The rift valley is 24 kilometers (15 mi) wide and 9 kilometers (6 mi) deep—about 7 kilometers (4 mi) deeper than the Grand Canyon!

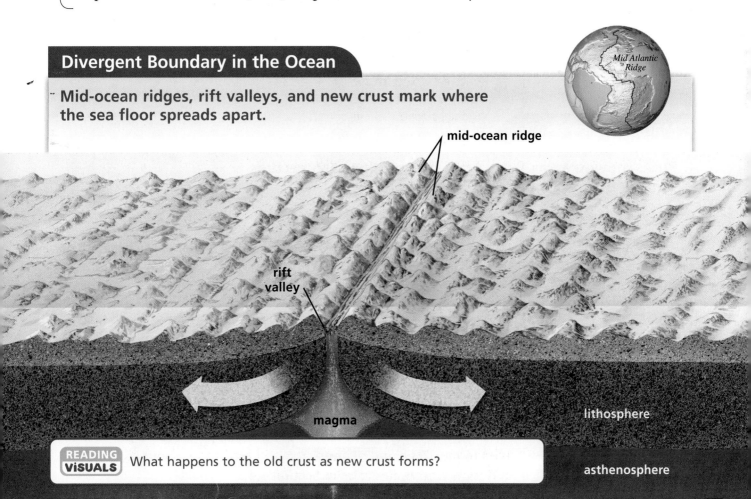

Divergent Boundary in the Ocean

Mid-ocean ridges, rift valleys, and new crust mark where the sea floor spreads apart.

Mid Atlantic Ridge

mid-ocean ridge

rift valley

magma

lithosphere

asthenosphere

READING VISUALS What happens to the old crust as new crust forms?

Sea-Floor Rock and Magnetic Reversals

You read earlier that the sea floor is younger near a mid-ocean ridge and older farther away. As scientists continued to study the sea-floor rock, they made a surprising discovery about Earth's magnetic field.

To understand Earth's magnetic field, you can compare the planet to a bar magnet, which has a north and a south pole. Earth's magnetic field affects the entire planet, as shown in the diagram below. Notice that Earth's geographic and magnetic poles are not in the same place.

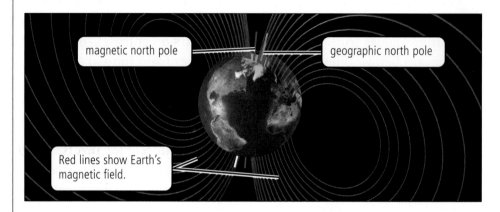

magnetic north pole

geographic north pole

Red lines show Earth's magnetic field.

Unlike a bar magnet, however, Earth's magnetic poles switch places every so often. The north pole becomes the south pole and the south pole becomes the north pole. This switch in direction is called a **magnetic reversal.** Such reversals are caused by changes in Earth's magnetic field. As yet, no one knows why these changes happen. In contrast, Earth's geographic poles never change places.

Magnetic Reversals

Rocks moving away from a mid-ocean ridge carry records of magnetic reversals.

mid-ocean ridge

rocks formed when magnetic field reversed

magma

rocks formed when magnetic field was normal

normal magnetic field

reversed magnetic field

Scientists found that each magnetic reversal is recorded in the sea-floor rock. These records are especially clear at some mid-ocean ridges. As the molten material rises and cools, some magnetic minerals line up with the Earth's magnetic field. When the material hardens, these minerals are permanently fixed like tiny compass needles pointing north and south. Whenever the magnetic field reverses, the cooling minerals record the change.

As shown in the diagram on page 24, the records of magnetic reversals line up like stripes in the rock. As the two plates move away from a mid-ocean ridge, each plate carries a record of magnetic reversals with it. The records are the same on either side of the ridge.

As scientists continued to map the ocean floor, they found more records of these reversals. By dating the rock, scientists had further evidence of plate movement. The youngest rock records the most recent reversal, which happened only about 760,000 years ago. The oldest rock, farthest from the mid-ocean ridge, records reversals that happened more than 150 million years ago.

CHECK YOUR READING Explain how records of magnetic reversals show that plates move apart.

INVESTIGATE Magnetic Reversals

How can you map magnetic reversals?

PROCEDURE

(1) Wrap one end of the string around the middle of the bar magnet. Tape the string in place as shown.

(2) Place a small piece of tape on one end of the magnet. Label the tape "N" to represent north.

(3) Hold the bar magnet over one end of the sea-floor model as shown. Move the magnet SLOWLY toward the other end of the sea-floor model. Record your observations.

WHAT DO YOU THINK?

• What did the magnet reveal about the sea-floor model? Draw a diagram showing any pattern that you might have observed.

• Which part of the model represents the youngest sea floor? Which part represents the oldest sea floor?

CHALLENGE If Earth's magnetic field had never reversed in the past, how would the sea-floor model be different?

SKILL FOCUS
Modeling

MATERIALS
• string
• bar magnet
• masking tape
• marking pen
• sea-floor model

TIME
20 minutes

Continents split apart at divergent boundaries.

SUPPORTING MAIN IDEAS
Use this diagram to help you take notes on how continents split apart.

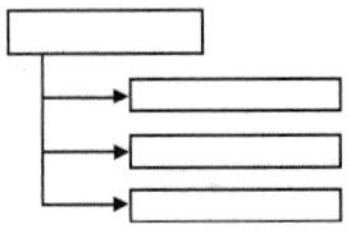

Like the sea floor, continents also spread apart at a divergent boundary. The boundary begins to form when hot material rises from deep in the mantle. This heat causes the crust to bulge upward. The crust cracks as it is stretched, and a rift valley forms, as shown in the diagram below. Magma rises through the cracked, thinned crust, forming volcanoes. As the rift valley grows wider, the continent begins to split apart.

If the rift valley continues to widen, the thinned valley floor sinks lower and lower until it is below sea level. Water from nearby oceans or rivers may fill the valley and form a sea or a lake. In the Middle East, for example, the Arabian Plate and African Plate have been moving apart for several million years. Over time, the waters of the Indian Ocean gradually filled the rift valley, forming the Red Sea. This sea is slowly getting wider as the plates continue to move apart.

CHECK YOUR READING What happens when the floor of a rift valley sinks below sea level?

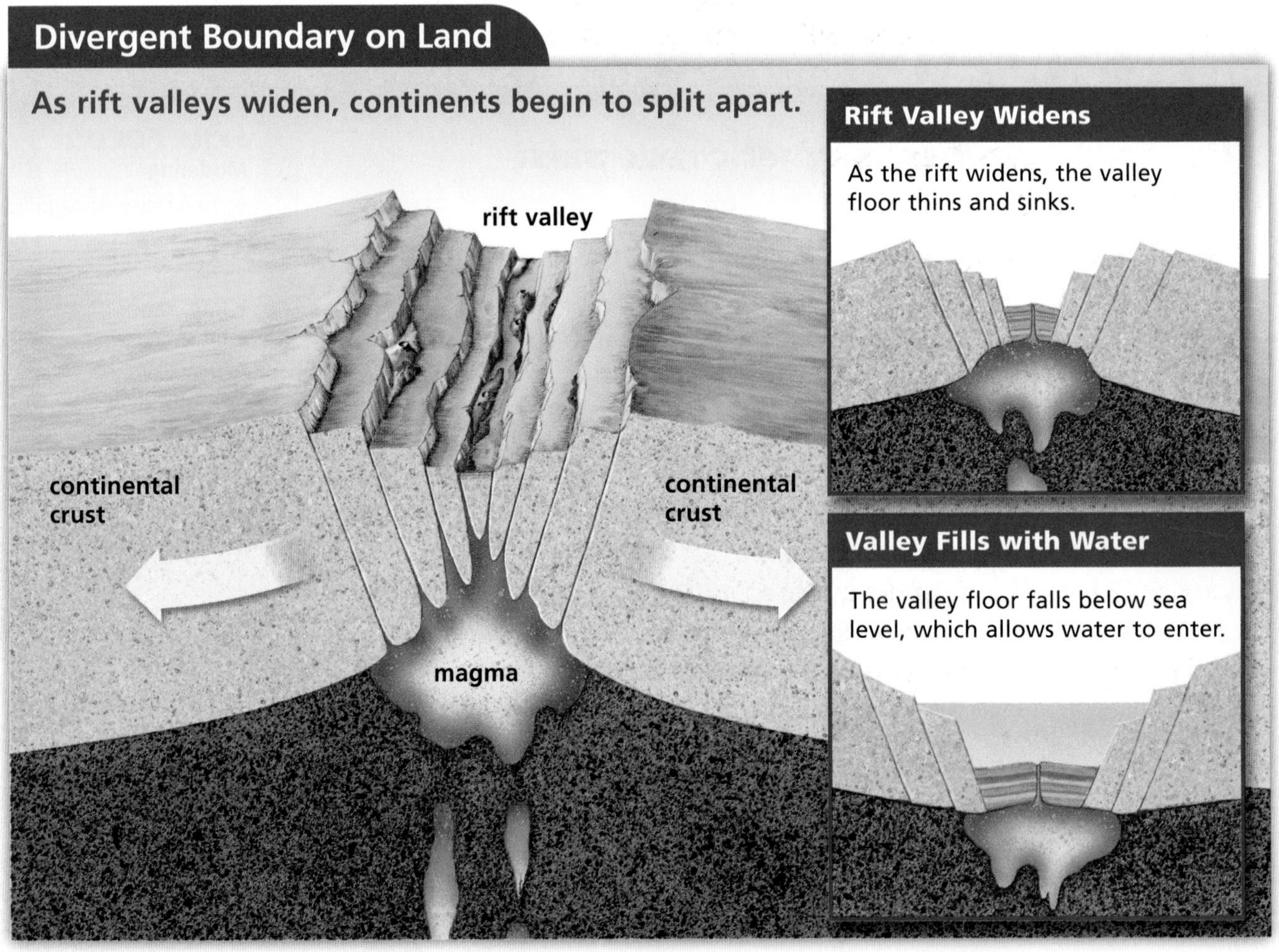

Divergent Boundary on Land

As rift valleys widen, continents begin to split apart.

rift valley

continental crust

continental crust

magma

Rift Valley Widens

As the rift widens, the valley floor thins and sinks.

Valley Fills with Water

The valley floor falls below sea level, which allows water to enter.

The Great Rift Valley in eastern Africa, shown in the photograph above, is a good example of a continental rift valley. It is getting wider as the African Plate splits apart. This huge valley is thousands of kilometers long and as much as 1800 meters (5900 ft) deep.

PREDICT Rift valleys, like the Great Rift Valley in Africa, occur where plates are moving apart. What will happen to the Rift Valley when it gets low enough?

Hot spots can be used to track plate movements.

In some places, called **hot spots,** heated rock rises in plumes, or thin columns, from the mantle. Volcanoes often develop above the plume. Although most hot spots occur far from plate boundaries, they offer a way to measure plate movement. This is because a hot spot generally stays in one place while the tectonic plate above it keeps moving.

At a hot spot, the heat from the plume partly melts some of the rock in the tectonic plate above it. It is like holding a candle under a wax tablet. Eventually, the wax above the flame will melt. Likewise, if the plate stays over the hot spot long enough, the rock above it will melt.

In time, a volcano will form at the surface of the plate. The volcano may become high enough to rise above the sea as an island. For example, the Hawaiian Islands are being built as the Pacific Plate moves slowly over a hot spot.

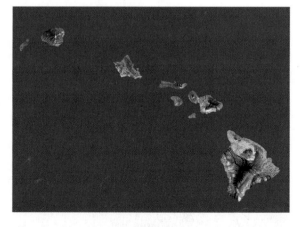

The Hawaiian islands are located in the middle of the Pacific Plate. The largest island, Hawaii, is still over the hot spot.

Hot Spots

Tectonic plates move over hot spots in the mantle.

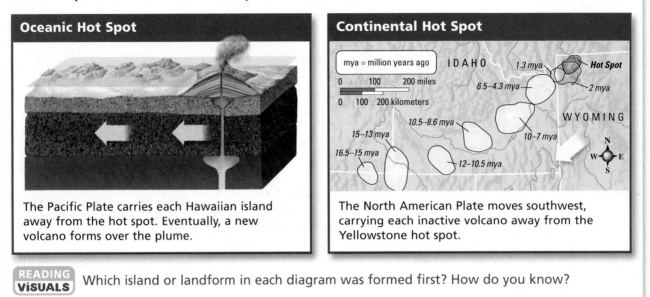

Oceanic Hot Spot

The Pacific Plate carries each Hawaiian island away from the hot spot. Eventually, a new volcano forms over the plume.

Continental Hot Spot

mya = million years ago

IDAHO

0   100   200 miles

0   100   200 kilometers

1.3 mya
6.5–4.3 mya
2 mya
Hot Spot

WYOMING

10.5–8.6 mya
15–13 mya
10–7 mya
16.5–15 mya
12–10.5 mya

N W E S

The North American Plate moves southwest, carrying each inactive volcano away from the Yellowstone hot spot.

READING VISUALS Which island or landform in each diagram was formed first? How do you know?

When the plate moves on, it carries the first volcano away from the hot spot. Heat from the mantle plume will then melt the rock at a new site, forming a new volcano. The diagram on the left shows this process.

Many hot spots provide a fixed point that scientists can use to measure the speed and direction of plate movements. For example, the Yellowstone hot spot under the North American Plate has formed a chain of inactive volcanoes, as shown in the diagram on the right. Scientists estimate that the North American Plate is moving southwest at about 2.3 cm (1 in.) per year.

CHECK YOUR READING How does a hot-spot volcano form?

1.3 Review

KEY CONCEPTS

1. Name and describe the three types of plate movements.

2. Create a two-column chart with the headings: Divergent boundary; Features. Fill in the chart for divergent boundaries at sea and on land.

3. How are hot spots used to track plate motion?

CRITICAL THINKING

4. **Predict** Suppose a magnetic reversal occurred today. How would new rocks at mid-ocean ridges differ from rocks that formed last year?

5. **Infer** A huge crack runs through Iceland, an island that lies above the Mid-Ocean Ridge. What do you think is happening to this country?

CHALLENGE

6. **Hypothesize** Look carefully at the diagram above and the Hawaiian Islands picture on page 27. Notice that some hot spot islands or landforms are larger than other islands or landforms in the same chain. Develop a hypothesis, based on plate movement, that might explain this fact.

MATH TUTORIAL
CLASSZONE.COM
Click on Math Tutorial for more help with rates.

Tracking Tectonic Plates

Scientists use lasers to track the movements of tectonic plates. They bounce laser light off satellites and measure the distance from each satellite to the ground. As the plates move, the distance changes. With this tracking system, scientists know exactly how much tectonic plates move each year.

You can use equivalent rates to predict how far two divergent plates will move over a given time. A rate is a ratio of two measures expressed in different units, such as

$$\frac{10 \text{ cm}}{4 \text{ yr}}$$

This 0.61-meter-wide satellite is covered with mirrors to reflect laser light back to Earth.

Example

If Boston, Massachusetts, and Lisbon, Portugal, are moving apart at an average rate of 10 cm every 4 years, how much farther apart will they move in 20 years?

Solution

Write an equivalent rate.

$$\frac{10 \text{ cm}}{4 \text{ yr}} = \frac{?}{20 \text{ yr}}$$

> Divide 20 yr by 4 yr to get 5, then multiply 10 cm by 5.

$$20 \div 4 = 5$$
$$10 \times 5 = 50$$

$$\frac{10 \text{ cm}}{4 \text{ yr}} = \frac{50 \text{ cm}}{20 \text{ yr}}$$

ANSWER Boston and Lisbon will move 50 centimeters farther apart in 10 years.

Answer the following questions.

1. If New York, New York, and London, England, are moving apart at an average rate of 5 cm every 2 years, how much farther apart will they move in 8 years?

2. If Miami, Florida, and Casablanca, Morocco, are moving apart at an average rate of 25 cm every 10 years, how much farther apart will they move in 30 years?

3. If Portland, Maine, and Dublin, Ireland, are moving apart at an average rate of 50 cm every 20 years, how much farther apart will they move in 10 years?

CHALLENGE If Halifax, Nova Scotia, and Birmingham, England, are moving apart at an average rate of 5 cm every 2 years, how long will it take them to move 35 cm farther apart?

Arabian Plate

Red Sea

African Plate

This satellite photograph shows where the Arabian Plate and the African Plate are moving apart. As a result, the Red Sea is slowly growing wider.

1.4 Plates converge or scrape past each other.

◀ BEFORE, you learned

- Plates move apart at divergent boundaries
- In the oceans, divergent boundaries mark where the sea floor spreads apart
- On land, continents split apart at divergent boundaries

▶ NOW, you will learn

- What happens when two continental plates converge
- What happens when an oceanic plate converges with another plate
- What happens when one plate scrapes past another plate

VOCABULARY

subduction p. 30
continental-continental collision p. 31
oceanic-oceanic subduction p. 32
oceanic-continental subduction p. 33

EXPLORE Tectonic Plates

What happens when tectonic plates collide?

PROCEDURE

1. Arrange six square napkins in two rows.
2. Slowly push the two rows of napkins together. Observe what happens.

WHAT DO YOU THINK?
- In what ways did the napkin edges move?
- How might your observations relate to the movement of tectonic plates?

MATERIALS
6 square napkins

Tectonic plates push together at convergent boundaries.

You read earlier that new crust forms at divergent boundaries where plates move apart. At convergent boundaries, where plates push together, crust is either folded or destroyed.

When two plates with continental crust collide, they will crumple and fold the rock between them. A plate with older, denser oceanic crust will sink beneath another plate. The crust melts in the asthenosphere and is destroyed. When one plate sinks beneath another, it is called **subduction.** The word is based on the Latin prefix *sub-,* meaning "under," and the Latin *ducere,* meaning "to lead." Therefore, subduction is a process in which one plate is "led under" another.

There are three types of convergent boundaries: where two continental plates meet, where two oceanic plates meet, or where an oceanic plate and a continental plate meet. Major geologic events occur at all three types of boundaries.

VOCABULARY
Remember to make a description wheel for the terms in this section.

Continental-Continental Collision

A **continental-continental collision** occurs where two plates carrying continental crust push together. Because both crusts are the same density, neither plate can sink beneath the other. If the plates keep moving, their edges crumple and fold, as in the diagram below.

You can see the same effect if you put two blocks of clay on a table and push them together. If you push hard enough, one or both of the blocks will buckle. One cannot sink under the other, so the clay folds under the pressure.

In some cases, the folded crust can be pushed up high enough to form mountains. Some of the world's largest mountains appear along continent-continent boundaries. For instance, the European Alps, shown in the photograph at right, are found where the African and European plates are colliding. The tallest mountains in the world, the Himalayas, first formed when the Indian Plate began colliding with the European Plate.

The Himalayas and the Alps are still forming today. As long as the plates keep moving, these mountains will keep rising higher.

The European Alps began rising nearly 40 million years ago as a section of the African Plate collided with the European Plate.

CHECK YOUR READING Explain how colliding plates form mountain ranges.

Convergent Boundary—Collision

Rocks crumple and fold to form mountains.

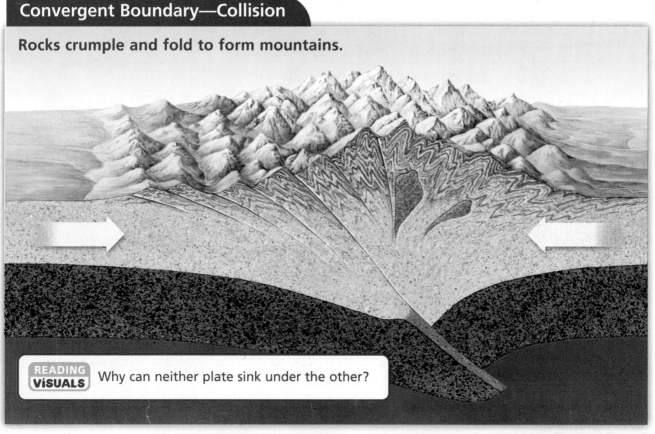

READING VISUALS Why can neither plate sink under the other?

Oceanic-Oceanic Subduction

An **oceanic-oceanic subduction** occurs where one plate with oceanic crust sinks, or subducts, under another plate with oceanic crust. The older plate sinks because it is colder and denser than the younger plate. When the older crust reaches the asthenosphere, it melts in the intense heat. Two main features form at oceanic-oceanic subductions: deep-ocean trenches and island arcs.

Deep-Ocean Trenches These trenches are like deep canyons that form in the ocean floor as a plate sinks. Most deep-ocean trenches are found in the Pacific Ocean. For example, at the Mariana Trench, the Pacific Plate is sinking under the Philippine Plate. This trench is the deepest place in the world's oceans, extending nearly 11,000 meters (36,000 ft) into the sea floor.

Island Arcs There are chains of volcanic islands that form on the top plate, parallel to a deep-ocean trench. As oceanic crust of the sinking plate melts, magma rises through the top plate. Over time, the flows build up a series of islands. Island arcs include the Philippine Islands, the Aleutian Islands of Alaska, and the islands of Japan.

Convergent Boundaries—Subduction

Sinking plates form deep-ocean trenches, island arcs, and coastal mountains.

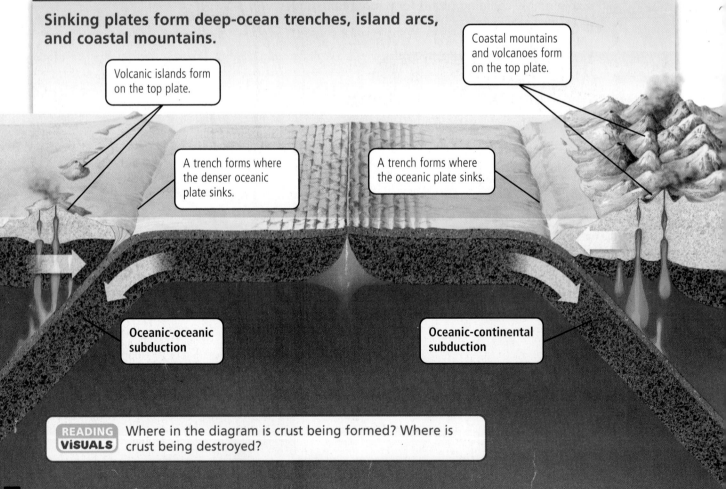

Volcanic islands form on the top plate.

Coastal mountains and volcanoes form on the top plate.

A trench forms where the denser oceanic plate sinks.

A trench forms where the oceanic plate sinks.

Oceanic-oceanic subduction

Oceanic-continental subduction

READING VISUALS Where in the diagram is crust being formed? Where is crust being destroyed?

Oceanic-Continental Subduction

An **oceanic-continental subduction** occurs when ocean crust sinks under continental crust, as shown in the diagram on page 32. The oceanic crust sinks because it is colder and denser than the continental crust. At these sites, deep-ocean trenches also form, along with coastal mountains.

Deep-Ocean Trenches Some of the world's youngest trenches are in the eastern Pacific Ocean. Here, for example, the Pacific Plate is sinking under the North American Plate. As the oceanic crust moves, it often causes underwater earthquakes.

Coastal Mountains As oceanic crust sinks under a continent, the continental crust buckles to form a range of mountains. These mountains, like island arcs, parallel a deep-ocean trench. As the diagram on page 32 shows, some of these mountains are volcanoes, which form as melted oceanic crust rises through the top plate.

The Cascade Mountains in Oregon and Washington are an example of coastal mountains. They began forming as the Juan de Fuca Plate began sinking under the North American Plate. Some of these peaks, such as Mount St. Helens in Washington, are active volcanoes.

VISUALIZATION
CLASSZONE.COM
Explore what happens along plate boundaries.

CHECK YOUR READING Why do deep-ocean trenches form at both types of subduction?

INVESTIGATE Convergent Boundaries

How can you model converging plates?

Tectonic plates move so slowly and are so large that it may be hard to visualize exactly how they move. Use what you know to design models showing how converging plates collide and subduct.

DESIGN
— YOUR OWN —

PROCEDURE

(1) Design your models using the materials listed. You can use the diagrams on pages 31–32 as a guide.

(2) Add more clay to your models if you need it.

WHAT DO YOU THINK?

• Describe how your models worked. You can draw a picture of each model to go along with your description.

• How well did your models represent each type of zone? Did each model work? Why or why not?

• How would you modify your designs now that you have seen the results?

SKILL FOCUS
Designing models

MATERIALS
• clay in three or more colors
• poster board
• marker pens

TIME
30 minutes

Tectonic plates scrape past each other at transform boundaries.

You learned that crust is formed at a divergent boundary and folded or destroyed at a convergent boundary. However, at a transform boundary, crust is neither formed nor destroyed. Here, two plates move past each other in opposite directions, as shown in the diagram below. As the plates move, their edges scrape and grind against each other.

This long crack in the earth reveals the transform boundary known as the San Andreas Fault.

Transform boundaries occur mostly on the sea floor near mid-ocean ridges. They also occur on land, where some are clearly visible as long cracks in Earth's surface. The San Andreas Fault in California is a transform boundary that runs from the Gulf of California through the San Francisco area. It marks where the Pacific Plate and part of the North American Plate are moving in opposite directions. If the plates keep moving at their present rate, Los Angeles will be a suburb of San Francisco in about 10 million years.

 CHECK YOUR READING What makes the San Andreas Fault a transform boundary?

Transform Boundary

Plate edges grind and scrape past each other. Crust is neither formed nor destroyed.

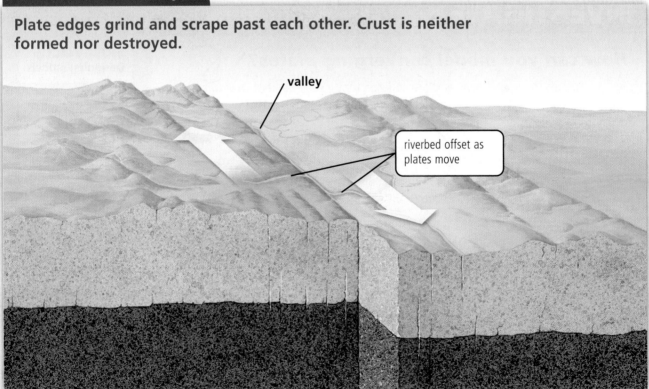

valley

riverbed offset as plates move

Tectonic Plate Boundaries

There are three types of plate boundaries: transform, divergent, and convergent. Major geologic events occur at all three types.

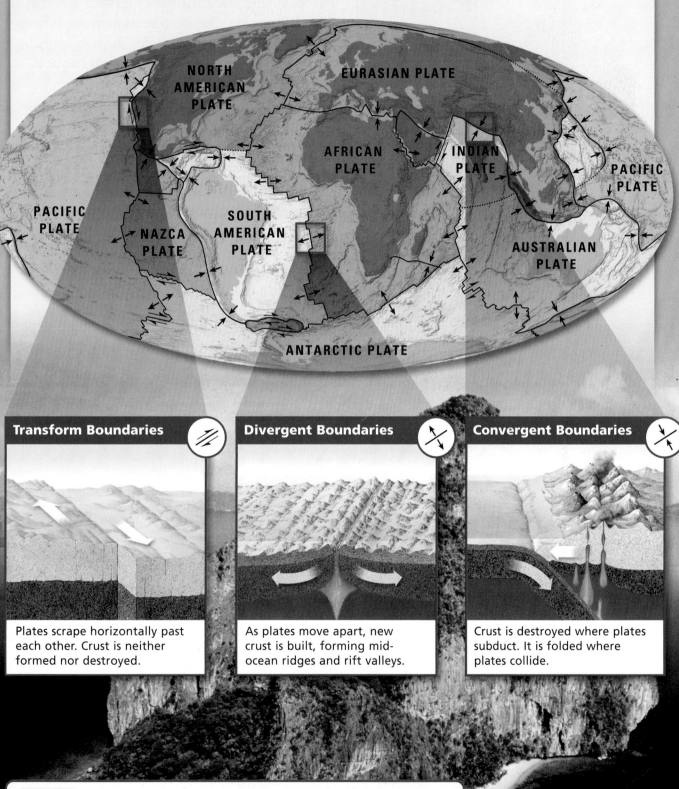

NORTH AMERICAN PLATE

EURASIAN PLATE

AFRICAN PLATE

INDIAN PLATE

PACIFIC PLATE

PACIFIC PLATE

NAZCA PLATE

SOUTH AMERICAN PLATE

AUSTRALIAN PLATE

ANTARCTIC PLATE

Transform Boundaries

Plates scrape horizontally past each other. Crust is neither formed nor destroyed.

Divergent Boundaries

As plates move apart, new crust is built, forming mid-ocean ridges and rift valleys.

Convergent Boundaries

Crust is destroyed where plates subduct. It is folded where plates collide.

READING VISUALS Where else on the map above can you find a transform, divergent, and convergent boundary?

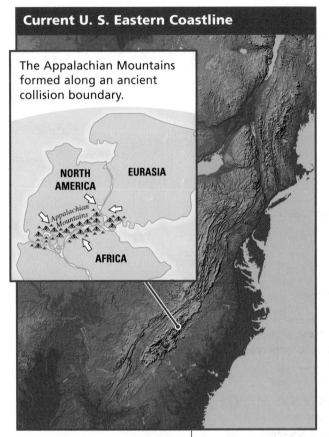

Current U. S. Eastern Coastline

The Appalachian Mountains formed along an ancient collision boundary.

NORTH AMERICA

EURASIA

Appalachian Mountains

AFRICA

The theory of plate tectonics helps geologists today.

The theory of plate tectonics changed the way that scientists view Earth. They learned that the planet's lithosphere has been in motion for millions of years. Today, the theory helps them to explain Earth's past and to predict what might happen along plate boundaries in the future.

By studying rock layers and using the theory, geologists can uncover the history of any region on Earth. For example, in the eastern United States, the deformed and folded rocks in the Appalachian Mountains are evidence of an ancient convergent boundary. Geologists discovered that these rocks are the same type and age as rocks in northwest Africa. These facts reveal that the mountains formed when North America collided with Africa and Eurasia as part of Pangaea. Where the plates eventually pulled apart, the rift valleys formed part of the current U. S. eastern coastline.

The theory of plate tectonics also gives scientists a way to study and predict geologic events. Scientists can predict, for example, that there are likely to be more earthquakes where plates slide past each other. They can look for volcanic activity where plates are sinking beneath other plates. And they can predict that mountains will continue to rise where plates push together.

 CHECK YOUR READING What future events can scientists predict using the theory of plate tectonics? Give two examples.

1.4 Review

KEY CONCEPTS

1. What are the three types of convergent boundaries?

2. Describe what happens at a transform boundary.

3. Why is the theory of plate tectonics so important to geologists?

CRITICAL THINKING

4. **Compare and Contrast** Use a Venn diagram to compare and contrast oceanic-oceanic and oceanic-continental subduction boundaries.

5. **Interpreting Visuals** Look again at the map on page 35. Identify the plates and type of boundary that formed the Andes Mountains on the west coast of South America.

○ CHALLENGE

6. **Synthesize** Sketch a diagram of the following landscape and label all the features. A plate with oceanic crust is sinking beneath a plate with continental crust. Further inland on the continent, a transform boundary can be seen in Earth's crust.

What on Earth Is Happening Here?

When tectonic plates move, they cause major changes in Earth's surface. Among other things, the earth shakes, magma erupts on the surface, crust is built or destroyed, and mountains or islands form. Read the observations about plate movements below, then evaluate the conclusions given.

▶ Observations

Scientists made these observations about a region known for the movement of two major tectonic plates.

a. The region is on the coast of a landmass.

b. Along the coast is a deep-ocean trench.

c. The mountains on the coast are volcanic.

d. A line connecting these mountains is fairly straight.

e. The mountains are getting higher.

f. Far out at sea, a mid-ocean ridge is forming.

▶ Conclusions

Here are three possible conclusions about the movement of tectonic plates in the region.

- One plate is pulling away from the other.
- One plate is sinking under the other.
- One plate is scraping past the other.

▶ Evaluate Each Conclusion

On Your Own Decide how well the observations support each conclusion. Note any observations that indicate that a conclusion is not justified.

As a Group Decide which conclusion is most reasonable. Discuss your ideas in a small group, and see if the group can agree.

CHALLENGE What further observations would support or weaken each conclusion? How could you make these observations? What other phenomena might this conclusion help explain?

A volcanic coastal mountain spews out ash.

RESOURCE CENTER
CLASSZONE.COM

Learn more about the effects of plate movement.

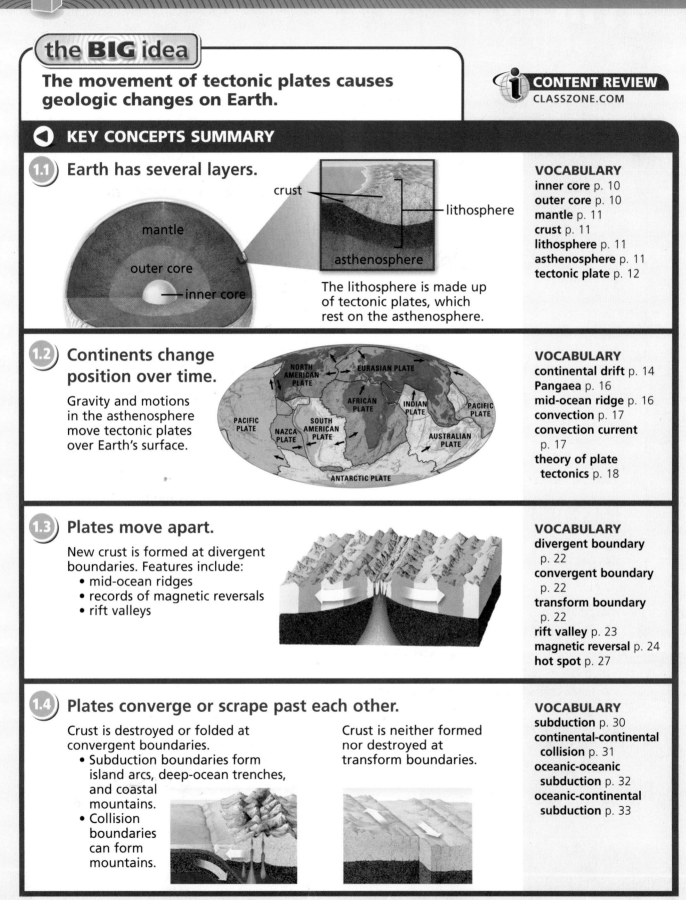

the **BIG** idea

The movement of tectonic plates causes geologic changes on Earth.

CONTENT REVIEW
CLASSZONE.COM

◀ KEY CONCEPTS SUMMARY

1.1 Earth has several layers.

crust
lithosphere
mantle
outer core
inner core
asthenosphere

The lithosphere is made up of tectonic plates, which rest on the asthenosphere.

VOCABULARY
inner core p. 10
outer core p. 10
mantle p. 11
crust p. 11
lithosphere p. 11
asthenosphere p. 11
tectonic plate p. 12

1.2 Continents change position over time.

Gravity and motions in the asthenosphere move tectonic plates over Earth's surface.

NORTH AMERICAN PLATE
EURASIAN PLATE
AFRICAN PLATE
INDIAN PLATE
PACIFIC PLATE
PACIFIC PLATE
NAZCA PLATE
SOUTH AMERICAN PLATE
AUSTRALIAN PLATE
ANTARCTIC PLATE

VOCABULARY
continental drift p. 14
Pangaea p. 16
mid-ocean ridge p. 16
convection p. 17
convection current p. 17
theory of plate tectonics p. 18

1.3 Plates move apart.

New crust is formed at divergent boundaries. Features include:
• mid-ocean ridges
• records of magnetic reversals
• rift valleys

VOCABULARY
divergent boundary p. 22
convergent boundary p. 22
transform boundary p. 22
rift valley p. 23
magnetic reversal p. 24
hot spot p. 27

1.4 Plates converge or scrape past each other.

Crust is destroyed or folded at convergent boundaries.
• Subduction boundaries form island arcs, deep-ocean trenches, and coastal mountains.
• Collision boundaries can form mountains.

Crust is neither formed nor destroyed at transform boundaries.

VOCABULARY
subduction p. 30
continental-continental collision p. 31
oceanic-oceanic subduction p. 32
oceanic-continental subduction p. 33

Reviewing Vocabulary

Make a magnet word diagram for each of the vocabulary terms listed below. Write the term in the magnet. Write other terms or ideas related to it on the lines around the magnet.

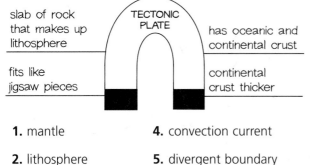

slab of rock that makes up lithosphere

TECTONIC PLATE

has oceanic and continental crust

fits like jigsaw pieces

continental crust thicker

1. mantle

2. lithosphere

3. mid-ocean ridge

4. convection current

5. divergent boundary

6. convergent boundary

Reviewing Key Concepts

Multiple Choice *Choose the letter of the best answer.*

7. Which of the following best describes Earth's mantle?
   a. the densest of Earth's layers
   b. the home of all life on Earth
   c. the thickest layer of hot rock
   d. the thinnest and hottest layer

8. Tectonic plates make up Earth's
   a. lower mantle
   b. lithosphere
   c. asthenosphere
   d. inner core

9. Why did many scientists reject Wegener's continental drift hypothesis?
   a. He could not explain how the continents moved.
   b. The geology of continents did not support his hypothesis.
   c. Fossil evidence showed that the continents were never joined.
   d. The climates of the continents have remained the same.

10. What evidence from the sea floor shows that tectonic plates move?
    a. The sea floor is much older than any of the continents.
    b. The sea floor is youngest near a mid-ocean ridge and older farther away.
    c. Mid-ocean ridges circle Earth like seams in a baseball.
    d. The sea floor is thinner than continental crust.

11. A mid-ocean ridge forms where plates
    a. move apart   c. scrape past each other
    b. push together   d. subduct

12. Plate motion is caused partly by
    a. magnetic reversals
    b. convection currents
    c. continental drift
    d. volcanic hot spots

13. Which of the following is formed at a collision zone?
    a. mountain range
    b. volcanic island chain
    c. deep-ocean trench
    d. continental rift valley

14. What happens when two oceanic plates meet?
    a. Both plates sink into the asthenosphere.
    b. The colder, denser plate sinks.
    c. Both plates fold the rock between them.
    d. One plate slides past the other.

15. Where is crust neither formed nor destroyed?
    a. mid-ocean ridge
    b. continental rift valley
    c. transform boundary
    d. subduction zone

Short Answer *Write a short answer to each question.*

16. How does the theory of plate tectonics help geologists predict future geologic events?

17. How do rocks record changes in Earth's magnetic field?

18. Explain what happens when a continental plate splits apart.

Thinking Critically

Use the diagram to answer the questions below.

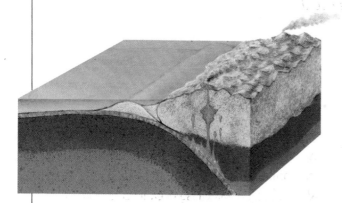

19. ANALYZE Write your own explanation of how the coastal mountains formed.

20. PREDICT Would you expect the volcanoes on this coastline to continue to be active? Why or why not?

21. APPLY Looking at the map above, why do you think the coastal mountains are in a fairly straight line?

22. APPLY On the map above, where would you expect to find a deep ocean trench? Why?

23. APPLY A friend looks at the diagram and tells you that there should be an island arc forming off the coast. Use your own knowledge and the map above to support or reject your friend's statement.

24. SYNTHESIZE On a separate piece of paper, extend the diagram to the left. Draw the type of plate boundary that someone might find far out at sea.

25. PREDICT Will the Andes Mountains on the west coast of South America become taller or shorter in the future? Use the theory of plate tectonics to explain your answer.

APPLY Copy the chart below. Fill in the type of boundary—divergent, convergent, or transform—where each formation is likely to appear.

Formation	Type of Boundary
26. Mid-ocean ridge	
27. Volcanic island arc	
28. Rift valley on land	
29. Mountains	
30. Deep-ocean trench	
31. Hot-spot volcano	

the BIG idea

32. IDENTIFY CAUSE AND EFFECT Look again at the photograph on pages 6–7. Now that you have finished the chapter, explain what may be forming this crack in Earth's surface.

33. PREDICT Use the map on page 19, which shows Earth's tectonic plates and the directions in which they are moving. Based on the plate movements, where do you think the continents might be in a few million years? Draw a map that illustrates your prediction. You might want to give your landmasses names.

UNIT PROJECTS

If you are doing a unit project, make a folder for your project. Include in your folder a list of the resources you will need, the date on which the project is due, and a schedule to keep track of your progress. Begin gathering data.

Standardized Test Practice

For practice o
state test, go
TEST PRAC
CLASSZONE.CO

Analyzing a Diagram

The diagram shows several tectonic plates. The arrows indicate the direction each plate is moving. Study the diagram and answer the questions below.

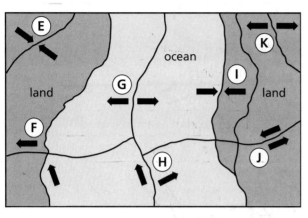

1. Where is an ocean trench most likely to form?

a. F   c. H

b. G   d. I

2. Where is a continental rift valley most likely to form?

a. E   c. J

b. F   d. K

3. Where would you find a convergent boundary?

a. E   c. H

b. F   d. K

4. Where is a mid-ocean ridge most likely to form?

a. G   c. I

b. H   d. F

5. What is a good example of a transform boundary?

a. E   c. J

b. I   d. K

6. Which is most likely to happen at I?

a. Island arcs will form parallel to a trench.

b. A spreading center will create a rift valley.

c. Continental crust will be destroyed.

d. Subduction will cause oceanic crust to melt.

7. Why are earthquakes likely to occur at J?

a. Two plates are spreading away from each other.

b. Two plates are colliding with each other.

c. Two plates are scraping past each other.

d. One plate is sliding under another plate.

8. Why are mountains likely to form at E?

a. A rift valley is forming.

b. Two plates are colliding.

c. Magma is flowing upward.

d. One plate is sinking.

9. Which is most likely to happen at G?

a. Rising magma will create new crust.

b. Subduction will cause a deep trench.

c. Colliding plates will cause rocks to crumple.

d. Moving plates will create island arcs.

Extended Response

Answer the two questions below in detail. Include some of the terms shown in the word box. In your answer, underline each term you use.

tectonic plates	subduction	magma	crust
continental drift	hot spot	mantle	

10. Two island chains are separated by a deep ocean trench. Although they are close to each other, the islands have very different fossils and types of rock. Explain why these island chains have such different geologic features.

11. Andrea lives near a chain of mountains located far from plate boundaries. The closest mountain is an active volcano. The other mountains used to be volcanoes. The farther away a mountain is in the chain, the older it is. Explain these facts.

2 Earthquakes

the **BIG** idea

Earthquakes release stress that has built up in rocks.

Key Concepts

SECTION

2.1 Earthquakes occur along faults.
Learn how rocks move along different kinds of faults.

SECTION

2.2 Earthquakes release energy.
Learn how energy from an earthquake is used to determine its location and size.

SECTION

2.3 Earthquake damage can be reduced.
Learn how structures are built to better withstand earthquakes.

Internet Preview

CLASSZONE.COM

Chapter 2 online resources: Content Review, two Visualizations, three Resource Centers, Math Tutorial, Test Practice

What caused these rails to bend, and how long did it take?

EXPLORE (the **BIG** idea)

Can You Bend Energy?

Put a clear glass filled with water on a table. Holding a flashlight at an angle to the glass, shine light through the water so that an oval of light forms on the table.

Observe and Think Did the light, which is a form of energy, travel in a straight line through the layers of air and water? Do you think other forms of energy travel in straight lines through layers inside Earth?

How Can Something Move Forward, Yet Sideways?

Put a stack of cards on a table and hold them as shown in the photograph. Slide the entire stack forward, tilting your fingers from side to side to fan the cards back and forth.

Observe and Think Compare the direction of movement of the entire stack of cards with the directions of movement of individual cards. How might this be similar to how energy can travel in waves?

Internet Activity: Earthquakes

Go to **ClassZone.com** to see maps of recent earthquakes around the world, in the United States, and in your own area.

Observe and Think Where and when did the largest earthquakes occur?

NSTA
scilinks.org
SCI LINKS

Earthquakes **Code: MDL053**

Getting Ready to Learn

◀ CONCEPT REVIEW

- Earth's lithosphere is broken into tectonic plates.
- Tectonic plates pull apart, push together, and scrape past one another.
- Major geologic events occur along tectonic plate boundaries.

◀ VOCABULARY REVIEW

lithosphere p. 11

tectonic plate p. 12

mid-ocean ridge p. 16

subduction p. 30

 **CONTENT REVIEW**
CLASSZONE.COM
Review concepts and vocabulary.

▶ TAKING NOTES

MAIN IDEA AND DETAIL NOTES

Make a two-column chart. Write the main ideas, such as those in the blue headings, in the column on the left. Write details about each of those main ideas in the column on the right.

VOCABULARY STRATEGY

For each vocabulary term, make a **magnet word** diagram. Write other terms or ideas related to that term around it.

See the Note-Taking Handbook on pages R45–R51.

SCIENCE NOTEBOOK

MAIN IDEAS	DETAIL NOTES
1. Rocks move along faults.	1. Blocks of rock can move past one another slowly and constantly.
	1. Blocks of rock can get stuck and then break free, causing earthquakes.
2. Most faults are located along tectonic plate boundaries.	2.
	2.
	2.

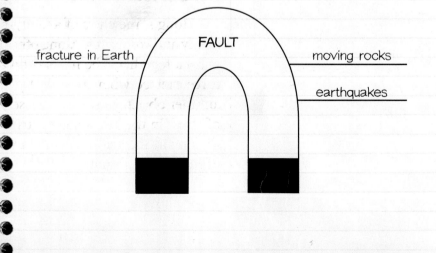

fracture in Earth   **FAULT**   moving rocks

earthquakes

2.1 Earthquakes occur along faults.

◀ **BEFORE, you learned**

- The crust and uppermost mantle make up the lithosphere
- The lithosphere is cold and rigid
- Tectonic plates move over hotter, weaker rock in the asthenosphere

▶ **NOW, you will learn**

- Why earthquakes occur
- Where most earthquakes occur
- How rocks move during earthquakes

VOCABULARY

fault p. 45
stress p. 45
earthquake p. 45

EXPLORE Pressure

How does pressure affect a solid material?

PROCEDURE

1. Hold a wooden craft stick at each end.
2. Bend the stick very slowly. Continue to put pressure on the stick until it breaks.

WHAT DO YOU THINK?

- How did the stick change before it broke?
- How might rocks react to pressure?

MATERIALS
wooden craft stick

VOCABULARY
Add magnet word diagrams for *fault, stress,* and *earthquake* to your notebook.

Rocks move along faults.

Sometimes when you pull on a drawer, it opens smoothly. At other times, the drawer sticks shut. If you pull hard enough, the drawer suddenly flies open. Rocks along faults behave in a similar way. A **fault** is a fracture, or break, in Earth's lithosphere, along which blocks of rock move past each other.

Along some parts of a fault, the rock on either side may slide along slowly and constantly. Along other parts of the fault, the rocks may stick, or lock together. The rocks bend as stress is put on them. **Stress** is the force exerted when an object presses on, pulls on, or pushes against another object. As stress increases, the rocks break free. A sudden release of stress in the lithosphere causes an earthquake. An **earthquake** is a shaking of the ground caused by the sudden movement of large blocks of rock along a fault.

Most faults are located along tectonic plate boundaries, so most earthquakes occur in these areas. However, the blocks of rock that move during an earthquake are much smaller than a tectonic plate. A plate boundary can be many thousands of kilometers long. During even a very powerful earthquake, blocks of rock might move only a few meters past each other along a distance of several hundred kilometers. The strength of an earthquake depends in part on

• how much stress builds up before the rocks move
• the distance the rocks move along the fault

About 80 percent of all earthquakes occur in a belt around the edges of the Pacific Ocean. In the United States, the best-known fault in this belt is the San Andreas (san an-DRAY-uhs) Fault in California. It forms part of the boundary between the North American Plate and the Pacific Plate. Unlike many other faults, parts of the San Andreas Fault can be seen on the surface of the ground.

A small percentage of earthquakes occur along faults within plates. As you read in Chapter 1, a tectonic plate is rigid. Therefore, stress along a plate's boundary can cause rocks to break and move along weak areas toward the middle of the plate.

Where Earthquakes Occur

This map shows the locations of moderate to intense earthquakes from 1993 through 2002.

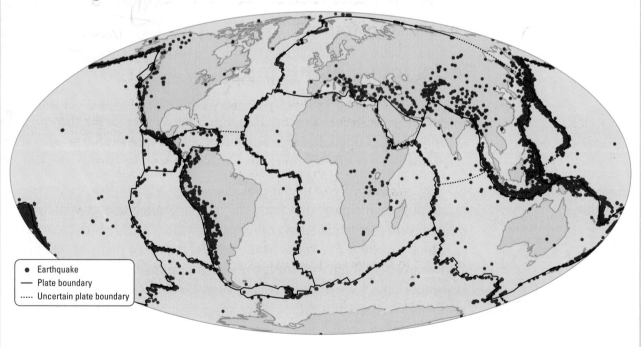

• Earthquake
— Plate boundary
..... Uncertain plate boundary

READING VISUALS   Why do most earthquakes in North America and South America occur near the continents' western coasts?

All earthquakes occur in the lithosphere. To understand why, you might compare a tectonic plate to a piece of cold, hard caramel. Like cold caramel, the plate is rigid and brittle. The rocks can break and move suddenly, causing an earthquake. Now compare the asthenosphere below the plate to warm, soft caramel. In the asthenosphere, hot rock bends and flows rather than breaks. A few earthquakes occur far below the normal depth of the lithosphere only because tectonic plates sinking in subduction zones are still cold enough to break.

 CHECK YOUR READING Why don't earthquakes occur in the asthenosphere?

Faults are classified by how rocks move.

The blocks of rock along different types of faults move in different directions, depending on the kinds of stress they are under. Scientists classify a fault according to the way the rocks on one side move with respect to the rocks on the other side.

The three main types of faults are normal faults, reverse faults, and strike-slip faults. More than one type of fault may be present along the same plate boundary. However, the type of fault that is most common along a boundary depends on whether plates are pulling apart, pushing together, or scraping past one another at that boundary.

MAIN IDEA AND DETAILS Record information about each type of fault in your notebook.

INVESTIGATE Faults

How can rocks move along faults?

PROCEDURE

1. Place one triangular block of wood against the other to form a rectangle.

2. Put two pieces of masking tape across both blocks. Draw a different pattern on each piece of tape. Break the tape where it crosses the blocks.

3. Keep the blocks in contact and slide one block along the other.

4. Repeat step 3 until you find three different ways the blocks can move relative to each other. Draw diagrams showing how the blocks moved. Include the tape patterns.

WHAT DO YOU THINK?

- How can you use the tape patterns to find the relative directions in which the blocks were moved?

- In each case, what sort of stress (such as pulling) did you put on the blocks?

CHALLENGE Compare the ways you moved the blocks with the ways tectonic plates move at their boundaries.

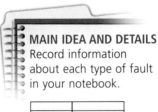

SKILL FOCUS
Modeling

MATERIALS
- 2 triangular blocks of wood
- masking tape
- marker

TIME
15 minutes

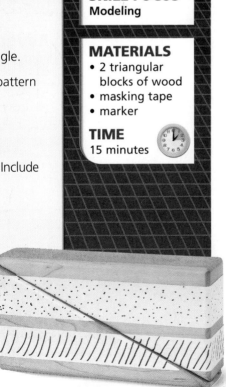

READING TiP

The word *plane* comes from the Latin word *planum,* which means "flat surface."

The illustrations on this page and page 49 show that a fault forms a plane that extends both horizontally and vertically. Blocks of rock move along the fault plane during an earthquake. Along a normal or reverse fault, the movement of the blocks is mainly vertical—the blocks move up or down. Along a strike-slip fault, the movement is horizontal—the blocks move sideways.

Normal Faults

Along a normal fault, the block of rock above the fault plane slides down relative to the other block. Stress that pulls rocks apart causes normal faults. Earthquakes along normal faults are common near boundaries where tectonic plates are moving apart, such as in the Great Rift Valley of Africa.

READING TiP

Compare the directions of the arrows in the diagrams with the directions of the arrows on the photographs.

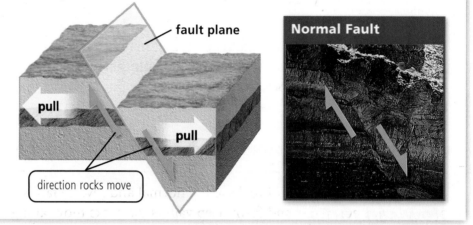

As rocks are pulled apart (white arrows), normal faults form. The block on the right has moved down with respect to the block on the left.

fault plane

pull

pull

direction rocks move

Normal Fault

Reverse Faults

Along a reverse fault, the block of rock above the fault plane moves up relative to the other block. Stress that presses rocks together causes reverse faults. These faults can occur near collision-zone boundaries

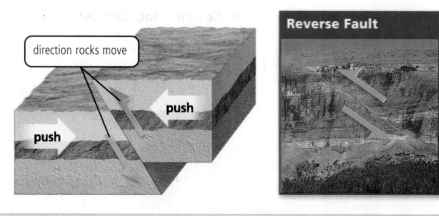

As rocks are pushed together (white arrows), reverse faults form. The block on the right has moved up with respect to the block on the left.

direction rocks move

push

push

Reverse Fault

between plates. The Himalaya Mountains, which rise in the area where the Indian Plate is pushing into the Eurasian Plate, have many earthquakes along reverse faults.

○ CHECK YOUR READING What type of stress produces reverse faults?

Strike-Slip Faults

Along a strike-slip fault, blocks of rock move sideways on either side of the fault plane. Stresses that push blocks of rock horizontally cause earthquakes along strike-slip faults. These faults can occur where plates scrape past each other. The San Andreas Fault is a strike-slip fault.

VISUALIZATION
CLASSZONE.COM
Explore animations showing fault motion.

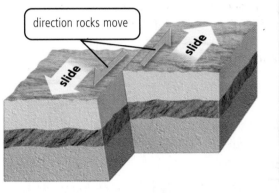

As rocks are pushed horizontally in opposite directions, strike-slip faults form. The block on the right has moved to the right with respect to the block on the left.

direction rocks move

slide

slide

Strike-Slip Fault

Over time, movement of rocks along normal and reverse faults can push up mountains and form deep valleys. As rocks move along strike-slip faults, rocks that were once in continuous layers can become separated by hundreds of kilometers.

2.1 Review

KEY CONCEPTS

1. What causes earthquakes?

2. Why do most earthquakes occur along tectonic plate boundaries?

3. What is the main direction of stress on blocks of rock at normal faults, reverse faults, and strike-slip faults?

CRITICAL THINKING

4. **Compare and Contrast** Make a chart showing the similarities and differences between normal and reverse faults.

5. **Connect** Japan is near a subduction zone. What type of faults would you expect to be responsible for many of the earthquakes there? Explain.

○ CHALLENGE

6. **Analyze** What evidence from rock layers could show a scientist that earthquakes had occurred in an area before written records were kept?

EXTREME SCIENCE

A landslide caused by the 1964 Alaskan earthquake tore this school in Anchorage apart. Fortunately, school was not in session.

In Anchorage, almost 120 km from the center of the earthquake, the ground shook for about three minutes, causing severe damage.

When Earth Shakes

Alaskan Earthquake Sinks Louisiana Boats

The most powerful earthquake ever recorded in the United States struck Prince William Sound in Alaska on March 27, 1964. Plates that had been moving a few centimeters per year lurched 9 meters (30 ft), causing the ground to shake for more than three minutes. When energy from the earthquake reached Louisiana, more than 5000 kilometers (3000 mi) away, it caused waves high enough to sink fishing boats in a harbor.

Wall of Water Higher than 20-Story Building

The 1964 Alaskan earthquake caused buildings to crumble and collapse. It also produced tsunamis—water waves caused by a sudden movement of the ground during an earthquake, landslide, or volcanic eruption. In Alaska's Valdez Inlet, a landslide triggered by the earthquake produced a tsunami 67 meters (220 ft) high—taller than a 20-story building.

Missouri Earthquakes Ring Massachusetts Bells

Earthquakes near New Madrid, Missouri, in 1811 and 1812 caused church bells in Boston, Massachusetts—nearly 1600 kilometers (1000 mi) away—to ring.

Five Largest Earthquakes Since 1900		
Location	Date	Moment Magnitude
Off the coast of Chile	1960	9.5
Prince William Sound, Alaska	1964	9.2
Andreanof Islands, Alaska	1957	9.1
Kamchatka Peninsula, Russia	1952	9.0
Off the coast of Sumatra	2004	9.0

Largest Earthquake Ever

The most powerful earthquake ever recorded hit Chile in 1960. This earthquake released almost 10 times as much energy as the 1964 earthquake in Alaska—and about 600 times the energy of the earthquake that destroyed much of San Francisco in 1906.

EXPLORE

1. **EXPLAIN** How were the 1964 Alaskan earthquake and the 1960 Chilean earthquake related to movements along tectonic plate boundaries?

2. **CHALLENGE** An inlet is a narrow body of water connected to a lake or ocean. Why might a tsunami be higher in an inlet than along the coastline around it?

2.2 Earthquakes release energy.

◀ BEFORE, you learned

- Most earthquakes occur along tectonic plate boundaries
- Different directions of stress cause normal, reverse, and strike-slip faults

▶ NOW, you will learn

- How energy from an earthquake travels through Earth
- How an earthquake's location is determined

VOCABULARY

seismic wave p. 51
focus p. 52
epicenter p. 52
seismograph p. 56

EXPLORE Movement of Energy

How does energy travel?

PROCEDURE

① On a flat surface, hold one end of a spring toy while a partner holds the other end. Stretch the spring, then squeeze some coils together and release them.

② Again, hold one end of the spring while your partner holds the other end. Shake your end of the spring back and forth.

MATERIALS
spring toy

WHAT DO YOU THINK?
- How did energy travel along the spring when you gathered and released some coils?
- How did energy travel along the spring when you shook one end back and forth?

Energy from earthquakes travels through Earth.

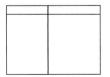

MAIN IDEA AND DETAILS
Record information about the energy released by earthquakes.

When you throw a rock into a pond, waves ripple outward from the spot where the rock hits the water. The energy released by an earthquake travels in a similar way through Earth. Unlike the pond ripples, though, earthquake energy travels outward in all directions—up, down, and to the sides. The energy travels as **seismic waves,** (SYZ-mihk) which are vibrations caused by earthquakes. Seismic waves from even small earthquakes can be recorded by sensitive instruments around the world.

All earthquakes start beneath Earth's surface. The **focus** of an earthquake is the point underground where rocks first begin to move. Seismic waves travel outward from the earthquake's focus. The **epicenter** (EHP-ih-SEHN-tuhr) is the point on Earth's surface directly above the focus. Scientists often name an earthquake after the city that is closest to its epicenter.

In general, if two earthquakes of equal strength have the same epicenter, the one with the shallower focus causes more damage. Seismic waves from a deep-focus earthquake lose more of their energy as they travel farther up to Earth's surface.

The depths of earthquakes along tectonic plate boundaries are related to the directions in which the plates move. For example, an earthquake along a mid-ocean spreading center has a shallow focus. There, the plates are pulling apart, and the new crust that forms is thin. Subduction zones have a wide range of earthquake depths, from shallow to very deep. Earthquakes can occur anywhere along the sinking plates.

Focus and Epicenter

Seismic waves spread out from the focus of an earthquake.

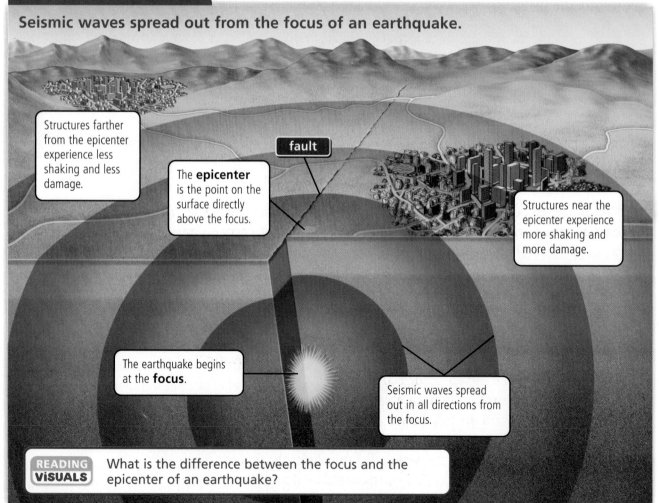

Structures farther from the epicenter experience less shaking and less damage.

fault

The **epicenter** is the point on the surface directly above the focus.

Structures near the epicenter experience more shaking and more damage.

The earthquake begins at the **focus**.

Seismic waves spread out in all directions from the focus.

READING VISUALS   What is the difference between the focus and the epicenter of an earthquake?

INVESTIGATE Subduction-Zone Earthquakes

Why are some earthquakes deeper than others?

PROCEDURE

1. Cut the first string into 4 pieces that are 4 cm long. Cut the second string into 3 pieces that are 8 cm long, and the third string into 4 pieces that are 15 cm long.

2. Use the key on the Earthquake Map to match string lengths with earthquake depths.

3. Tape one end of the pieces of string to the map at the earthquake locations, as shown in the photograph. Always cover the same amount of string with tape.

4. Hold the map upside down, with the strings hanging down. Observe the patterns of earthquake locations and depths.

WHAT DO YOU THINK?

- What patterns among the strings do you observe? How do you explain them?

- How might the earthquake depths relate to the sinking of a tectonic plate in a subduction zone?

CHALLENGE Draw a line on the map, showing where the subduction zone might be at Earth's surface. How might the depths of the earthquakes be different if the subduction zone were on the other side of the island?

SKILL FOCUS
Analyzing

MATERIALS
- different colors of string
- ruler
- scissors
- Earthquake Map
- tape

TIME
20 minutes

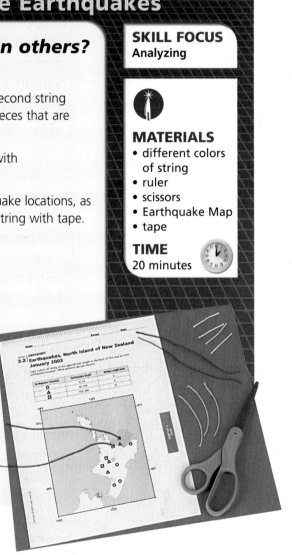

Waves and Energy

Waves are part of your everyday life. For example, music reaches your ears as sound waves. All waves, including seismic waves, carry energy from place to place. As a wave moves through a material, particles of the material move out of position temporarily, causing the particles next to them to move. After each particle moves, it returns to its original position. In this way, energy moves through the material, but matter does not.

On October 17, 1989, an earthquake stopped baseball's World Series at Candlestick Park in San Francisco. As the seismic waves arrived, fans heard a low rumble; then for about 15 seconds the stadium shook from side to side and up and down. About 20 minutes after the earthquake was felt at the stadium, the seismic waves had traveled to the other side of Earth. There, the waves did not shake the ground hard enough for people to notice. The waves could be detected only by scientific instruments.

Earthquakes produce three types of seismic waves: primary waves, secondary waves, and surface waves. Each type moves through materials differently. In addition, the waves can reflect, or bounce, off boundaries between different layers. The waves can also bend as they pass from one layer into another. Scientists learn about Earth's layers by studying the paths and speeds of seismic waves traveling through Earth.

Primary Waves

READING TiP

One meaning of *primary* is "first." Primary waves arrive before secondary waves.

The fastest seismic waves are called primary waves, or P waves. These waves are the first to reach any particular location after an earthquake occurs. Primary waves travel through Earth's crust at an average speed of about 5 kilometers per second (3 mi/s). Primary waves can travel through solids, liquids, and gases. As they pass through a material, the particles of the material are slightly pushed together and pulled apart. Buildings also experience this push and pull as primary waves pass through the ground they are built on.

Secondary Waves

VISUALIZATION
CLASSZONE.COM

Explore primary-wave and secondary-wave motion.

Secondary waves are the second seismic waves to arrive at any particular location after an earthquake, though they start at the same time as primary waves. Secondary waves travel through Earth's interior at about half the speed of primary waves. Secondary waves are also called S waves. As they pass through a material, the material's particles are shaken up and down or from side to side. Secondary waves rock small buildings back and forth as they pass.

Secondary waves can travel through rock, but unlike primary waves they cannot travel through liquids or gases. Look at the illustrations on page 55. As a primary wave passes through a material, the volume and density of the material change slightly. But as a secondary wave passes, the material changes slightly in shape. Liquids and gases do not have definite shapes. These materials flow—that is, particles in them do not return to their original positions after being moved. When scientists learned that secondary waves cannot pass through Earth's outer core, they realized that the outer core is not solid.

 CHECK YOUR READING Why can't secondary waves travel through liquids or gases?

Surface Waves

Surface waves are seismic waves that move along Earth's surface, not through its interior. They make the ground roll up and down or shake from side to side. Surface waves cause the largest ground movements and the most damage. Surface waves travel more slowly than the other types of seismic waves.

Seismic Waves

Earthquakes produce three types of seismic waves.

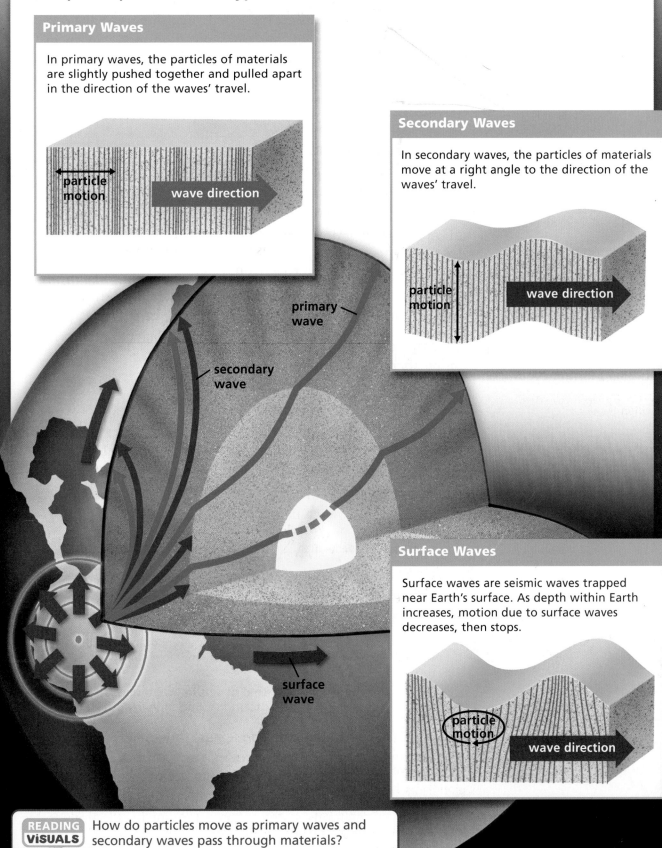

Primary Waves

In primary waves, the particles of materials are slightly pushed together and pulled apart in the direction of the waves' travel.

particle motion

wave direction

Secondary Waves

In secondary waves, the particles of materials move at a right angle to the direction of the waves' travel.

particle motion

wave direction

primary wave

secondary wave

surface wave

Surface Waves

Surface waves are seismic waves trapped near Earth's surface. As depth within Earth increases, motion due to surface waves decreases, then stops.

particle motion

wave direction

READING VISUALS How do particles move as primary waves and secondary waves pass through materials?

Seismic waves can be measured.

Without listening to the news, scientists at seismic stations all over the world know when an earthquake occurs. Seismic stations are places where ground movements are measured. A **seismograph** (SYZ-muh-GRAF) is an instrument that constantly records ground movements. The recording of an earthquake looks like a group of wiggles in a line. The height of the wiggles indicates the amount of ground movement produced by seismic waves at the seismograph's location.

Using Seismographs

Separate seismographs are needed to record side-to-side movements and up-and-down movements. A seismograph that measures side-to-side movements has a heavy weight hanging from a wire. The weight remains almost still as the ground moves back and forth beneath it. A pen attached to the weight records the movements. A seismograph that records up-and-down movements has a heavy weight hanging from a spring. As the ground moves, the weight stays almost still as the spring absorbs the movement by getting longer or shorter. A pen attached to the weight records the changes in distance between the ground and the weight.

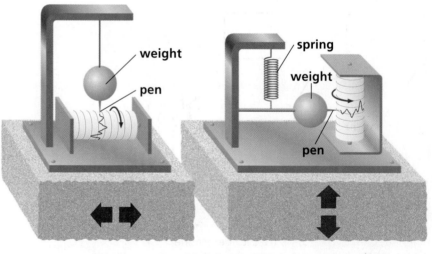

This seismograph records side-to-side movements.

This seismograph records up-and-down movements.

CHECK YOUR READING Why is more than one kind of seismograph needed to record all the movements of the ground during an earthquake?

Scientists use seismographs to measure thousands of earthquakes, large and small, every year. Some seismographs can detect ground movements as small as one hundred-millionth of a centimeter. The recording produced by a seismograph is called a seismogram. By studying seismograms, scientists can determine the locations and strengths of earthquakes.

Locating an Earthquake

To locate the epicenter of an earthquake, scientists must have seismograms from at least three seismic stations. The procedure for locating an epicenter has three steps:

1 Scientists find the difference between the arrival times of the primary and the secondary waves at each of the three stations.

2 The time difference is used to determine the distance of the epicenter from each station. The greater the difference in time, the farther away the epicenter is.

3 A circle is drawn around each station, with a radius corresponding to the epicenter's distance from that station. The point where the three circles meet is the epicenter.

Finding an Epicenter

Seismograms provide data used to find an earthquake's epicenter.

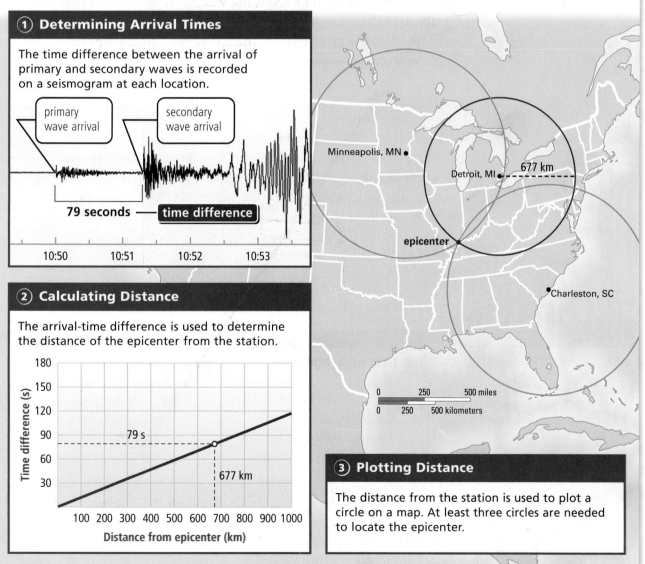

① Determining Arrival Times

The time difference between the arrival of primary and secondary waves is recorded on a seismogram at each location.

primary wave arrival

secondary wave arrival

79 seconds — time difference

10:50   10:51   10:52   10:53

② Calculating Distance

The arrival-time difference is used to determine the distance of the epicenter from the station.

Time difference (s)

180
150
120
90   79 s
60
30
          677 km

100 200 300 400 500 600 700 800 900 1000
Distance from epicenter (km)

Minneapolis, MN

Detroit, MI   677 km

epicenter

Charleston, SC

0   250   500 miles
0   250   500 kilometers

③ Plotting Distance

The distance from the station is used to plot a circle on a map. At least three circles are needed to locate the epicenter.

Scientists can also use seismograph data to locate the focus of an earthquake. They study seismograms to identify waves that have reflected off boundaries inside Earth. Some of these waves help the scientists to determine the earthquake's depth.

A seismogram records the time when the first primary wave arrives. This wave travels by a direct path. The data also show when the first reflected primary wave arrives. After leaving the focus, this wave reflects from Earth's surface and then travels to the seismic station. The reflected wave takes a longer path, so it arrives slightly later. The difference in arrival times indicates the depth of the focus. Scientists can make the necessary calculations, but more commonly a computer is used to calculate the location of an earthquake's epicenter and focus.

An earthquake's depth is determined from the difference in arrival times of direct and reflected seismic waves.

seismic station

reflected wave

fault

focus

direct wave

READING TiP

The word *magnitude* comes from the Latin word *magnitudo,* meaning "greatness."

Scientists also use seismograms to determine earthquakes' magnitudes, or strengths. The more energy an earthquake releases, the greater the ground movement recorded. The greatest movement determines the earthquake's strength on a magnitude scale. Stronger earthquakes get higher numbers. You will read more about earthquake magnitude scales in the next section.

2.2 Review

KEY CONCEPTS

1. Why does the greatest shaking of the ground occur near an earthquake's epicenter?

2. What information do you need to completely describe where an earthquake started?

3. What types of information can a scientist get by studying seismograms?

CRITICAL THINKING

4. **Compare and Contrast** How are primary and secondary waves similar? How are they different?

5. **Apply** What information could you get about an earthquake's location from only two seismic stations' data? Explain.

○ CHALLENGE

6. **Apply** Why might an earthquake's primary waves, but not its secondary waves, reach a location on the other side of the world from the epicenter?

MATH TUTORIAL
CLASSZONE.COM
Click on Math Tutorial
for more help with
multiplication.

Earthquake Energy

Seismologists use the moment magnitude scale to describe the energies of earthquakes. Because earthquakes vary from quite weak to very strong, the scale is designed to cover a wide range of energies. Each whole number increase in magnitude represents the release of about 32 times as much energy. For example, a magnitude 5 earthquake releases about 32 times as much energy as a magnitude 4 earthquake.

Magnitude	1	2	3	4	5	6	7	8	9	10
Energy		×32	×32	×32	×32	×32	×32	×32	×32	×32

Similarly, a magnitude 6 earthquake releases about 32 times as much energy as a magnitude 5 earthquake, and a magnitude 7 earthquake releases about 32 times as much energy as a magnitude 6 earthquake. You can use multiplication to compare the energies of earthquakes.

Example

Compare the energy of a magnitude 4 earthquake to the energy of a magnitude 7 earthquake. Give your answer to the nearest 1000.

SOLUTION

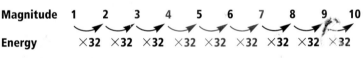

Magnitude	1	2	3	4	5	6	7	8	9	10
Energy		×32	×32	×32	×32	×32	×32	×32	×32	×32

(1) Multiply: $32 \times 32 \times 32 =$ **32,768**

(2) Round your answer to the nearest 1000: **33,000**

ANSWER A magnitude 7 earthquake releases about 33,000 times as much energy as a magnitude 4 earthquake.

Compare the energies of two earthquakes:

1. Magnitude 4 and magnitude 6; give your answer to the nearest 100

2. Magnitude 5 and magnitude 9; give your answer to the nearest 100,000

3. Magnitude 3.3 and magnitude 4.3

CHALLENGE What is the magnitude of an earthquake that releases about 1000 times the energy of a magnitude 2 earthquake?

2.3 Earthquake damage can be reduced.

BEFORE, you learned

- Seismic waves travel through Earth
- An earthquake's location and magnitude can be determined

NOW, you will learn

- How an earthquake's magnitude is related to the damage it causes
- How structures are built to withstand most earthquakes
- How scientists estimate the earthquake risk in an area

VOCABULARY

aftershock p. 62
liquefaction p. 62
tsunami p. 62

EXPLORE Shaking

What happens as materials are shaken?

PROCEDURE

1. Pour a pile of sand on a newspaper. Place a metal washer on top of the sand. Shake the paper and observe what happens to the sand and the washer.

2. Now place the washer on top of a flat rock. Shake the rock and observe what happens.

WHAT DO YOU THINK?

- How did the washer, the sand, and the rock react differently to shaking?
- How might the washer, the sand, and the rock model what happens to buildings and land during earthquakes?

MATERIALS

- sand
- newspaper
- flat rock
- washer

Earthquakes can cause severe damage and loss of life.

MAIN IDEA AND DETAILS
Record information about the effects of earthquakes in your notebook.

Every year, on average, an extremely powerful earthquake—one with a magnitude of 8 or higher—strikes somewhere on Earth. Such an earthquake can destroy almost all the buildings near its epicenter and cause great loss of life.

Earthquakes are most dangerous when they occur near areas where many people live. Most injuries and deaths due to earthquakes are not directly caused by the movement of the ground. They are caused by collapsing buildings and other structures and by fires. After an earthquake, fires may start due to broken natural-gas lines, broken electrical power lines, or overturned stoves.

Earthquake Magnitude

A very powerful earthquake can release more energy than 1 million weak earthquakes combined. Earthquake magnitude scales give scientists and engineers a simple way to describe this huge range in energy.

The first scale of earthquake magnitude was developed in California during the 1930s by the scientists Charles Richter (RIHK-tuhr) and Beno Gutenberg. In this scale, called the Richter scale, an earthquake's magnitude is based on how fast the ground moves at a seismic station. However, most scientists today prefer to use a newer, more accurate scale: the moment magnitude scale. This scale is based on the total amounts of energy released by earthquakes. The moment magnitude scale is used for all earthquake magnitudes given in this chapter.

Both the Richter scale and the moment magnitude scale are often shown with a top value of 10, but neither actually has a maximum value. On each scale, an increase of one whole number indicates an increase of 32 times more energy. For example, a magnitude 5 earthquake releases 32 times as much energy as a magnitude 4 earthquake and about 1000 times as much energy as a magnitude 3 earthquake.

Magnitude and Effects Near Epicenter

More powerful earthquakes have higher magnitude values.

Magnitude	Effects Near Epicenter
0–3.9 Very Minor to Minor	rarely noticed
4.0–4.9 Light	slight damage
5.0–5.9 Moderate	some structures damaged
6.0–6.9 Strong	major damage to structures
7.0–7.9 Major	some well-built structures destroyed
8.0 and above Great	major to total destruction

Damage from Powerful Earthquake

This road collapsed during a magnitude 6.9 earthquake in California on October 17, 1989. About 140 earthquakes with magnitudes of 6 or higher occur each year around the world.

VOCABULARY
Add magnet word diagrams for *aftershock* and *liquefaction* to your notebook.

The moment magnitude scale is more accurate for larger earthquakes than the Richter scale. Another advantage of the moment magnitude scale is that it can be used for earthquakes that occurred before seismographs were invented. Geologists can measure the strength of the rocks and the length they moved along a fault to calculate a past earthquake's magnitude. This information is important for geologists to know when they determine an area's earthquake risk.

 CHECK YOUR READING What are two advantages of the moment magnitude scale over the Richter scale?

Damage from Earthquakes

Movement of the blocks of rock on either side of a fault can crack roads, buildings, dams, and any other structures on the fault. As blocks of rock move, they can also raise, lower, or tilt the ground surface. Sometimes structures weakened by an earthquake collapse during shaking caused by aftershocks. An **aftershock** is a smaller earthquake that follows a more powerful earthquake in the same area. Also, fires that break out can cause great damage if broken water pipes keep firefighters from getting water. In the 1906 San Francisco earthquake, fires caused more than 90 percent of the building damage.

Earthquakes can cause major damage by affecting the soil and other loose materials. For example, landslides often occur as a result of earthquakes. A landslide is a movement of soil and rocks down a hill or mountain. Earthquakes can cause soil **liquefaction,** a process in which shaking of the ground causes soil to act like a liquid. For a short time the soil becomes like a thick soup. Liquefaction occurs only in areas where the soil is made up of loose sand and silt and contains a large amount of water. As the shaking temporarily changes the wet soil, structures either sink down into the soil or flow away with it. Shaking of the ground also affects areas that have mixtures of soils. Some soil types pack together more than others when shaken.

This building in Venezuela tilted and sank as the ground beneath it collapsed during an earthquake in 1967.

 CHECK YOUR READING List five ways in which earthquakes can cause damage.

Damage from Tsunamis

If you sit on an ocean beach, you can watch the depth of the water change as waves come in. If you watch for a longer time, you may notice bigger changes as the tide rises or falls. A special type of wave, however, can make water rise more than the height of a 20-story building. This wave, known as a **tsunami** (tsu-NAH-mee), is a water wave triggered by an earthquake, volcanic eruption, or landslide. Tsunamis are

sometimes called tidal waves, but they are not caused by the forces that produce tides. A tsunami may not be a single wave but several waves that can have different heights and can arrive hours apart.

Tsunamis move quickly and can travel thousands of kilometers without weakening. In deep water, they can reach speeds of about 700 kilometers per hour (430 mi/h). A tsunami in the deep water of the open ocean may be less than one meter (3 ft) in height at the surface. As a tsunami reaches shallow water around an island or continent, however, it slows down, and its height greatly increases.

A 1946 earthquake on Alaska's coast caused a tsunami that swept across the entire Pacific Ocean. In Alaska the tsunami destroyed a new U.S. Coast Guard lighthouse that otherwise would have been able to send warnings to other areas. In less than five hours, the tsunami reached Hawaii as a series of waves. The highest wave was about 17 meters (55 ft) tall. Because people did not know of the danger, no one had evacuated, and 159 people were killed.

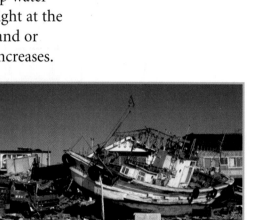

In 1993, a tsunami from a powerful earthquake in Japan threw boats onto land.

Many earthquakes occur around the edges of the Pacific Ocean. Therefore, Hawaii and other areas in and around this ocean are likely to be hit by tsunamis. The Pacific Tsunami Warning Center, located in Hawaii, was established in 1949. The center monitors earthquakes and issues warnings to areas that could be struck by tsunamis.

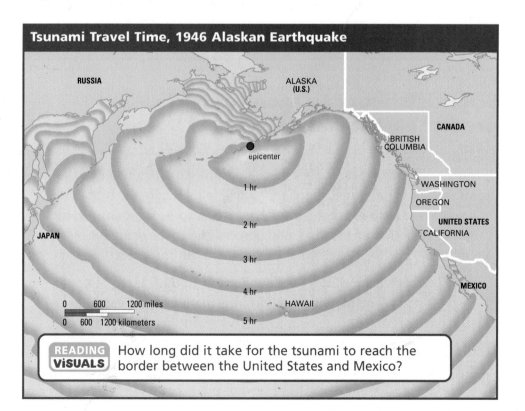

Tsunami Travel Time, 1946 Alaskan Earthquake

RUSSIA

ALASKA (U.S.)

epicenter

CANADA

BRITISH COLUMBIA

1 hr

WASHINGTON

OREGON

2 hr

UNITED STATES
CALIFORNIA

JAPAN

3 hr

4 hr

MEXICO

0   600   1200 miles

0   600   1200 kilometers

HAWAII

5 hr

READING VISUALS How long did it take for the tsunami to reach the border between the United States and Mexico?

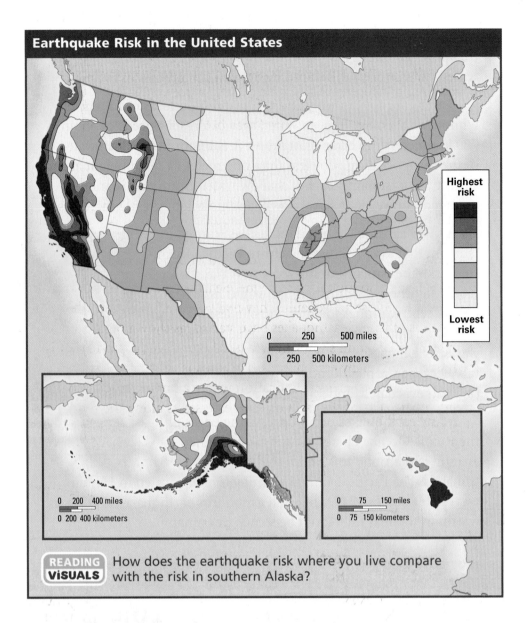

Earthquake Risk in the United States

0   250   500 miles
0   250   500 kilometers

Highest risk

Lowest risk

0   200   400 miles
0   200   400 kilometers

0   75   150 miles
0   75   150 kilometers

READING VISUALS How does the earthquake risk where you live compare with the risk in southern Alaska?

Scientists work to monitor and predict earthquakes.

READING TIP

A prediction is a statement about an event before it occurs. Scientists use their knowledge to make predictions about when earthquakes might occur.

Scientists cannot yet predict the day or even the year when an earthquake will occur. Sometimes there are signs years before an earthquake strikes, and sometimes there are none at all. Usually the best that scientists can do is to give long-term predictions. For example, they might state that an area has a 60 percent chance of being hit by an earthquake with a magnitude 7 or higher within the next 25 years.

The map above shows earthquake risks in the United States for the next 50 years. The map is based on information about earthquakes that have occurred since people began keeping records, along with evidence of earlier earthquakes preserved in rocks. Note that most areas with the highest earthquake risks are near the Pacific Ocean.

To learn more about earthquakes and to find ways of predicting them, scientists all over the world study seismic activity along faults. They monitor whether stress is building up in the rocks along faults. Such signs include

- tilts or changes in the elevation of the ground
- slow movements or stretching in rock
- the development of small cracks in the ground

An increase in small earthquakes can be a sign that stress is building up along a fault and that a large earthquake is likely to occur. But an increase in small earthquakes can also be a sign that a fault is releasing stress bit by bit, decreasing the likelihood of a major earthquake.

Scientists also look for areas where earthquakes have not occurred along an otherwise active fault. They make diagrams in which they plot the locations where earthquakes have started, as shown below. Sometimes such a diagram shows an area of few or no earthquakes that is surrounded by many earthquakes. This area is called a seismic gap. A seismic gap can indicate a location where a fault is stuck. Movement along other parts of the fault can increase stress along the stuck part. This stress could be released by a major earthquake.

CHECK YOUR READING Why can a lack of earthquakes in an area near an active fault cause concern?

Seismic Gaps

A seismic gap is a section of a fault with few earthquakes compared with sections of the fault on either side of the gap.

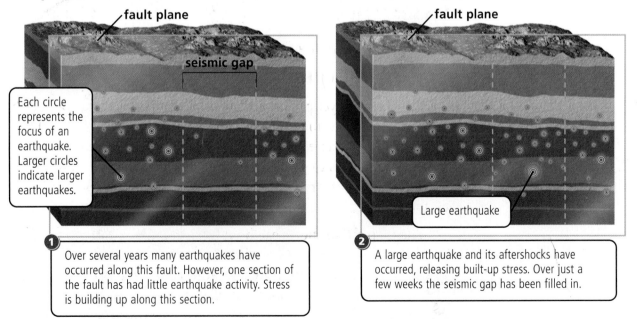

fault plane

seismic gap

Each circle represents the focus of an earthquake. Larger circles indicate larger earthquakes.

fault plane

Large earthquake

1 Over several years many earthquakes have occurred along this fault. However, one section of the fault has had little earthquake activity. Stress is building up along this section.

2 A large earthquake and its aftershocks have occurred, releasing built-up stress. Over just a few weeks the seismic gap has been filled in.

Structures can be designed to resist earthquake damage.

READING TiP

Here, the term *structure* refers to office buildings, homes, bridges, dams, factories—all the things that people build.

For safety, it might be best to be outdoors, far from any buildings, during an earthquake. But there is no way to tell just when or where an earthquake will occur. For this reason, the best way to reduce deaths, injuries, and damage from earthquakes is to build structures able to withstand strong ground shaking. The first step is to understand what the risks from earthquakes are in an area. The second step is to build structures that are appropriate for the area.

Scientists make maps of areas to show the locations of fault zones, past earthquakes, and areas likely to experience flooding, landslides, or liquefaction. In Japan, California, and other areas that have many earthquakes, planners use these maps to develop rules for building new structures and strengthening older ones. The maps are also used to select building locations that are stable—unlikely to experience landslides or liquefaction.

Earthquake damage to small buildings, such as most houses, often occurs when the buildings are shaken off their foundations. Small buildings are better protected when they are firmly fastened to their foundations. Also, their walls need to be strong. Some houses were built before modern safety rules were in place. The walls of these houses can be made stronger by adding supports. Supports are particularly important in brick walls, which can easily collapse in an earthquake. A special type of steel is commonly used for the supports because it is strong and is able to bend, then return to its original shape.

⚠ SAFETY TIPS

Earthquakes

Before

- Fasten heavy objects, such as bookcases, to floors or walls to keep them from falling.
- Put latches on cabinets to keep dishes from falling out.
- Identify safe spots in every room, such as the space under a strong table.
- Keep an emergency supply of bottled water.

During and After

- If you are inside a building, stay inside until the shaking stops. Objects falling from buildings cause many injuries.
- If you are outdoors, move away from buildings, poles, and trees.
- Make a family plan for contacting a person who lives in another town. As people call to say they are safe, this person can pass on the information.

Many of the methods used to make larger buildings and other structures safer are designed to reduce the amount they shake during an earthquake. One method is to use devices called base isolators, as shown in the illustration. Base isolators are placed between a building and its foundation. The isolators are made of flexible materials that are stacked in layers like pancakes. When an earthquake occurs, the isolators absorb much of the ground motion. Any shaking that does reach the building is slower and smoother.

A building may also have an open space, or moat, around it. The moat, which may be covered at the surface with sidewalks and landscaping, lets the building shake more gently than the ground during an earthquake.

Special walls, called shear walls, add strength to a structure. These walls contain steel supports. Shear walls in the center of a building are often built around a stairwell or an elevator shaft. These walls make up a part of the building known as the shear core.

Walls can also be made stronger by adding braces. Pairs of braces that form an **X** shape are called cross braces. They help a structure keep its shape while it is being shaken.

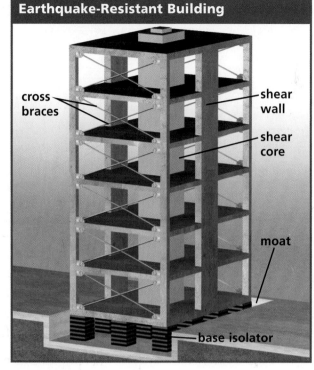

Earthquake-Resistant Building

cross braces

shear wall

shear core

moat

base isolator

CHECK YOUR READING Describe two methods used to make buildings stronger.

2.3 Review

KEY CONCEPTS

1. How is an earthquake magnitude scale related to the amounts of energy released by earthquakes?

2. What are the major dangers to people from an earthquake?

3. Name three methods of improving a building's safety before an earthquake.

CRITICAL THINKING

4. **Apply** What might people living next to the ocean do to protect themselves if they were given a two-hour warning of an approaching tsunami?

5. **Connect** If you lived in an area where earthquakes were common, what could you do to make your room safer?

CHALLENGE

6. **Analyze** Earthquakes release stress that has built up in rocks. Why do you think aftershocks occur?

How Structures React in Earthquakes

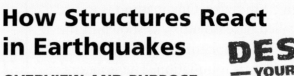

OVERVIEW AND PURPOSE

In 1989 a magnitude 6.9 earthquake struck the San Francisco Bay area, killing 62 people and leaving 12,000 homeless. In 1988 a magnitude 6.9 earthquake occurred near Spitak, Armenia. There, nearly 25,000 people died and 514,000 lost their homes. The difference in the effects of these two earthquakes was largely due to differences in construction methods. In this investigation you will

- build a structure and measure how long it can withstand shaking on a shake table provided by your teacher
- explore methods of building earthquake-resistant structures

MATERIALS
- modeling clay
- stirrer straws
- piece of thin cardboard 15 cm on each side
- scissors
- ruler
- shake table

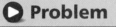

▶ Problem

How can structures be built to withstand most earthquakes?

▶ Hypothesize

Write a hypothesis to explain how structures can be built to withstand shaking. Your hypothesis should take the form of an "If . . . , then . . . , because . . ." statement.

▶ Procedure

1. Make a data table like the one shown on the next page.

2. Use stirrers joined with clay to build a structure at least 20 cm tall on top of the cardboard. Cut the stirrers if necessary.

3. Make a diagram of your structure.

step 2

4 Lift your structure by its cardboard base and place it on the shake-table platform. Pull the platform 2 centimeters to one side and release it.

step 4

5 Repeat step 4 until the structure begins to collapse.

▶ Observe and Analyze
Write It Up

1. **RECORD** Complete your data table and make notes about the collapse, including areas of possible weakness in your structure.

2. **INFER** Use your observations to design a structure that will better withstand shaking.

▶ Conclude
Write It Up

1. **INTERPRET** Compare your results with your hypothesis. Do your observations support your hypothesis?

2. **INFER** How would you use the shake table to model earthquakes of different magnitudes?

3. **IDENTIFY VARIABLES** How might your results differ if you always pulled the platform to the same side or if you pulled it to different sides?

4. **IDENTIFY LIMITS** In what ways might a building's behavior during an earthquake differ from the behavior of your structure on the shake table?

5. **COMPARE** Examine the diagrams of the three structures that lasted longest in your class. What characteristics, if any, did they have in common?

6. **APPLY** Based on your results, write a list of recommendations for building earthquake-resistant structures.

▶ INVESTIGATE Further

CHALLENGE Have a contest to see who can build the most earthquake-resistant structure. Design your structure as if you were an earthquake engineer. Make a model of your structure at least 30 centimeters tall, using the types of materials you used in this investigation. Test the structure on the shake table. What design features helped the winning structure to resist shaking the longest?

How Structures React in Earthquakes

Problem How can structures be built to withstand most earthquakes?

Hypothesize

Observe and Analyze

Table 1. Number of Trials Until Collapse of Structure

Trial	Distance Platform Pulled to Side (cm)	Notes
1	2	
2	2	
3	2	
4	2	

Conclude

Chapter Review

the BIG idea

Earthquakes release stress that has built up in rocks.

CONTENT REVIEW
CLASSZONE.COM

◀ KEY CONCEPTS SUMMARY

2.1 Earthquakes occur along faults.

Normal faults form as rocks are pulled apart.

Reverse faults form as rocks are pushed together.

Strike-slip faults form as rocks are pushed horizontally in opposite directions.

VOCABULARY
fault p. 45
stress p. 45
earthquake p. 45

2.2 Earthquakes release energy.

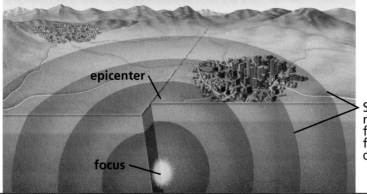

epicenter

focus

Seismic waves move out from the focus in all directions.

VOCABULARY
seismic wave p. 51
focus p. 52
epicenter p. 52
seismograph p. 56

2.3 Earthquake damage can be reduced.

A powerful earthquake releases more energy and causes more shaking of the ground than does a weak earthquake.

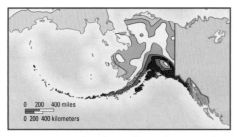

0 200 400 miles
0 200 400 kilometers

An area's risk of earthquakes can be predicted.

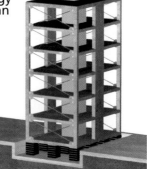

Structures can be designed for greater safety in an earthquake.

VOCABULARY
aftershock p. 62
liquefaction p. 62
tsunami p. 62

Reviewing Vocabulary

On a separate sheet of paper, draw a diagram to show the relationships among each set of words. One set has been done as an example.

seismograph, seismic waves, seismogram

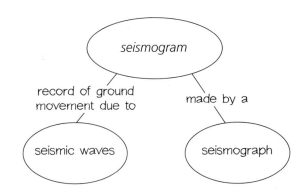

1. earthquake, epicenter, focus

2. earthquake, tsunami, liquefaction

3. fault, stress, earthquake, aftershock

4. tsunami, epicenter, seismogram

Reviewing Key Concepts

Multiple Choice *Choose the letter of the best answer.*

5. What causes an earthquake?
   a. a rise of magma in the mantle
   b. a sudden movement of blocks of rock
   c. a buildup of seismic waves
   d. a change in Earth's magnetic poles

6. Earthquakes release energy in the form of
   a. seismic waves
   b. faults
   c. stress lines
   d. seismograms

7. Most damage from an earthquake usually occurs
   a. below the focus
   b. far from the epicenter
   c. at the focus
   d. near the epicenter

8. To locate the epicenter of an earthquake, scientists need seismograms from at least _____ seismic stations.
   a. two   c. four
   b. three   d. five

9. The seismic waves that usually cause the most damage are
   a. surface waves
   b. tsunami waves
   c. primary waves
   d. secondary waves

10. Earthquakes release _____ that has built up in rocks.
    a. water   c. stress
    b. magnetism   d. electricity

11. About 80 percent of all earthquakes occur in a belt around the
    a. Pacific Ocean
    b. San Andreas Fault
    c. North American Plate
    d. African Rift Valley

12. In a strike-slip fault, blocks of rock move _____ along the fault plane.
    a. up
    b. down
    c. sideways
    d. up and down

13. One method of making a building earthquake resistant is to
    a. add sand under the foundation
    b. reduce the use of steel
    c. make the walls of brick
    d. use cross braces

Short Answer *Write a short answer to each question.*

14. Why do most earthquakes occur at or near tectonic plate boundaries?

15. How do data from seismic waves indicate that Earth's outer core is liquid?

16. What causes most of the injuries and deaths due to earthquakes?

Thinking Critically

Study the illustration below, showing the epicenter and focus of an earthquake, then answer the following six questions.

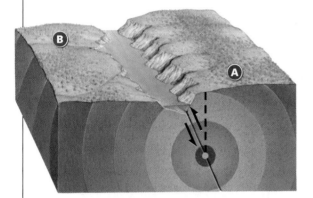

17. **APPLY** What type of fault is shown in the illustration? How do you know?

18. **APPLY** Where on the surface is the greatest shaking likely to occur?

19. **INFER** What does the set of circles around the focus represent?

20. **EXPLAIN** In what ways would the times of arrival of primary and secondary waves be different at points *A* and *B*?

21. **IDENTIFY EFFECTS** The land surface to the left of the fault is lower than the land surface to the right. How might this be related to movements along the fault?

22. **ANALYZE** What are the main directions of stress on the blocks of rock on either side of the fault?

23. **APPLY** A builder is planning to construct a new house near a fault along which earthquakes are common. Write a list of guidelines that the builder might use to decide where and how to build the house.

24. **ANALYZE** Identify two areas of the United States where earthquakes are most likely to occur. Explain your choices in terms of plate tectonics.

25. **IDENTIFY EFFECTS** A town has been struck by an earthquake with a magnitude of 5.8. The epicenter was 10 kilometers (6 mi) away, and the focus was shallow. What sort of damage would you expect to find in the town?

26. **ANALYZE** What role do earthquakes play in shaping Earth's surface?

27. **CALCULATE** If primary waves travel at a speed of about 5 kilometers per second, how long would it take them to arrive at a seismic station located 695 kilometers from an earthquake's focus?

the BIG idea

28. **CONNECT** Look again at the photograph of earthquake damage on pages 42–43. Explain how energy released by an earthquake can travel through rock and cause damage at Earth's surface.

29. **SYNTHESIZE** The illustration below shows convection in Earth's mantle. What are the relationships among the heat inside Earth, the movements of tectonic plates, and the occurrences of earthquakes?

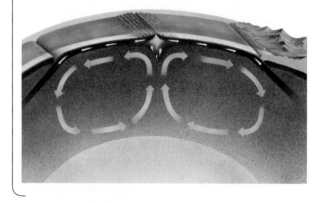

UNIT PROJECTS

If you need to do an experiment for your unit project, gather the materials. Be sure to allow enough time to observe results before the project is due.

Analyzing Data

The following tables show magnitudes and average numbers of earthquakes in the world per year, and states in which two or more major earthquakes have been recorded. Use the information in the tables to answer the questions below.

Earthquakes in the World per Year

Classification	Magnitude	Average Number per Year
Great	8.0 and higher	1
Major	7.0–7.9	18
Strong	6.0–6.9	120
Moderate	5.0–5.9	800
Light	4.0–4.9	6200
Minor	3.0–3.9	49,000

States That Have Recorded Two or More Major Earthquakes

State	Number of Major Earthquakes
Alaska	74
Arkansas	2
California	16
Hawaii	4
Missouri	2
Nevada	3

1. A major earthquake can have a magnitude of
   a. 6.0–6.9
   b. 6.0 and higher
   c. 7.4
   d. 8.2

2. The most major earthquakes have been recorded in which state?
   a. Arkansas
   b. Hawaii
   c. Missouri
   d. Nevada

3. A magnitude 3.2 earthquake is classified as
   a. major
   b. strong
   c. moderate
   d. minor

4. The world's most powerful earthquakes occur along reverse faults. In which state are reverse faults most likely to be common?
   a. Alaska
   b. California
   c. Hawaii
   d. Nevada

5. In which state is a tectonic plate boundary most likely to be located?
   a. Arkansas
   b. California
   c. Hawaii
   d. Nevada

6. Compared to the number of major earthquakes each year, the number of moderate earthquakes is
   a. about 40 times greater
   b. about 4 times greater
   c. about equal
   d. smaller

7. Alaska has recorded a total of 82 earthquakes with magnitudes of 7.0 and higher. How many of these earthquakes are classified as "great"?
   a. 0
   b. 8
   c. 56
   d. 74

8. An earthquake of which classification releases the most energy?
   a. great
   b. major
   c. strong
   d. minor

Extended Response

Answer the two questions below in detail. Include some of the terms shown in the word box. In your answers underline each term you use.

seismic waves	primary	secondary	surface
stress		fault	plate boundary

9. During an earthquake, Dustin felt a small amount of shaking. About 15 seconds later, he felt some more shaking. Then about 45 seconds later he felt the strongest shaking. Explain what happened.

10. The island of Sumatra is located in an area where the Pacific Plate sinks under the Eurasian Plate. Explain why Sumatra has many earthquakes.

Mountains and Volcanoes

the **BIG** idea

Mountains and volcanoes form as tectonic plates move.

Key Concepts

SECTION

3.1 Movement of rock builds mountains.
Learn how different types of mountains form.

SECTION

3.2 Volcanoes form as molten rock erupts.
Learn why there are different types of volcanoes and volcanic eruptions.

SECTION

3.3 Volcanoes affect Earth's land, air, and water.
Learn how volcanic eruptions affect land, air, and water.

Internet Preview

CLASSZONE.COM

Chapter 3 online resources: Content Review, Simulation, Visualization, two Resource Centers, Math Tutorial, Test Practice

How does new land form from molten rock?

EXPLORE the BIG idea

Making Mountains

Line up and hold a row of about ten checkers or coins on a table. Tilt the row, then let it go.

Observe and Think What happened to the height, length, and shape of the row? How do you think these changes might be similar to the processes by which some mountains and valleys form?

Under Pressure

Half fill two empty plastic bottles with a fresh carbonated beverage. Screw the caps on the bottles tightly. Put one bottle in hot tap water and one in ice water. Wait three minutes.

Observe and Think Slowly unscrew the caps from the bottles and observe how quickly gas bubbles form and escape. What is the role of pressure? How might gas bubbles cause pressure to build up in magma as they form?

Internet Activity: Volcanoes

Go to **ClassZone.com** to make a volcano erupt.

Observe and Think Why are some volcanic eruptions much more violent than others?

NSTA
scilinks.org
SCiLINKS

Explore Volcanoes **Code: MDL054**

Getting Ready to Learn

◀ CONCEPT REVIEW

- Earthquakes occur as blocks of rock move along faults.
- Tectonic plates pull apart, push together, or scrape past one another along their boundaries.

◀ VOCABULARY REVIEW

convergent boundary p. 22

subduction p. 30

fault p. 45

earthquake p. 45

magma *See Glossary.*

ⓘ CONTENT REVIEW
CLASSZONE.COM
Review concepts and vocabulary.

▶ TAKING NOTES

CONTENT FRAME

Organize your notes into a **content frame** for mountains. Make categories at the top that describe their types, features, and how they form. Then fill in the boxes for each type of mountain. Later in the chapter you will make content frames for other topics.

VOCABULARY STRATEGY

Draw a **word triangle** diagram for each new vocabulary term. On the bottom line, write and define the term. Above that, write a sentence that uses the term correctly. At the top, draw a small picture to show what the term looks like.

See the Note-Taking Handbook on pages R45–R51.

SCIENCE NOTEBOOK

TYPE OF MOUNTAINS	CHARACTERISTIC	WHERE THEY FORM	EXAMPLES
folded	rocks bent and folded	at convergent plate boundaries	Appalachians Himalayas
fault-block			

Fault-block mountains form as continental crust is pulled apart.

fault-block mountain:
a mountain pushed up or tilted along a fault

3.1 Movement of rock builds mountains.

◀ BEFORE, you learned

- Major geologic events occur at tectonic plate boundaries
- Most faults are located along plate boundaries

▶ NOW, you will learn

- How the folding of rock can form mountains
- How movement along faults can form mountains

VOCABULARY

folded mountain p. 80
fault-block mountain p. 82

EXPLORE Folding

How does rock fold?

PROCEDURE

① Make three flat layers of clay on top of a sheet of newspaper. Put a block at either end of the clay.

② Hold one block still. Push on the other block to slowly bring the blocks closer together.

WHAT DO YOU THINK?

- What happened to the clay when you pushed on the block?
- What shape did the middle layer of clay form?
- If a large block of rock reacted to pressure in a similar way, what kind of landform would result?

MATERIALS

- 2 or 3 colors of modeling clay
- 2 blocks
- newspaper

Most mountains form along plate boundaries.

A shallow sea once covered the area that is now Mount Everest, Earth's tallest mountain. If you were to climb Mount Everest, you would be standing on rocks containing the remains of ocean animals. Mount Everest also contains rocks that formed far away at a spreading center on the sea floor. How can rocks from the sea floor be on top of a mountain on a continent? Plate tectonics provides the answer.

Recall that an oceanic plate sinks when it collides with a continental plate. Some sea-floor material scrapes off the sinking plate and onto the continent. As continental mountains form, material once at the bottom of an ocean can be pushed many kilometers high.

Mountain Ranges and Belts

A mountain is an area of land that rises steeply from the land around it. A single mountain is rare. Most mountains belong to ranges—long lines of mountains that were formed at about the same time and by the same processes. Ranges that are close together make up mountain belts. For example, the Rocky Mountain belt in western North America contains about 100 ranges.

①
Mountains rise high above the land around them.

②
Most mountains are in groups called mountain ranges.

③
Closely spaced mountain ranges make up mountain belts.

Most of the world's major mountain belts are located along tectonic plate boundaries. But mountain belts like the Appalachians (AP-uh-LAY-chee-uhnz) in eastern North America are in the interior of plates. Mountains such as these were formed by ancient plate collisions that assembled the present-day continents.

Major Mountain Belts

Major mountain belts mark the locations of present or past plate boundaries.

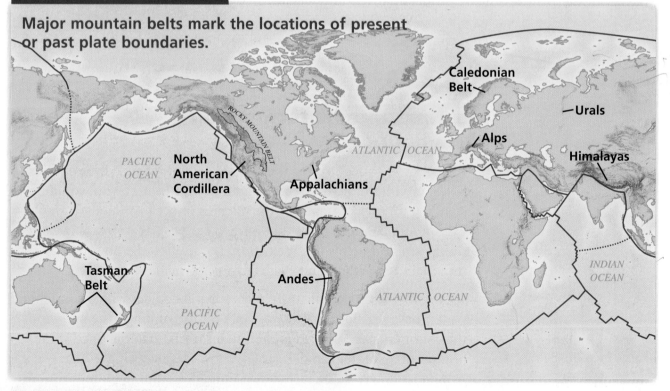

Mountains, Rocks, and Sediment

At the same time that some processes push mountains up, other processes wear them down. At Earth's surface, water and wind break rocks apart and move the pieces away. As long as mountains are pushed up faster than they wear down, they grow taller. For this reason, young mountains tend to be tall and steep. But eventually mountain-building processes slow, then end. Water and wind take over. Given enough time, all mountains become rounded hills, and then they are gone. Countless mountains have formed and worn away throughout Earth's long history.

Rocks break down into loose pieces that can be carried by water or wind. These pieces are called sediments. For example, sand on a beach is sediment. Thick layers of sediments can build up in low-lying areas, such as valleys, lakes, or the ocean. Pieces of sediments form sedimentary rock as they are pressed together or joined by natural cement.

The land becomes flatter as mountains wear down and valleys fill with sediments. If tectonic plates were to stop moving, eventually the surfaces of all the continents would be completely flat.

Mountains Wear Down

Mountains wear down as water and wind break their rocks into sediments and carry them away.

Young Mountains

Most young mountains are rugged. But even as they form, their rocks are being broken apart.

Old Mountains

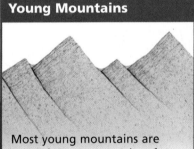

Most old mountains are rounded. Lower areas around them contain thick layers of sediments.

READING VISUALS How do mountains wear away?

Mountains can form as rocks fold.

Though people usually do not think of rocks as being able to bend and fold, they can. Think of a wax candle. If you bend a candle quickly, it will break. If you leave a candle propped up at an angle, over many days it will bend. If the candle is in a warm area, it will bend more quickly. Rocks also bend when stress is applied slowly. Rocks deep in the crust are at high temperatures and pressures. They are particularly likely to bend rather than break.

CHECK YOUR READING Under what conditions are rocks likely to bend and fold?

VOCABULARY
Make a word triangle for *folded mountain* in your notebook.

READING TiP
Eurasia is the landmass consisting of Europe and Asia.

Remember that tectonic plates move only a few centimeters each year. The edge of a continent along a convergent boundary is subjected to stress for a very long time as another plate pushes against it. Some of the continent's rocks break, and others fold. As folding continues, mountains are pushed up. A **folded mountain** is a mountain that forms as continental crust crumples and bends into folds.

Folded mountains form as an oceanic plate sinks under the edge of a continent or as continents collide. One example is the Himalaya (HIHM-uh-LAY-uh) belt, which formed by a collision between India and Eurasia. Its formation is illustrated on page 81.

❶ Convergent Boundary Develops At one time an ocean separated India and Eurasia. As India moved northward, oceanic lithosphere sank in a newly formed subduction zone along the Eurasian Plate. Along the edge of Eurasia, folded mountains formed. Volcanoes also formed as magma rose from the subduction zone to the surface.

❷ Continental Collision Begins Eventually the sea floor was completely destroyed, and India and Eurasia collided. Subduction ended. The volcanoes stopped erupting because they were no longer supplied with magma. Sea-floor material that had been added to the edge of Eurasia became part of the mountains pushed up by the collision.

❸ Collision Continues India and Eurasia continue to push together. Their collision has formed the Himalayas, the world's tallest mountains. They grow even higher as rock is folded and pushed up for hundreds of kilometers on either side of the collision boundary.

Earthquakes can also be important to the upward growth of folded mountains. A great deal of rock in the Himalaya belt has been pushed up along reverse faults, which are common at convergent boundaries.

Formation of Himalayas

The Himalayas are being pushed higher by an ongoing continental collision.

① Convergent Boundary Develops

As India began moving toward Eurasia 200 million years ago, a convergent boundary developed along the edge of Eurasia. The oceanic lithosphere between the two continents sank into a subduction zone.

India

Eurasia

Folded mountains formed as oceanic and continental plates pushed together.

Volcanoes formed as magma rose from the subduction zone to the surface.

② Continental Collision Begins

The sea floor was completely destroyed about 50 million years ago, and India and Eurasia collided.

Crust along the edges of both continents was crumpled and folded into mountains.

Subduction stopped after the continents collided. No more magma formed.

③ The Collision Continues

Currently, the Himalayas are growing more than one centimeter higher each year.

Himalayas

As the collision continues, the crust keeps folding. Also, earthquakes are common.

A remnant of sea floor crust remains deep under the mountains.

Himalayas

READING VISUALS In each illustration, where is the boundary between India and Eurasia?

Mountains can form as rocks move along faults.

CONTENT FRAME
Add information about fault-block mountains to your content frame.

In the southwestern United States and northwestern Mexico, hundreds of mountain ranges line up in rows. The ranges, as well as the valleys between them, formed along nearly parallel normal faults. Mountains that form as blocks of rock move up or down along normal faults are called **fault-block mountains.**

CHECK YOUR READING How can the movement of rocks along faults lead to the formation of mountains?

Fault-block mountains form as the lithosphere is stretched and pulled apart by forces within Earth. The rocks of the crust are cool and rigid. As the lithosphere begins to stretch, the crust breaks into large blocks. As stretching continues, the blocks of rock move along the faults that separate them. The illustrations on page 83 show how this process forms fault-block mountains.

INVESTIGATE Fault-Block Mountains

How do fault-block mountains form?

Fault-block mountains form along normal faults as blocks of continental crust are pulled apart. In this activity, you will use wooden blocks to demonstrate the processes that form fault-block mountains.

SKILL FOCUS
Modeling

MATERIALS
- 3 triangular blocks
- 3 rectangular blocks

TIME
15 minutes

PROCEDURE

1. Use the triangular blocks to demonstrate how movements along normal faults form two mountains separated by a valley. Start with the blocks arranged as shown. Move the outer blocks apart to form two mountains separated by a valley. Draw a diagram of your results.

2. Use the rectangular blocks to demonstrate how a row of tilted fault-block mountains forms along normal faults. (**Hint:** You can tilt the blocks as they move.) Draw a diagram of your results.

WHAT DO YOU THINK?

- How do your diagrams show that fault-block mountains form as the crust is being stretched?

- Along which type of plate boundary would fault-block mountains be most likely to form—divergent, convergent, or transform? Explain.

CHALLENGE Why do fault-block mountains not form at strike-slip faults?

① An area of the lithosphere can arch upward when, for example, it is heated by material rising in the mantle beneath it. As the crust stretches, it breaks into many blocks separated by faults.

② As the lithosphere is pulled apart, some blocks tilt. The edges of the blocks that tilt upward form mountains, and the edges that tilt downward form valleys. Other blocks drop down between faults, forming valleys. The edges of the blocks next to blocks that drop down are left standing high above the valleys as mountains.

Fault-block mountains form as stress repeatedly builds up in the crust and then is released during earthquakes. Even the most powerful earthquakes can move blocks of rock only a few meters up or down at one time. Fault-block mountains can be kilometers high. Millions of years and countless earthquakes are needed for them to form.

 Describe two ways that blocks of rock can move along faults and form mountains.

Fault-Block Mountains

Fault-block mountains form as the crust stretches and breaks into blocks that move along faults.

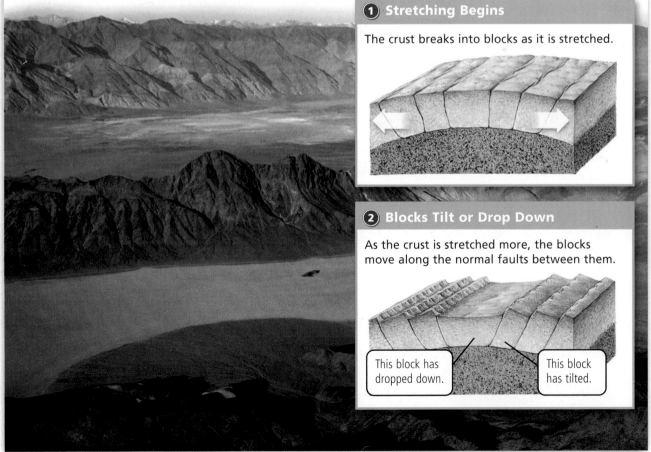

① Stretching Begins

The crust breaks into blocks as it is stretched.

② Blocks Tilt or Drop Down

As the crust is stretched more, the blocks move along the normal faults between them.

This block has dropped down.

This block has tilted.

The Sierra Nevada moved up along one side of the fault.

Approximate location of fault

The land on the other side of the fault dropped down.

The Sierra Nevada in California is a fault-block mountain range. The range moved up along a normal fault along its eastern edge. The block on the other side of the fault dropped down. This combination of upward and downward movement formed the steep eastern side of the Sierra Nevada. The western side of the range tilts down gently toward California's Central Valley.

In summary, both folded mountains and fault-block mountains form over millions of years. Folded mountains are pushed up by slow, continual stress that causes rock to gradually bend. Fault-block mountains form, earthquake by earthquake, as stress built up in the crust is released by the movement of rock. Folded mountains form where continental crust is being compressed, and fault-block mountains form where it is being stretched.

3.1 Review

KEY CONCEPTS

1. How is the formation of mountain belts related to tectonic plate boundaries?

2. How do folded mountains form?

3. How do fault-block mountains form?

CRITICAL THINKING

4. **Analyze** The Ural Mountain belt is no longer along the edge of a tectonic plate. Would you expect the Urals to be tall and steep or low and rounded? Why?

5. **Synthesize** How could it be possible for a mountain range to be continually pushed up but not get any higher?

⬤ CHALLENGE

6. **Analyze** This graph shows how the heights of two mountains changed as they formed. Which line shows the formation of a folded mountain? a fault-block mountain? Explain.

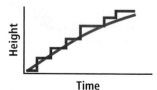

MATH TUTORIAL

CLASSZONE.COM

Click on Math Tutorial for more help finding the mean.

Comparing Mountain Heights

How do the tallest mountains in the United States compare with the tallest mountains in the world? The table shows the heights of the five tallest mountains in the world. All five are in Asia.

Mountain	Height (meters)
Everest	8850
K2	8611
Kanchenjunga	8586
Lhotse	8516
Makalu	8463

To describe data, you can find their average, or mean. The **mean** of a data set is the sum of the values divided by the number of values.

Example

To find the mean height of the five tallest mountains in the world, first add the heights.

$$
\begin{array}{r}
8{,}850 \\
8{,}611 \\
8{,}586 \\
8{,}516 \\
+8{,}463 \\
\hline
43{,}026
\end{array}
$$

Then divide by 5, the number of mountains.

$$\frac{43{,}026}{5} = 8605.2$$

Round your result to a whole number.

ANSWER The mean height of the five tallest mountains is 8605 meters.

Answer the following questions.

1. The table to the left shows the heights of the five tallest mountains in the United States. All five are in Alaska. Find the mean of the data.

2. What is the difference between the mean height of the three tallest mountains in the world and the mean height of the three tallest mountains in the United States?

3. Suppose Mount Everest were in the United States. What would the mean of the three tallest mountains in the United States then be?

CHALLENGE The mean height of all the land in the United States is 763 meters. Does knowing the mean height help you describe the shape of the land in the United States? Explain why or why not.

Mountain	Height (meters)
McKinley	6194
St. Elias	5489
Foraker	5304
Bona	5029
Blackburn	4996

Mount McKinley, Alaska, is the tallest mountain in North America.

KEY CONCEPT

3.2 Volcanoes form as molten rock erupts.

◀ BEFORE, you learned

- Magma is molten rock inside Earth
- Magma forms as a plate sinking in a subduction zone starts to melt
- Volcanoes can form over hot spots far from plate boundaries

▶ NOW, you will learn

- Where most volcanoes are located
- How volcanoes erupt
- What types of volcanoes there are

VOCABULARY

volcano p. 86
lava p. 87
pyroclastic flow p. 88

EXPLORE Eruptions

What happens when a volcano erupts?

PROCEDURE

① Add water to an empty film canister until it is three-fourths full.

② Drop an antacid tablet in the water and put the lid on the canister. Observe what happens.

WHAT DO YOU THINK?

- What happened to the water and to the canister lid?
- What caused the changes you observed?
- How might the events you observed be similar to the eruption of a volcano?

MATERIALS

- empty film canister
- effervescent antacid tablet
- water

VOCABULARY
Make a word triangle for *volcano* in your notebook.

Volcanoes erupt many types of material.

Earth's thin outer layer is made of cool rock, but most of Earth is made of extremely hot rock and molten metal. Some of the heat inside Earth escapes to the surface through volcanoes. A **volcano** is an opening in Earth's crust through which molten rock, rock fragments, and hot gases erupt. A mountain built up from erupted material is also called a volcano.

A volcano may erupt violently or gently. A violent eruption can cause tremendous destruction even if not much molten rock reaches the surface. For example, a volcano might throw out huge amounts of rock fragments that start fires where they land or fall in thick layers on roofs, causing them to collapse. A volcano can erupt gently yet pour out rivers of molten rock that flow long distances. The violence of an eruption depends mainly on the type of magma feeding the volcano.

Magma

A major portion of all magma is silica, which is a compound of silicon and oxygen. Magma also contains gases, which expand as the magma rises. Magma that is high in silica resists flowing, so expanding gases are trapped in it. Pressure builds up until the gases blast out in a violent, dangerous explosion. Magma that is relatively poor in silica flows easily, so gas bubbles move up through it and escape fairly gently. Though an eruption of silica-poor magma can throw lava high into the air, forming lava fountains, visitors can usually watch safely nearby.

Magma rises toward Earth's surface as long as it is less dense than the surrounding rock. Once magma stops rising, it can collect in areas called magma chambers. Magma can remain in a chamber until it cools, forming igneous rock, or it can erupt. Volcanic eruptions occur when, for example, a chamber is not large enough to hold additional magma that pushes in. When magma erupts, it is called lava. **Lava** is magma that has reached Earth's surface.

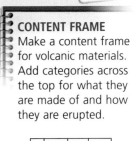

CONTENT FRAME
Make a content frame for volcanic materials. Add categories across the top for what they are made of and how they are erupted.

Structure of a Volcano

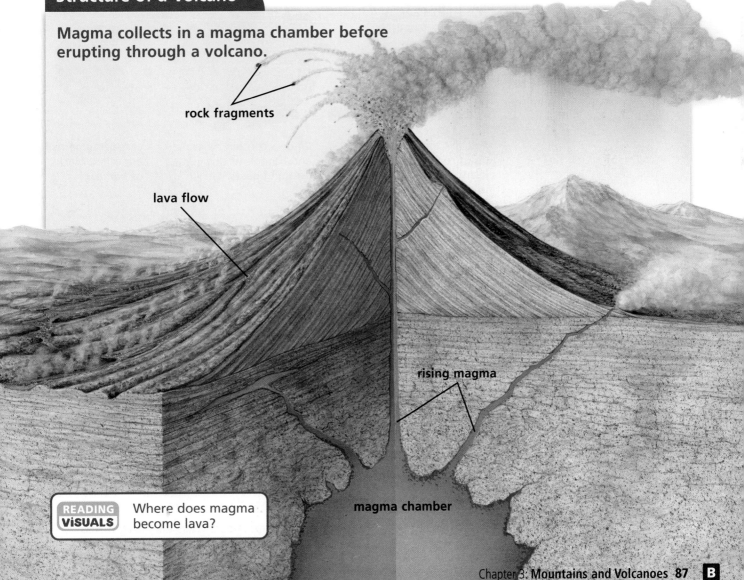

Magma collects in a magma chamber before erupting through a volcano.

rock fragments

lava flow

rising magma

magma chamber

READING VISUALS Where does magma become lava?

VISUALIZATION
CLASSZONE.COM

Watch clips of erupted volcanic material.

Rock Fragments

A great deal of material erupts from volcanoes as rock fragments. The fragments form as

- escaping gas bubbles pop, tearing magma apart
- larger pieces of lava are thrown into the air, cooling and hardening during their flight
- rocks of all sizes rip loose from volcanoes' walls during eruptions

Tiny rock fragments form volcanic ash, which consists of particles ranging from the size of dust to about the size of rice grains. Volcanic cinders are somewhat larger. The largest fragments are volcanic bombs and blocks. Bombs are molten when they are thrown out and often have streamlined shapes. Blocks, which can be the size of houses, erupt as solid pieces of rock. Large rock fragments fall quickly, but ash can be carried long distances by winds—even all the way around Earth.

ash

cinders

block

Volcanic ash is made up of rock fragments less than 2 millimeters in diameter.

Cinders contain holes and tunnels left by escaping gases.

Large fragments are called blocks or bombs.

Volcanic Gases

What looks like smoke rising from a volcano is actually a mixture of ash and gases. The main gases in magma are water vapor and carbon dioxide. Some volcanic gases combine with water in the air to form acids—you will read about these in the next section.

During an eruption, volcanic gases can mix with rock fragments and stay near the ground. The mixture forms a **pyroclastic flow** (PY-roh-KLAS-tihk), which is a dense cloud of superhot gases and rock fragments that races downhill. Such a flow can be as hot as 800°C (1500°F) and can travel faster than 160 kilometers per hour (100 mi/h). Pyroclastic flows are the most dangerous type of volcanic eruption.

READING **TiP**

The prefix *pyro-* means "heat," and *clastic* means "made up of rock fragments."

CHECK YOUR
READING What are two reasons why pyroclastic flows are dangerous?

Most volcanoes form along plate boundaries.

Volcanoes are common along tectonic plate boundaries where oceanic plates sink beneath other plates. As a plate sinks deep into a subduction zone, it heats and begins to melt, forming magma. If the magma reaches the surface it can build tall volcanic mountains.

Volcanoes are also common along tectonic boundaries where plates pull apart, allowing magma to rise from the mantle. Some of these volcanoes are in Africa's Great Rift Valley. However, much of Earth's volcanic activity takes place underwater. Magma erupts along spreading centers in the ocean and cools to form new lithosphere.

Less commonly, a volcano can form over a hot spot far from a plate boundary. Heat carried by material rising from deep in the mantle melts some of the rock in the lithosphere above it. Eruptions over a hot spot built the Hawaiian Islands.

More than 400 volcanoes—about 80 percent of all active volcanoes above sea level—are along subduction zones in the Pacific Ocean. An active volcano is one that is erupting or has erupted in recorded history. The volcanoes around the Pacific Ocean form a belt called the Ring of Fire. Some of these volcanoes are in the western United States.

Ring of Fire

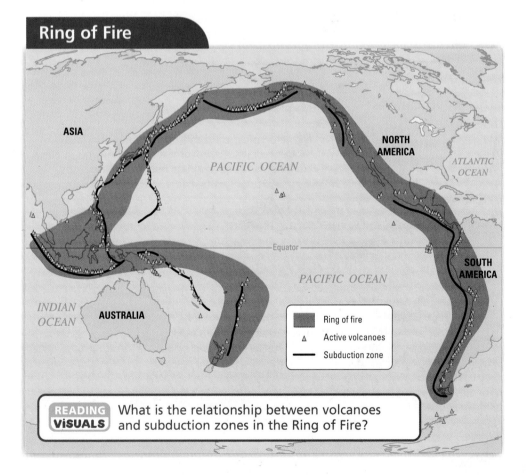

ASIA

PACIFIC OCEAN

NORTH AMERICA

ATLANTIC OCEAN

Equator

SOUTH AMERICA

PACIFIC OCEAN

INDIAN OCEAN

AUSTRALIA

Ring of fire

△ Active volcanoes

— Subduction zone

READING VISUALS What is the relationship between volcanoes and subduction zones in the Ring of Fire?

Volcanoes can have many shapes and sizes.

CONTENT FRAME
Make a content frame for types of volcanoes. Add categories for shape, size, makeup, and examples.

RESOURCE CENTER
CLASSZONE.COM

Learn more about historic and current volcanic eruptions.

Mount St. Helens is a cone-shaped volcano in Washington. Its eruption in 1980 killed 57 people. One side of the volcano exploded, blasting out a mixture of hot rock, ash, and gases that destroyed trees tens of kilometers away. Since 1980, this volcano has had many smaller eruptions.

Volcanoes can have many shapes, including steep cones and nearly flat land. Most volcanoes erupt from openings in bowl-shaped pits called craters. Some volcanoes erupt from long cracks in the ground. The type of magma feeding a volcano determines its shape.

❶ Shield Volcano A shield volcano is shaped like a broad, flat dome. It is built up by many eruptions of lava that is relatively low in silica and therefore flows easily and spreads out in thin layers. The largest volcano on Earth, Mauna Loa (MOW-nuh LOH-uh), is a shield volcano. It makes up much of the island of Hawaii. The total height of this volcano is about 17 kilometers (10.5 mi), but only about 4 kilometers (2.5 mi) are above sea level. At the top of Mauna Loa is a crater that is 5 kilometers (3 mi) across at its widest point. Mauna Loa is one of Earth's most active volcanoes.

❷ Cinder Cone A cinder cone is a steep, cone-shaped hill formed by the eruption of cinders and other rock fragments that pile up around

Three Types of Volcanoes

Two types of material form volcanoes: rock fragments that fall close to the openings they erupted from and lava flows that have cooled and hardened.

❶ Shield Volcano

A shield volcano is built up of many thin layers of hardened lava. Rangitoto, a shield volcano in New Zealand, is broad and has gently sloping sides.

shield volcano

a single crater. Cinders form as gas-rich magma erupts. Escaping gases throw small chunks of lava into the air, where they harden before landing. Cinder cones are tens to hundreds of meters tall. Many of them form on the sides of other types of volcanoes.

❸ Composite Volcano A composite volcano is a cone-shaped volcano built up of layers of lava and layers of rock fragments. Its magma is high in silica, and therefore is pasty. A composite volcano is steep near the top and flattens out toward the bottom. Because hardened lava flows add strength to the structure of a composite volcano, it can grow much larger than a cinder cone.

READING **TiP**

The word *composite* comes from a Latin word meaning "put together." Something that is composite is made of distinct parts.

Composite volcanoes have violent eruptions for two reasons. First, expanding gases trapped in rising magma tend to cause explosions. Second, hardened lava from earlier eruptions often plugs openings in these volcanoes. This rock must be blown out of the way before any more magma can escape. Mount St. Helens is a composite volcano. Though its 1980 eruption was devastating, many composite volcanoes have exploded with much greater power.

 CHECK YOUR READING List the three main types of volcanoes. What questions do you have about how they form?

❷ Cinder Cone

A cinder cone, like this one in Arizona, has steep sides and is a loose pile of volcanic rock fragments.

❸ Composite Volcano

A composite volcano is usually cone-shaped and is built up of layers of hardened lava and of rock fragments. Mount St. Helens is a typical composite volcano.

composite volcano

cinder cone

Crater Lake fills the caldera of a composite volcano.

A huge eruption removed much of the magma from the magma chamber.

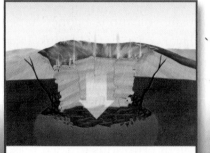

The volcano collapsed, creating a caldera 8 kilometers in diameter and 1.6 kilometers deep.

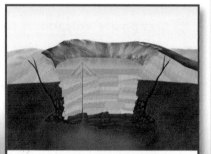

New eruptions built a small cone in the caldera. The caldera filled with water from rain and snow.

Both shield volcanoes and composite volcanoes can form features called calderas (kal-DAIR-uhz). A caldera is a huge crater formed by the collapse of a volcano when magma rapidly erupts from underneath it. The crater at the top of Mauna Loa in Hawaii is a caldera. Crater Lake in Oregon fills a caldera formed by a composite volcano about 7700 years ago. A violent eruption emptied much of its magma chamber, and the top of the volcano collapsed into it. The caldera now holds the deepest lake in the United States.

Scientists monitor volcanoes.

CONTENT FRAME
Make a content frame for types of data used to predict eruptions. Include categories for current activity and history.

Before Mount Pinatubo (PIHN-uh-TOO-boh) in the Philippines erupted in 1991, most people living in the area did not realize that it was a composite volcano. It had not erupted in about 500 years, and erosion had changed its shape. Fortunately, scientists in the Philippines knew that the volcano was becoming active months before it exploded. They were able to warn the government and ask people to leave the area. Their efforts probably saved tens of thousands of lives.

As the 1991 eruption of Mount Pinatubo shows, volcanoes can go hundreds of years between eruptions. Before Pinatubo's eruption, scientists noticed warning signs that included the occurrence of many small earthquakes followed by explosions of steam near the volcano's top. Researchers brought in equipment to monitor the volcano's activity. Although they could not stop the eruption, they were able to tell when people should leave.

Scientists monitor volcanoes around the world for signs of eruptions. Indications that magma is moving underneath a volcano include earthquake activity and changes in the tilt of the ground. Scientists also monitor the temperatures at openings, springs, and lakes on volcanoes, as well as the amounts and types of gases given off by the volcanoes. Rising temperatures and changes in volcanic gases can indicate that fresh magma has moved into a shallow magma chamber.

Scientists study the ages and types of volcanic rocks around a volcano to understand the volcano's history, including how much time has passed between eruptions and how violent the eruptions have been. This information gives clues about possible future eruptions.

Even with close monitoring, most property damage from volcanic eruptions cannot be prevented. But warning people to move away from a volcano that is about to erupt can save lives. Many of the active volcanoes that are closely monitored are located near major cities. Among these are Mount Rainier (ruh-NEER), which is near Seattle, Washington, and Mount Vesuvius (vih-SOO-vee-uhs), which is near Naples (NAY-puhlz), Italy.

The robot Dante II is about to enter the crater of Mt. Spurr, Alaska, where it will collect video data as well as water and gas samples.

CHECK YOUR READING   What is the purpose of monitoring volcanoes?

3.2 Review

KEY CONCEPTS

1. Where are most volcanoes located, and why are they located there?

2. How does the type of material that erupts from a volcano determine the shape of the volcano?

3. What conditions do scientists examine when they monitor volcanoes?

CRITICAL THINKING

4. **Compare and Contrast** How do the three main types of volcanoes differ?

5. **Infer** Volcanic ash can be deposited in areas many kilometers away from the volcano that produced it. What are two ways in which the ash can reach these areas?

⬤ CHALLENGE

6. **Analyze** Draw diagrams showing how a composite volcano might change in shape by getting larger or smaller with repeated eruptions.

Make Your Own Volcanoes

OVERVIEW AND PURPOSE Scientists who have never been to a particular volcano can estimate how steep a climb it would be to its top. All they need to know is what type of volcano it is. Volcanoes vary not only in size but also in slope, or the steepness of their sides. The three main types of volcanoes—cinder cones, shield volcanoes, and composite volcanoes—are very different in size and shape. In this activity you will
- make models of volcanoes and measure their slopes
- determine how the types of materials that form a volcano affect how steep it can get

MATERIALS
- 375 mL plaster of Paris
- 180 mL water
- 500 mL gravel
- 3 cardboard pieces
- two 250 mL paper cups
- stirrer
- ruler
- protractor

▶ Problem

Write It Up

What does a volcano's slope reveal about the materials that formed it?

▶ Hypothesize

Write It Up

Write a hypothesis to explain how a volcano's slope is related to the materials it is made of. Your hypothesis should take the form of an "If . . . , then . . . , because . . ." statement.

▶ Procedure

1. Make a data table like the one shown in the sample notebook on page 95.

2. Mix 125 mL of plaster of Paris with 60 mL of water in a paper cup. Stir the mixture well. Work quickly with the mixture, because it will harden quickly.

3. Pour the mixture onto a piece of cardboard from a height of 2–3 cm. Write "cone A" on the cardboard and set it aside.

4. Fill another paper cup with gravel. Slowly pour the gravel onto a second piece of cardboard from a height of about 10 cm. Label this model "cone B" and set it aside.

step 3

5 In a cup, mix the rest of the plaster of Paris with the rest of the water. Fill the other paper cup with gravel. Pour a small amount of the plaster mixture onto the third piece of cardboard, then pour some gravel on top. Repeat until all the plaster mixture and gravel have been used. Label this model "cone C" and set it aside until the plaster in both cone A and cone C has hardened (about 20 min).

▶ Observe and Analyze

Write It Up

1. **MEASURE** Use the protractor to measure the approximate slope of each cone.

2. **RECORD** Complete your data table.

3. **OBSERVE** Compare the appearances of the cone. Record your observations in your **Science Notebook**.

4. **COMPARE** How different are the slopes of the cones?

▶ Conclude

Write It Up

1. **CONNECT** Which volcanic materials do the plaster mixture and the gravel represent?

2. **IDENTIFY VARIABLES** What is the relationship between the cones' slopes and the materials they are made of?

3. **ANALYZE** Compare your results with your hypothesis. Do your data support your hypothesis?

4. **INTERPRET** Which type of volcano does each model represent?

5. **DRAW CONCLUSIONS** Which of your models represents a volcano that cannot grow as large as the others? Explain.

6. **APPLY** What factors might cause the slopes of real volcanoes to be different from those of your models?

7. **APPLY** If you were a scientist, what information, in addition to slope, might you need in order to determine a volcano's type?

8. **APPLY** How could the method you used to make a model of a cinder cone be used to show how the slope of a hill or mountain contributes to a landslide?

▶ INVESTIGATE Further

CHALLENGE Calculate the slopes of your models using the formula $y = mx + b$. In this formula, y and x are graph coordinates of a point on a straight line. The slope of the line is m. The intersection of the line with the y-axis of the graph is b. For example, if the height of a model is 1.6 cm, and the distance from its edge to its center is 4 cm, then the equation becomes $1.6 = m4 + 0$.

The slope is $\frac{1.6}{4}$, or 0.4.

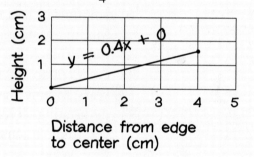

Distance from edge to center (cm)

Make Your Own Volcanoes
Table 1. Volcano Model and Slope

Cone	Drawing of Cone	Slope (degrees)
A.		
B.		
C.		

3.3 Volcanoes affect Earth's land, air, and water.

◄ **BEFORE, you learned**

- Rock fragments, lava, and gases erupt from volcanoes
- Some volcanoes have explosive eruptions

▶ **NOW, you will learn**

- How volcanic eruptions affect Earth's surface
- How volcanic gases affect the atmosphere
- How volcanic activity affects water

VOCABULARY

acid rain p. 100
geyser p. 101

THINK ABOUT

Which volcano is more dangerous?

Mauna Loa is a shield volcano that forms a large part of the island of Hawaii. It is one of the most active volcanoes on Earth, frequently producing large amounts of lava that flow long distances. Mount Shasta is a composite volcano in California. It has erupted at least once every 600 to 800 years for the past 10,000 years. Mount Shasta can erupt with devastating violence. Which volcano do you think it is more dangerous to live near. Why?

Mauna Loa

Mount Shasta

CONTENT FRAME
Add a content frame for how eruptions affect Earth's land and air. Include categories for what dangers are caused and how long the dangers last.

Volcanic eruptions affect the land.

A volcanic eruption can knock down forests and clog rivers with volcanic ash. Damage can occur far from the volcano. But volcanoes build as well as destroy. Material erupted from volcanoes can form new land. Over time, lava flows can form new, rich soil.

Many towns and cities are located close to volcanoes. The people of Goma in the eastern Democratic Republic of the Congo experienced an eruption of a nearby volcano in 2002. A lava flow cut the city in half and destroyed the homes of tens of thousands of people, either by flowing into the homes or by starting fires. Hilo (HEE-loh), the largest city on the island of Hawaii, is built in part on young lava flows. The city is at high risk from future volcanic activity.

Immediate Effects

The effects of a volcanic eruption largely depend on how much material and what types of material the volcano ejects. Near a volcano, lava flows can cover the land with new rock. A much larger area can be affected by events such as ash falls, landslides, mudflows, pyroclastic flows, and steam explosions.

Lava Flows Most lava moves slowly enough that people can move away and not be hurt. But even a slow-moving lava flow will knock down, cover, or burn nearly everything in its path.

Volcanic Ash Near a volcanic eruption, the weight of fallen volcanic ash can cause the roofs of buildings to collapse. Volcanic ash is heavy because it is made of tiny pieces of rock. Ash makes roads slippery, and it clogs up machinery, including cars and airplanes. Large amounts of falling ash can suffocate plants, animals, and people.

Mudflows Mudflows are landslides that occur when loose rocks and soil are mixed with water. Heat from an eruption melts any ice and snow on the volcano very quickly. Mudflows form as the water mixes with volcanic ash and other loose particles. Mudflows also form as ash mixes into rivers flowing from a volcano. Fast-moving mudflows have buried entire towns tens of kilometers from an eruption.

Pyroclastic flows As a pyroclastic flow rushes downhill, it can knock down or burn everything in its way. Pyroclastic flows tend to follow valleys. However, a particularly fast-moving flow can sweep up and over hills, then race down a neighboring valley. As a flow passes, it can leave a thick layer of volcanic rock fragments. Pyroclastic flows are extremely dangerous. In 1902, a pyroclastic flow from an eruption in the West Indies completely destroyed the city of Saint Pierre (SAYNT PEER). Almost 30,000 people were killed within a few minutes.

Landslides Part of a volcano can collapse and start a landslide— a rapid downhill movement of rock and soil. The collapse may be caused by magma moving underground, an eruption, an earthquake, or even heavy rainfall. A landslide can cause a tsunami if a large amount of material falls into the ocean.

Lava Flow

Trees catch fire as a lava flow moves through a forest in Hawaii in 1999.

Volcanic Ash

Large piles of volcanic ash from the 1991 eruption of Mt. Pinatubo line a street in Olongapo, Philippines, at the start of the cleanup effort.

REMINDER

A tsunami is a water wave caused by an earthquake, a volcanic eruption, or a landslide.

RESOURCE CENTER
CLASSZONE.COM

Find out more about
the effects of volcanic
eruptions.

Steam Explosions Though relatively uncommon, steam explosions can be devastating. They occur when magma comes near water or into contact with it. A steam explosion may have caused the destruction of a volcanic island in Indonesia. The entire island of Krakatau (KRACK-uh-TOW) exploded in 1883, causing a tsunami that destroyed hundreds of towns and killed more than 36,000 people.

 CHECK YOUR READING What are two ways a volcanic eruption can result in damage to areas hundreds of kilometers away?

Long-term Effects

Volcanic eruptions can be tremendously destructive. But even after an eruption ends, a volcano can remain dangerous for many years.

The explosive eruption of Mount Pinatubo in 1991 threw out huge amounts of volcanic ash and rock fragments. The area the volcano is in gets heavy rains each year. Mudflows have formed as large amounts of rainwater mixed with ash and other loose material on the sides of the volcano. Since the eruption, mudflows have destroyed the homes of more than 100,000 people.

This school bus was partly buried by a mudflow from Mount St. Helens. No one was in the bus when the mudflow hit.

Another possible source of water for mudflows was a lake that began filling the volcano's crater. The upper part of the crater is weak, and the lake level was rising. A collapse of the crater could have emptied the lake of much of its water. In 2001, people dug a channel to lower the level of the lake, greatly decreasing the chance of a collapse.

 CHECK YOUR READING Why can volcanic ash be dangerous for years after an eruption?

Even though volcanoes are dangerous, over time they can have positive effects. When a lava flow cools, it forms a layer of hard rock on which no plants can grow. However, over many years, this rock can break down to form rich soil. Volcanic ash can smother plants, but the tiny pieces of rock break down quickly and make soil richer. Highly productive farmland surrounds some active volcanoes.

Over time, repeated volcanic eruptions can build a magnificent landscape of mountains and valleys. People may choose to live in a volcanic area in part for its natural beauty. Many other people may visit the area, supporting a tourist industry.

INVESTIGATE Mudflows

How does the shape of the land affect mudflows?

PROCEDURE

(1) Look at the map of Mount Rainier mudflows. Observe the relationship between the paths of rivers and the paths of the mudflows.

(2) Write the number of towns shown within the boundaries of mudflow areas.

(3) Write the differences in elevation between the following locations: the top of Mount Rainier and the point where the West Fork joins the White River, the point where the rivers join and the town of Buckley, and the towns of Buckley and Auburn. Where is the land steepest?

(4) On the back of the paper, explain why in some areas mudflows have followed rivers and in other areas mudflows have spread out.

WHAT DO YOU THINK?

- What three factors are most important in causing mudflows to start near the top of Mount Rainier and flow long distances?

- How likely are future mudflows to follow the same paths as earlier mudflows?

CHALLENGE The largest mudflow starting on Mount Rainier moved at about 22 kilometers per hour (14 mi/h) and covered the land to an average depth of 6 meters (20 ft). Describe the steps you would take to protect people from a similar mudflow in the same area.

SKILL FOCUS
Analyzing

MATERIAL
Map of Mount Rainier Mudflows

TIME
25 minutes

Volcanic gases and ash affect the air.

If you visit a volcano, you might notice some unpleasant odors. These odors come from gases released into the air from magma. Some of these gases contain the element sulfur. Hydrogen sulfide gas smells like rotten eggs. Sulfur dioxide gas is what you smell when you strike a match. The volcano might also be releasing carbon dioxide, a gas you would not notice because it has no color or odor. Volcanoes release gases before, during, and after eruptions.

Many gases from volcanoes are dangerous. They can make breathing difficult and damage the lungs of people and animals. Carbon dioxide can be fatal. In West Africa, a sudden release of carbon dioxide killed 1700 people in 1986. The gas came from a volcano at the bottom of a lake. Carbon dioxide built up in the water until a large amount escaped at once. Pipes are now being used to release carbon dioxide from the bottom of the lake so that the gas will not build up again.

> **READING TiP**
> An element is a substance that contains only one type of atom.

A cloud of hot gases and ash rises high into the atmosphere during an eruption of Mount Etna in Italy.

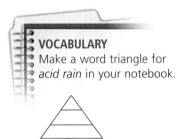

VOCABULARY
Make a word triangle for *acid rain* in your notebook.

Some gases, such as sulfur dioxide, form acids when they mix with water in the air. These acids fall to Earth's surface in rain, snow, or sleet. Rain that contains large amounts of acid is called **acid rain.** Volcanoes are sources of acid-forming gases, but a bigger source is human activity. For example, the burning of coal in electrical power plants adds acid-forming gases to the air. In some areas, acid rain has damaged forests and killed fish in lakes.

Large amounts of volcanic gases in the atmosphere can change weather worldwide. The 1991 eruption of Mount Pinatubo released enough sulfur dioxide to form a haze high in the atmosphere around the entire planet. The haze decreased the amount of sunlight reaching Earth's surface and lowered average world temperatures in 1992 and 1993.

Volcanic gases can lift ash high above an erupting volcano. Winds can then carry the ash far away. During the May 1980 eruption of Mount St. Helens, ash falling 400 kilometers (250 mi) away in Spokane, Washington, blocked so much sunlight that nighttime street-lights were turned on during the day. The smallest ash particles can remain in the air for years, circling Earth many times. These particles also reflect sunlight and can lower Earth's temperature.

 CHECK YOUR READING Describe two ways sulfur dioxide can affect the atmosphere.

Volcanic activity affects water.

Yellowstone National Park in the western United States is famous for its hot springs—places where heated water flows to Earth's surface. Yellowstone is a volcanic region, and its hot springs sit in a huge caldera. The springs' heat comes from a hot spot under the North American Plate.

Geysers

Rainwater can sink through cracks in rock. If it is heated within Earth, it can rise to form hot springs and geysers.

broken rock

Cold water moves down.

Water collects until it erupts.

Heated water rises.

heat source

Old Faithful geyser in Yellowstone National Park erupts more often than any other large geyser. Heated water is forced up into the air through a narrow channel.

Hot Springs, Geysers, and Fumaroles

Most hot springs are in areas where magma or hot rock is near Earth's surface. Water moves down through the ground, gets heated, and rises at a hot spring. At most hot springs, the water flows out into a calm pool. But at a type of hot spring called a **geyser,** water shoots into the air. A geyser forms where water collects in an underground chamber, then erupts through a narrow channel. Old Faithful, a geyser in Yellowstone National Park, erupts every 35 minutes to 2 hours. Most geysers erupt less predictably.

In addition to the United States, countries with many hot springs and geysers include New Zealand and Iceland. Beneath Iceland, which sits on an ocean spreading center, is magma that rises as plates pull apart. People in Iceland use hot underground water as an energy source to heat their capital city, Reykjavík (RAY-kyuh-VEEK).

A feature known as a fumarole (FYOO-muh-ROHL) is similar to a hot spring. Instead of liquid water, though, a fumarole releases steam and other gases. Changes in hot springs and fumaroles located on the sides of a volcano can show that the volcano is becoming more active. As magma moves close to the surface, water temperatures get higher, and fumaroles can release more or different gases.

CONTENT FRAME
Make a content frame for features formed by heated water. Include categories for how they form and where they form.

CHECK YOUR READING   Why might fumaroles and hot springs be monitored?

Deep-Sea Vents

Deep-sea vents are hot springs that form at spreading centers in the ocean. In these places, the ocean floor has many cracks through which cold seawater sinks to depths of several kilometers. The sea water gets heated by hot rock and magma, then rises again. The hot water coming out of the ocean floor is rich in dissolved minerals and gases from the rock and magma.

At some deep-sea vents, warm water flows gently from cracks in the ocean floor. At others, water at temperatures that can be higher than 350°C (660°F) shoots out of chimney-like vents. The water looks black because it contains large amounts of dissolved minerals. As the hot water mixes with cold water, dissolved minerals form into solid minerals again, building up the vent chimneys.

This deep-sea vent is more than 3 kilometers (2 mi) below the surface of the Atlantic Ocean. A black cloud of mineral-rich water rises from the vent.

Deep-sea vents support such unusual life forms as blind crabs and tubeworms that measure up to 3 meters (10 ft) long. These animals feed on one-celled organisms that get their energy from chemicals in the vent water. Unlike other one-celled organisms, these organisms do not need sunlight to make their food.

 CHECK YOUR READING Why do chimneys form around some deep-sea vents?

3.3 Review

KEY CONCEPTS

1. Describe how a heavy ash fall from a volcanic eruption can affect Earth's surface.

2. Describe how large amounts of volcanic gases can affect weather around Earth.

3. Why do hot springs occur in volcanic areas?

CRITICAL THINKING

4. **Compare and Contrast** What do geysers and deep-sea vents that form chimneys have in common? How are they different?

5. **Evaluate** Which is more dangerous, a pyroclastic flow or a mudflow? Explain.

▲ CHALLENGE

6. **Analyze** Ice in Greenland and Antarctica contains layers of ash from eruptions that occurred many thousands of years ago. How do you think the ash reached the ice, and why is it preserved?

JOB

Rangers at Yellowstone

Rangers at Yellowstone National Park help monitor volcanic activity. The hot spot that is now under Yellowstone has powered some of the largest volcanic eruptions on Earth. The amount of volcanic ash and lava produced by Yellowstone's three giant eruptions could fill the Grand Canyon. The last giant eruption occurred 640,000 years ago. At least 30 smaller eruptions have occurred since. Most of Yellowstone's hot springs and geysers sit in the caldera produced by the last giant eruption.

Beware Volcanic Gases

Park rangers must be aware of the effects of volcanic gases given off by hot springs. Here, volcanic gases are bubbling up through mud. Carbon dioxide, a common volcanic gas, is heavier than air. It sinks and fills low areas. Rangers sometimes find the body of a small animal that entered a shallow cave and died for lack of oxygen.

On Thin Ground

It is dangerous to walk up to the edge of Yellowstone's springs, some of which contain scalding hot water. The ground might be a layer of rock too thin to support a person's weight. Park rangers make sure visitors know to stay on safe walkways, and they inform the public about the science of hot springs.

Tracking Yellowstone's Temperature

Park rangers measure the temperatures of hot springs every month. Increases in temperatures or in hot-spring and geyser activity might indicate increasing volcanic activity.

EXPLORE

1. **ANALYZE** Why do you think Yellowstone is sometimes called a supervolcano? What do you think the characteristics of supervolcanoes might be?

2. **CHALLENGE** A geyser's activity often changes after an earthquake. Draw diagrams showing how changes to a geyser's underground system could cause its water to shoot higher when it erupts.

Chapter Review

the BIG idea

Mountains and volcanoes form as tectonic plates move.

CONTENT REVIEW
CLASSZONE.COM

◀ KEY CONCEPTS SUMMARY

3.1 Movement of rock builds mountains.

Folded mountains form as plates push together.

Fault-block mountains form as the lithosphere is stretched.

VOCABULARY
folded mountain p. 80
fault-block mountain p. 82

3.2 Volcanoes form as molten rock erupts.

Volcanoes erupt molten rock, rock fragments, and gases. Different types of erupted materials build up different types of volcanoes.

A cinder cone is made up of loose rock fragments and cinders that form as gas-rich magma erupts.

A shield volcano is made up of many layers of low-silica lava.

A composite volcano consists of layers of erupted rock fragments and cooled flows of high-silica lava.

VOCABULARY
volcano p. 86
lava p. 87
pyroclastic flow p. 88

3.3 Volcanoes affect Earth's land, air, and water.

Materials erupted from volcanoes, as well as heat from molten rock underground, affect Earth's surface.

Land	Air	Water
• lava	• poisonous gases	• hot springs
• volcanic ash	• adds to acid rain	• geysers
• landslides	• haze	• fumaroles
• mudflows	• lower temperatures	• deep-sea vents
• pyroclastic flows		

VOCABULARY
acid rain p. 100
geyser p. 101

Reviewing Vocabulary

Draw a Venn diagram to compare and contrast each pair of features. Example:

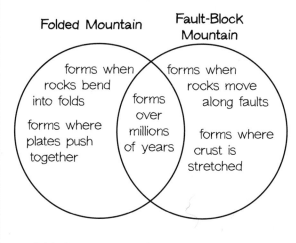

Folded Mountain   Fault-Block Mountain

- forms when rocks bend into folds
- forms where plates push together

- forms over millions of years

- forms when rocks move along faults
- forms where crust is stretched

1. folded mountain, volcano

2. lava, pyroclastic flow

3. volcano, geyser

Reviewing Key Concepts

Multiple Choice *Choose the letter of the best answer.*

4. In areas where the lithosphere is being pulled apart, the crust
  a. folds and crumples into mountains
  b. breaks into blocks separated by faults
  c. slides down into the mantle
  d. develops a subduction zone

5. When two plates carrying continental crust collide, the rock of the continents
  a. folds   **c.** expands
  b. melts   **d.** stretches

6. The movement of huge blocks of rock along a fault can produce
  a. lava plugs   **c.** fault-block mountains
  b. volcanoes   **d.** folded mountains

7. Volcanoes in the Ring of Fire are supplied with magma rising from
  a. spreading centers   **c.** rift valleys
  b. hot spots   **d.** subduction zones

8. Before magma erupts it collects under a volcano in a
  a. chamber   **c.** crater
  b. caldera   **d.** vent

9. The explosiveness of a volcanic eruption depends mostly on the _____ of the magma.
  a. gas content   **c.** amount
  b. silica content   **d.** temperature

10. The type of magma erupting from a volcano determines the volcano's
  a. size   **c.** shape
  b. age   **d.** location

11. Volcanic ash can be carried thousands of kilometers from an eruption by
  a. lava flows   **c.** landslides
  b. pyroclastic flows   **d.** winds

12. In a volcanic region, water moving through the ground gets _____ by magma or hot rock.
  a. melted   **c.** erupted
  b. dissolved   **d.** heated

Short Answer *Write a short answer to each question.*

13. Describe how an old mountain belt located in the center of a continent most likely formed.

14. How are the locations of volcanoes related to tectonic plate boundaries?

15. What causes a shield volcano to be shaped like a broad dome?

16. By what processes can a volcanic eruption affect temperatures around the world?

Thinking Critically

This photograph shows a volcanic eruption. The volcano produces rivers of lava that flow long distances. Use the photograph to answer the next six questions.

17. INFER What kind of volcano is shown in the photograph? How do you know?

18. APPLY Is this eruption likely to produce large amounts of ash that could lead to dangerous mudflows for many years afterward? Why or why not?

19. IDENTIFY EFFECTS How might volcanic gases affect the health of people and animals living near the volcano?

20. ANALYZE What would be likely to happen if a large amount of water reached the volcano's magma chamber?

21. COMPARE AND CONTRAST How could this volcano affect nearby farmland during the eruption? many years after the eruption?

22. SYNTHESIZE What types of changes would let scientists monitoring the volcano know that an eruption was likely to occur?

23. COMPARE AND CONTRAST How does the stress on continental crust in areas where folded mountains form differ from that in areas where fault-block mountains form?

24. APPLY Draw a diagram showing how one magma chamber can supply magma to a shield volcano and to a cinder cone on the side of the shield volcano.

25. INFER Many of the volcanoes in the Ring of Fire erupt explosively. Would you expect these volcanoes to be cinder cones, shield volcanoes, or composite volcanoes? Explain your answer.

26. PREDICT How might an area with many hot springs and geysers be affected as magma and hot rock near the surface cooled?

27. ANALYZE Why do volcanoes form along boundaries where oceanic plates are pushing into other plates but not along boundaries where continents are pushing together?

28. APPLY Explain why shield volcanoes, composite volcanoes, and cinder cones have different sizes and shapes.

the BIG idea

29. INFER How would you expect tectonic plates to be moving at a plate boundary where folded mountains are being pushed up and volcanoes are erupting?

30. PREDICT If tectonic plates continue to move as they are moving today, the continents of Australia and Antarctica will collide in the far future. What will happen after the sea floor that is now between the continents is destroyed?

UNIT PROJECTS

Check your schedule for your unit project. How are you doing? Be sure that you have placed data or notes from your research in your project folder.

Standardized Test Practice

For practice on your
state test, go to . . .
TEST PRACTICE
CLASSZONE.COM

Analyzing Data

The graph below shows the amounts of lava, rock, and other materials released in four large volcanic eruptions. Study the graph, then answer the questions below.

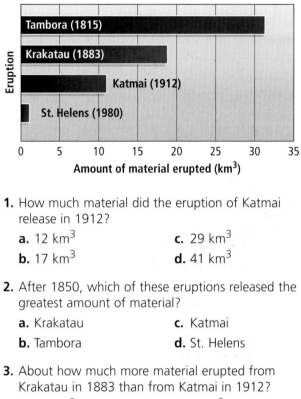

Eruption

Tambora (1815)
Krakatau (1883)
Katmai (1912)
St. Helens (1980)

0   5   10   15   20   25   30   35
Amount of material erupted (km³)

1. How much material did the eruption of Katmai release in 1912?

 a. 12 km³   **c.** 29 km³
 b. 17 km³   **d.** 41 km³

2. After 1850, which of these eruptions released the greatest amount of material?

 a. Krakatau   **c.** Katmai
 b. Tambora   **d.** St. Helens

3. About how much more material erupted from Krakatau in 1883 than from Katmai in 1912?

 a. 28 km³   **c.** 6 km³
 b. 12 km³   **d.** 2 km³

4. Katmai, a large mountain built of layers of hardened lava flows and of rock fragments, is a

 a. cinder cone   **c.** pyroclastic cone
 b. shield volcano   **d.** composite volcano

5. How much material did the 1815 eruption of Tambora produce compared with the 1883 eruption of Krakatau?

 a. less than one-half the amount
 b. a nearly equal amount
 c. almost two times the amount
 d. almost four times the amount

6. All of the eruptions shown in the graph created calderas—craters formed by the collapse of volcanoes—because the eruptions were large enough to

 a. mostly empty the volcanoes' magma chambers
 b. produce lava that flowed long distances
 c. produce lava that had a low silica content
 d. form dangerous pyroclastic flows and mudflows

7. The average temperature of Earth can decrease for several years when a huge volcanic eruption adds to the atmosphere large amounts of

 a. acid rain   **c.** volcanic cinders
 b. energy   **d.** volcanic gases

8. A thick layer of volcanic ash can be heavy enough to collapse the roofs of buildings because ash

 a. is produced as rocks burn
 b. is made up of tiny pieces of rock
 c. becomes heavier as it cools
 d. can hold large amounts of water

Extended Response

Answer the two questions below in detail. Include some of the terms shown in the word box. In your answers, underline each term you use.

boundaries	hot spots	rising
subduction	magma	heat
spreading centers		

9. Petra is marking the locations of active volcanoes on a map of the world. Explain how the locations of the volcanoes are related to the locations of tectonic plates.

10. Scientists regularly check the temperature of a lake on a volcano. Explain how this information might help them learn whether the volcano is becoming more active.

4

Views of Earth's Past

the **BIG** idea

Rocks, fossils, and other types of natural evidence tell Earth's story.

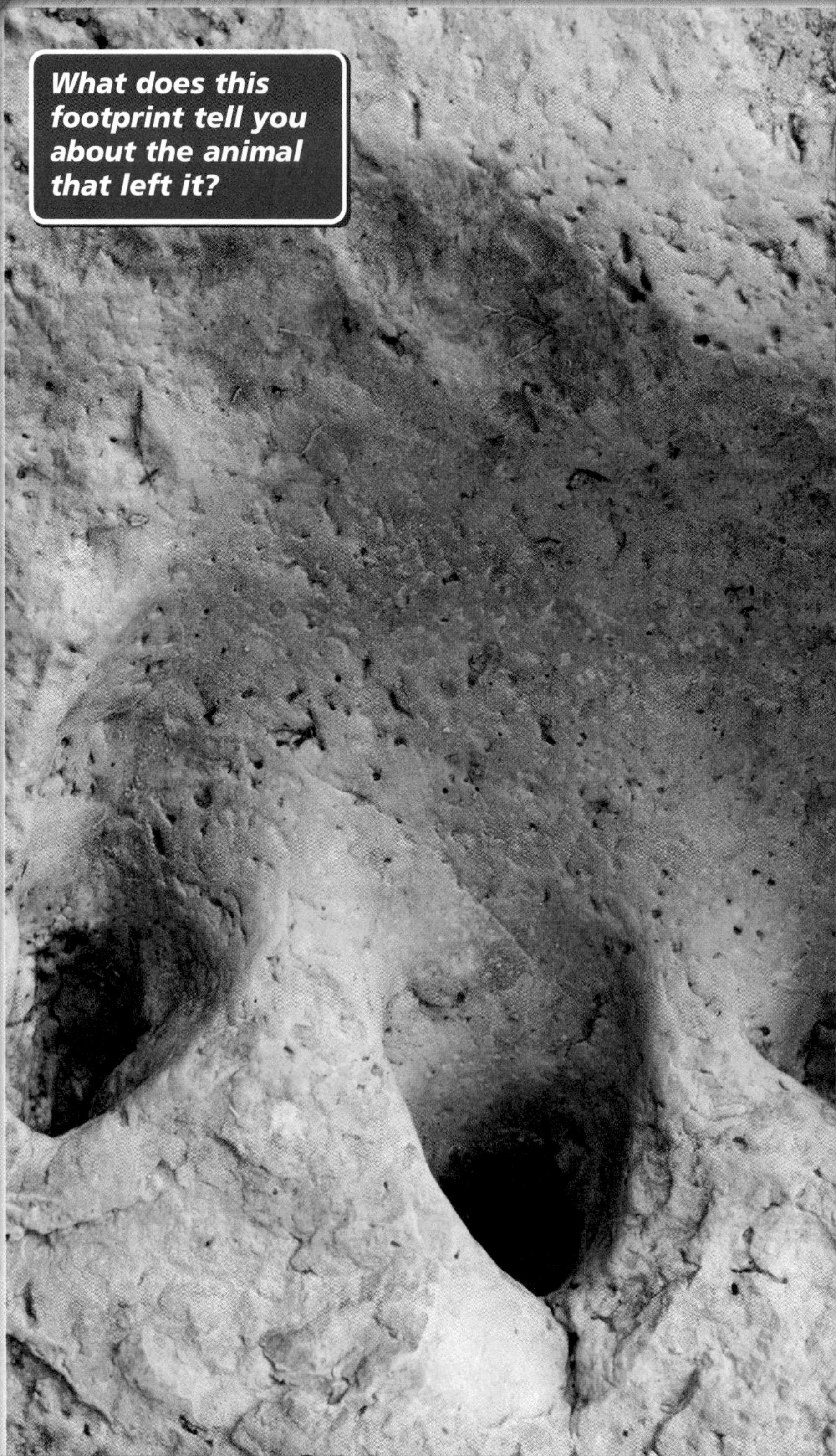

What does this footprint tell you about the animal that left it?

Key Concepts

SECTION

4.1 Earth's past is revealed in rocks and fossils.
Learn about different kinds of fossils and what they tell about Earth's past.

SECTION

4.2 Rocks provide a timeline for Earth.
Learn how information from rocks tells about Earth's past.

SECTION

4.3 The geologic time scale shows Earth's past.
Learn about 4.6 billion years of Earth's history.

Internet Preview

CLASSZONE.COM

Chapter 4 online resources: Content Review, two Visualizations, three Resource Centers, Math Tutorial, Test Practice

EXPLORE the BIG idea

How Do You Know What Happened?

Observe an area around your neighborhood to find evidence of a past event. For example, you might see tracks from tires or a stump from a tree. Record your observations.

Observe and Think
What evidence did you find? What does the evidence suggest about the past?

How Long Has That Been There?

Look inside a cabinet or refrigerator and choose one item to investigate. See if you can tell where the item was made, where it was purchased, how long it has been in the cabinet or refrigerator, and when it was last used.

Observe and Think How did you figure out the history of the item?

Internet Activity: Earth's History

Go to **ClassZone.com** to discover how scientists pieced together information to figure out the story of the dinosaurs.

Observe and Think
What kinds of evidence did scientists use?

NSTA
scilinks.org
SCiLINKS

Earth's Story Code: MDL055

Getting Ready to Learn

◀ CONCEPT REVIEW

- Earth has layers that change over time.
- Movement of rock builds mountains.
- Volcanoes form as molten rock erupts.

◀ VOCABULARY REVIEW

crust p. 11

continental drift p. 15

lava p. 87

CONTENT REVIEW
CLASSZONE.COM
Review concepts and vocabulary.

▶ TAKING NOTES

OUTLINE

As you read, copy the headings on your paper in the form of an outline. Then add notes in your own words that summarize what you read.

CHOOSE YOUR OWN STRATEGY

Take notes about new vocabulary terms, using one or more of the strategies from earlier chapters—**four square, word magnet,** and **word triangle.** Mix and match the strategies, or use an entirely different strategy.

See the Note-Taking Handbook on pages R45–R51.

SCIENCE NOTEBOOK

I. Earth's past is revealed in rocks and fossils.

  A. Rocks, fossils, and original remains give clues about the past.

    1. Original Remains

      a.

      b.

      c.

    2. Fossil Formation

      a.

      b.

      c.

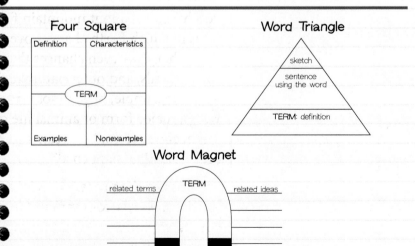

Four Square

Definition	Characteristics
TERM	
Examples	Nonexamples

Word Triangle

sketch

sentence using the word

TERM: definition

Word Magnet

related terms   TERM   related ideas

Earth's past is revealed in rocks and fossils.

4.1

◀ BEFORE, you learned

- The slow, continuous movement of tectonic plates causes large changes over time
- Molten rock cools to form solid rock

▶ NOW, you will learn

- How different kinds of fossils show traces of life from Earth's past
- How ice cores and tree rings reveal conditions and changes in the environment

VOCABULARY

fossil p. 111
original remains p. 112
ice core p. 117

EXPLORE Rocks

What can we learn from a rock?

PROCEDURE

① Use a hand lens to examine the rock sample.

② Make a sketch of any shapes you see in the rock.

WHAT DO YOU THINK?

- What do you think those shapes are?
- How did they get there?

MATERIALS

- rock sample
- hand lens
- paper and pencil

Rocks, fossils, and original remains give clues about the past.

OUTLINE
Remember to take notes on this section in outline form.

I. Main idea
  A. Supporting idea
    1. Detail
    2. Detail
  B. Supporting idea

You have read about mountain formation, earthquakes, and other ways in which Earth changes over time. Scientists have learned about these changes—even changes that happened long ago—by studying rocks, fossils, and other natural evidence. Two hundred million years ago, for example, huge dinosaurs walked on Earth. These giant reptiles were a major form of animal life on the planet for millions of years. Then, about 65 million years ago, the dinosaurs became extinct, or died out. What happened?

To solve the mystery of why dinosaurs disappeared, scientists look for clues. Fossils, for example, are important clues about past events. **Fossils** are traces or remains of living things from long ago. Dinosaur bones and footprints preserved in stone are examples of fossils.

Using fossils and other natural evidence, scientists have formed a theory about why the dinosaurs disappeared. They now think that some major event, such as the crashing of one or more giant asteroids into Earth, led to rapid changes that caused the dinosaurs to become extinct.

Fossils also tell us about organisms, such as dinosaurs, that are now extinct. Even though no one has ever seen a dinosaur, people have some idea about what dinosaurs looked like and how they behaved because of fossils.

Fossils exist in many different forms. Most fossils are hardened animal remains such as shells, bones, and teeth. Minerals replace the remains, forming a fossil of the hard skeletal body parts. Other fossils are impressions or other evidence of an organism preserved in rock. Sometimes, an actual organism—or part of an organism—can be preserved and become a fossil.

Original Remains

Fossils that are the actual bodies or body parts of organisms are called **original remains.** Usually, soft parts of dead animals and plants decay and disappear. But soft parts can become fossil evidence if they are sealed in a substance that keeps out air and tiny organisms. Original remains are found in places where conditions prevent the decomposition, or breakdown, that normally occurs. Original remains are important because they give direct evidence of forms of life that lived long ago.

1 Ice Ice is one of the best preservers of the remains of prehistoric life. Huge ice fields in Siberia and Alaska contain the bodies of 10,000-year-old mammoths and prehistoric rhinos, with bones, muscle, skin, and even hair still in place. The ice preserved the animals after they died.

2 Amber Another natural substance that preserves the remains of some living things is amber. Amber forms from resin, a sticky substance inside trees that flows like syrup and protects the tree by trapping insects. If the tree gets buried after it dies, the resin can harden into amber. Amber can contain the remains of insects and other small organisms.

3 Tar The original remains of animals have also been found in places where there were pools of tar—a thick, oily liquid. Saber-toothed cats and other animals were trapped in the tar and preserved.

Original Remains

1 Ice

This frozen mammoth body was found in Siberia.

2 Amber

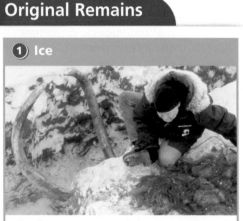

These insects, which are related to flies and mosquitoes, were trapped and preserved in amber 40 million years ago.

3 Tar

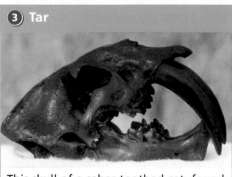

This skull of a saber-toothed cat, found in the La Brea Tar Pits in California, was preserved in the tar for 10,000 to 40,000 years.

Fossil Formation

VISUALIZATION
CLASSZONE.COM

Explore how fossils form.

Conditions have to be just right for a fossil to form in rock. The organism or trace of the organism must be preserved before it decomposes or disappears. Usually, the soft parts of an organism decay too quickly to be preserved in rock. For that reason, many rock fossils reveal traces or shapes of only the hard parts of animals or plants. Hard parts, such as shells, bones, teeth, and stems or tree trunks, decompose slowly, so they are more likely to be preserved as fossil evidence. Most organisms that lived in the past died and decomposed without leaving any traces. An organism that has no hard parts, such as a mushroom or a slug, rarely leaves fossil evidence.

Rock fossils form in sedimentary rock. Sedimentary rock forms from layers of sediment, such as sand or mud. Sometimes, the sediment builds up around animal and plant remains, which can leave fossils in the rock. If sedimentary rocks are changed by heat or pressure, their fossils can be destroyed. Igneous rocks never contain fossils. The heat of the molten rock—from which igneous rock cools—destroys any traces of plants or animals.

CHECK YOUR READING Why do rock fossils form in sedimentary rock rather than in igneous rock?

Theropod Fossil

Artist's Drawing of Theropod

CHINA

This 130-million-year-old skeleton of a small theropod dinosaur, found between two slabs of rock in China, contains well-preserved featherlike structures. The fossil is about a meter (3 ft) long.

Fossils in Rocks

If an organism is covered by or buried in sediment, it may become a fossil as the sediments become rock. Many rock fossils are actual body parts, such as bones or teeth, that were buried in sediment and then replaced by minerals and turned to stone.

Some fossils are not original remains or actual body parts that have turned to stone. Instead, these fossils are impressions or traces made of rock and provide indirect evidence that the organisms were there, just as a shoeprint can reveal much about the shoe that made it. Rocks can contain detailed shapes or prints of plants, animals, and even organisms too small to see without a microscope. Fossils in rock include molds and casts, petrified wood, carbon films, and trace fossils.

1 **Molds and Casts** Some fossils that form in sedimentary rock are mold fossils. A mold is a visible shape that was left after an animal or plant was buried in sediment and then decayed away. In some cases, a hollow mold later becomes filled with minerals, producing a cast fossil. The cast fossil is a solid model in the shape of the organism. If you think of the mold as a shoeprint, the cast would be what would result if sand filled the print and hardened into stone.

2 **Petrified Wood** The stone fossil of a tree is called petrified wood. In certain conditions, a fallen tree can become covered with sediments. Over time, water passes through the sediments and into the tree's cells. Minerals that are carried in the water take the place of the cells, producing a stone likeness of the tree.

3 **Carbon Films** Carbon is an element that is found in every living thing. Sometimes when a dead plant or animal decays, its carbon is left behind as a visible layer. This image is called a carbon film. Carbon films can show details of soft parts of animals and plants that are rarely seen in other fossils.

4 **Trace Fossils** Do you want to know how fast a dinosaur could run? Trace fossils might be able to tell you. These are not parts of an animal or impressions of it, but rather evidence of an animal's presence in a given location. Trace fossils include preserved footprints, trails, animal holes, and even feces. By comparing these clues with what is known about modern animals, scientists can learn how prehistoric animals may have lived, what they ate, and how they behaved. For instance, dinosaur tracks can be studied to learn how fast dinosaurs ran.

RESOURCE CENTER
CLASSZONE.COM
Learn more about fossils.

These ancient logs in the Painted Desert Wilderness in Arizona have been preserved as petrified wood for around 225 million years. Minerals replaced the wood to make the stone logs.

CHECK YOUR READING What do carbon film fossils show that trace fossils do not show?

Fossils in Rocks

Rock fossils show shapes and traces of past life.

① Molds and Casts

A mold and cast are formed in the steps below.

An organism dies and falls into soft sediment.

Over time, the sediment becomes rock and the organism decays, leaving a mold.

Minerals fill the mold and make a cast of the organism.

② Petrified Wood

In this close-up, you can see the minerals that replaced the wood, forming petrified wood.

③ Carbon Films

This carbon film of a moth is about 10 million years old. Carbon films are especially useful because they can show details of the soft parts of organisms.

④ Trace Fossils

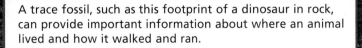

A trace fossil, such as this footprint of a dinosaur in rock, can provide important information about where an animal lived and how it walked and ran.

READING VISUALS What is similar about mold-and-cast fossils and petrified wood?

Fossils and other natural evidence show changes in life and the environment.

Fossils reveal that Earth has undergone many changes over billions of years. Scientists study fossils to learn what organisms and animals once lived in places where the fossils were found. Today the land around the South Pole is mostly covered by ice, but fossils show that crocodiles, dinosaurs, and palm trees once lived on that land. The land was once much closer to the equator.

The earliest fossils are of tiny one-celled organisms that lived in an environment without oxygen. Three billion years ago, humans or the land animals we know today could not have breathed the air on Earth. Fossils also record the disappearance of many species.

Tree Rings

The rings in tree trunks are also a tool for studying the past. The width of tree rings varies, depending on how much the tree grows in various years. In dry years, a tree does not grow very much and the rings for those years are thin. A thick ring is a sign of a good year for growth, with enough rainfall. By analyzing the tree rings of many old trees, scientists can develop an accurate history of overall weather patterns over time.

INVESTIGATE Learning from Tree Rings

What do tree rings tell about the past?

1. Examine the photograph of a cross section of a tree trunk.

2. Count the dark and light rings in the cross section.

3. Compare the rings with one another. Record your observations.

WHAT DO YOU THINK?

- Rings in a tree trunk form as the tree grows each year. The number of rings tells the tree's age. A light ring forms in the early part of the growing season, and a dark ring in the later part. How old was the tree when it was cut down?

- In what year did the tree first grow?

- During dry years, trees don't grow as much. Which year was very dry where this tree grew?

CHALLENGE During what part of the growing season was this tree probably cut down? How do you know?

SKILL FOCUS
Observing

MATERIALS
- Tree Cross Section Datasheet
- hand lens

TIME
20 minutes

These scientists are removing an ice core from a thick ice sheet in Antarctica. Ice at the bottom end is oldest.

Scientists study tiny specks of dirt in the ice, looking for signs of past microscopic organisms.

Ice Cores

In Greenland and Antarctica, snowfall has built up gigantic layers of ice that can be much deeper than the height of skyscrapers and as much as 530,000 years old at the bottom. Scientists drill into the ice and remove ice cores for study. An **ice core** is a tubular sample that shows the layers of snow and ice that have built up over thousands of years. The layers serve as a vertical timeline of part of Earth's past.

Scientists analyze air trapped in the ice to learn how the atmosphere has changed. Increases in dust or ash in the ice show when major volcanic eruptions occurred somewhere on Earth. Differences in the air content at different levels of the ice indicate how much temperatures went up and down, showing how long ice ages and warm periods lasted. This information can help scientists understand how Earth's climate might be changing now and how it might change in the future.

CHECK YOUR READING How does an ice core provide information about Earth's history?

4.1 Review

KEY CONCEPTS

1. What can rock fossils and original remains show about Earth's past?

2. Why do rock fossils form in sedimentary rock and not in igneous rock?

3. How do tree rings and ice cores help scientists understand how Earth has changed over time?

CRITICAL THINKING

4. **Infer** If you uncovered fossils of tropical fish and palm trees, what could you say about the environment at the time the fossils formed?

5. **Synthesize** Why might ancient lake and sea beds be rich sources of fossils?

⚠ CHALLENGE

6. **Rank** Which evidence—a fossil, a tree ring, or an ice core—would be most helpful to a historian studying how the Pilgrims grew food at Plymouth Colony in 1620? Explain your reasoning.

Could *T. Rex* Win a Race?

If you want to know how fast a dinosaur ran, study a chicken. Two scientists, John Hutchinson and Mariano Garcia, did just that. They wanted to know if *Tyrannosaurus rex* was actually as fast on its feet as some people said it was.

To find the answer, the scientists worked to figure out how strong the dinosaur's legs were. What they needed to know was how much muscle the giant dinosaur had in its legs. Yet they couldn't study *T. rex's* muscle mass directly, because there are no complete remains of dinosaur muscle, just bones. This is where the chicken comes in.

Fossils and Fowls

The bone fossils of dinosaurs suggest that birds and dinosaurs have some similarities. Using the chicken as a model for *T. rex,* the scientists found that a chicken needs at least one-tenth of its body mass to be leg muscle. They measured chickens and found they have even more than that, about one-fifth.

The scientists used a computer program to learn if a chicken the size of a 5900 kilogram (10,000 lb) *T. rex* would be able to run. The computer model showed that a chicken that size would need 90 percent of its body mass in its legs to run fast. By connecting their knowledge of dinosaur fossils and chickens, the two scientists showed that *T. rex* was not a fast runner.

Still, the giant dinosaur was not exactly a slowpoke. The scientists also calculated that with its 2.5 meter (8 ft) legs *T. rex* could travel at a rate of about 24 kilometers per hour (15 mi/h). For many people, that's running speed.

EXPLORE

1. **SYNTHESIZE** Based on what you have read, what might be the relationship between the size of an animal and its speed?

2. **DRAW CONCLUSIONS** Why do you think some scientists think that *T. rex*, a meat eater, mostly ate animals already dead instead of live prey?

4.2 Rocks provide a timeline for Earth.

◀ BEFORE, you learned

- Fossils contain information about the past
- Fossils, ice cores, and tree rings record conditions and changes in the environment

▶ NOW, you will learn

- What the relative ages of rock layers reveal about Earth
- How index fossils are used to determine the ages of rock layers
- How the absolute ages of rocks are determined

VOCABULARY

relative age p. 119
index fossil p. 121
absolute age p. 123
half-life p. 123

THINK ABOUT

How old are these bicycles?

You might not know exactly when each of the bicycles shown was made, but you can probably tell which is the oldest. How could you arrange these bikes in order of their ages without knowing how old each is?

Layers of sedimentary rocks show relative age.

VOCABULARY
Remember to add *relative age* to your notebook, using the vocabulary strategy of your choice.

Fossils are clues in the story of Earth's past. But for the story to make sense, the clues need to be arranged in order. **Relative age** is the age of an event or object in relation to other events or objects. You probably know relative ages for many things in your life. For example, if a friend tells you she has an older brother and a younger brother, you know the relative ages of her brothers even if you don't know their exact ages.

Until the beginning of the 1900s, geologists didn't have a way to determine the exact ages of objects that existed in Earth's past. Instead, they reconstructed Earth's story based on the relative ages of different clues. Today there are still many parts of Earth's history that cannot be given exact ages. Determining relative age continues to be an important way of piecing together the puzzle of Earth's past.

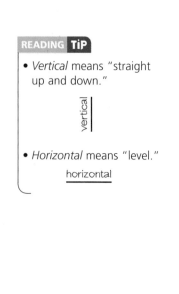

READING TiP

• *Vertical* means "straight up and down."

vertical

• *Horizontal* means "level."

horizontal

Sedimentary rock layers contain information about the relative ages of events and objects in Earth's history. As you read earlier, sedimentary rocks form from the sediments that fall to the bottom of lakes, rivers, and seas. Over time, the sediments pile up to form horizontal layers of sedimentary rocks. The bottom layer of rock forms first, which means it is oldest. Each layer above that is younger, and the top layer is youngest of all. This ordering is relative because you cannot be sure exactly when each layer formed, only that each layer is younger then the one below it.

When horizontal layers of sedimentary rock are undisturbed, the youngest layer is always on top, as shown in the photograph on the left below. But over millions of years, the movement of tectonic plates can disturb rock layers. A whole set of layers can get turned on its side. Rock layers can get bent, or even folded over, like taco shells that begin as flat tortillas. If a set of rock layers has been disturbed, the youngest layer may no longer be on top. One way scientists determine the original order is to compare the disturbed rock layers with a similar but undisturbed stack of layers.

 CHECK YOUR READING | When might the youngest layer in a set of sedimentary rock layers not be on top?

Rock Layers

Undisturbed Layers

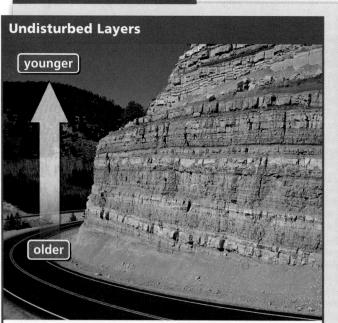

younger

older

Because sedimentary rock forms in layers, the oldest layer of undisturbed sedimentary rock will be on the bottom and the youngest on top.

Disturbed Layers

older

younger

If the rock layers are bent, they may no longer be in order from oldest to youngest.

READING VISUALS | Where are the youngest layers in each photo?

Igneous Rock and Sedimentary Layers

Sedimentary rock layers can also be disturbed by igneous rock. Molten rock from within Earth can force its way up through the layers above it, cooling and forming igneous rock. Because the sedimentary rock layers have to be present before the molten rock cuts through them, the igneous rock must be younger than the layers it cuts through.

VISUALIZATION
CLASSZONE.COM

Watch molten rock cut through layers of sedimentary rock.

① Over time, sand and silt form horizontal layers of sedimentary rock.

Deep underground, molten rock cuts through the sedimentary rock layers.

③ A river gradually wears away the rock, exposing the younger igneous rock.

If the molten rock erupts and flows onto the surface, it forms a layer of igneous rock on top of the layers of sedimentary rock. Over time, more sedimentary rock layers may form on top of the igneous rock. The igneous rock layer is younger than the sedimentary layers under it and older than the sedimentary layers that form on top of it.

CHECK YOUR READING Why is igneous rock always younger than any rock it cuts through?

Index Fossils

Fossils contained within sedimentary rock can offer clues about the age of the rock. An organism that was fossilized in rock must have lived during the same time span in which the rock formed. Using information from rocks and other natural evidence, scientists have determined when specific fossilized organisms existed. If people know how long ago a fossilized organism lived, then they can figure out the age of the rock in which the fossil was found.

Fossils of organisms that were common, that lived in many areas, and that existed only during specific spans of time are called **index fossils.** These characteristics of index fossils make them especially useful for figuring out when rock layers formed.

This rock contains the index fossil *Arnioceras semicostatum,* an organism that lived between 206 million and 144 million years ago.

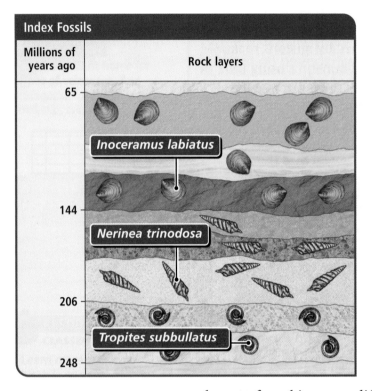

Index Fossils

Millions of years ago	Rock layers
65	*Inoceramus labiatus*
144	*Nerinea trinodosa*
206	*Tropites subbullatus*
248	

Index fossils can be used to estimate the ages of the rocks in which they are found.

The mollusk *Inoceramus labiatus*, for example, is a kind of sea animal that appeared 144 million years ago and went extinct 65 million years ago. So, if you find a rock that contains a fossil of this mollusk, the rock must be between 144 million and 65 million years old because this mollusk lived during that time span.

The chart shows a cross section of rock layers in which *Inoceramus labiatus* and two other index fossils are found. *Nerinea trinodosa* is a kind of sea animal that lived between 206 million and 144 million years ago. *Tropites subbullatus* is a kind of sea animal that lived between 248 million and 206 million years ago.

Remember that one characteristic of index fossils is that they are widespread—they are found in many different parts of the world. Because they are widespread, index fossils can be used to compare the ages of rock layers in different parts of the world.

INVESTIGATE Relative and Absolute Age

How can newspapers model rock layers?

PROCEDURE

1. Have one person in your group arrange the newspapers in a pile with the oldest newspaper on the bottom and the newest on top.

2. After the newspapers are stacked, place one pencil between two newspapers and the other pencil between two different newspapers. Use the model to answer the questions below.

WHAT DO YOU THINK?

- If the newspapers were really placed on the stack on the days they were published, which pencil has probably been there longer?

- Look at the dates on the newspapers. Now what can you say about when the pencils were placed on the stack?

CHALLENGE How does what you could tell about the "ages" of the pencils before looking at the dates differ from what you could tell after looking?

SKILL FOCUS
Making models

MATERIALS
- 5 or more newspapers with different dates
- 2 pencils

TIME
20 minutes

Radioactive dating can show absolute age.

Think again about the friend who tells you that she has two brothers, one older than she is and one younger. You know the order in which they were born—that is, their relative ages. The older brother, however, might be 1 year older or 20 years older. The exact age of the younger brother is also still a mystery. To find out how much older or younger your friend's brothers are, you need to know their actual ages. The actual age of an event or object is called its **absolute age.**

 CHECK YOUR READING What is the difference between relative age and absolute age? Use an example in your explanation.

Half-Life

Because scientists can't ask a rock its age, they have had to find a different way of determining the absolute ages of rocks. The solution lies in the smallest unit of matter, the atom. Atoms make up everything on Earth, including you and rocks. The atoms of many chemical elements exist in various forms. Some of these forms are unstable and break down over time into another form. This breakdown—called radioactivity—is a very useful clock because a particular unstable form of an element always breaks down at the same rate into the same other form.

The rate of change of a radioactive element is measured in half-lives. A **half-life** is the length of time it takes for half of the atoms in a sample of a radioactive element to change from an unstable form into another form. Different elements have different half-lives, ranging from fractions of a second to billions of years.

Just as a ruler is not a very useful tool for measuring the distance between planets, elements with very short half-lives are not very useful for measuring the ages of rocks. Instead, elements with half-lives of

Over time, a radioactive element breaks down at a constant rate into another form.

millions to billions of years are used to date rocks. For example, uranium 235 has a half-life of 704 million years. Uranium 235 is an unstable element found in some igneous rocks. Over time, uranium 235 breaks down into lead 207. Using information from radioactive dating of rocks, scientists estimate that Earth is around 4.6 billion years old.

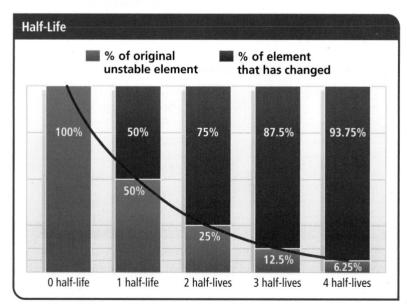

Half-Life

■ % of original unstable element ■ % of element that has changed

| 0 half-life | 1 half-life | 2 half-lives | 3 half-lives | 4 half-lives |

100% | 50% / 50% | 75% / 25% | 87.5% / 12.5% | 93.75% / 6.25%

Radioactive Breakdown and Dating Rock Layers

Igneous rocks contain radioactive elements that break down over time. This breakdown can be used to tell the ages of the rocks.

① 1408 Million Years Ago

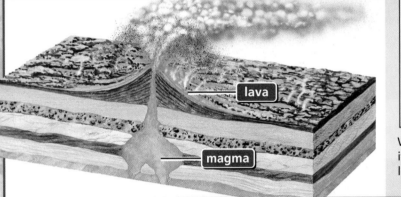

lava

magma

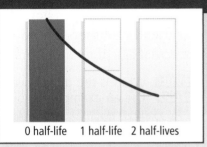

0 half-life 1 half-life 2 half-lives

When magma first hardens into rock, it contains some uranium 235 and no lead 207.

② 704 Million Years Ago

Over time, the rock formed by the volcano wore away and new sedimentary rock layers formed.

igneous rock

0 half-life 1 half-life 2 half-lives

After 704 million years, or one half-life, half of the uranium 235 in the igneous rock has broken down into lead 207.

③ Today

Radioactive dating shows that this igneous rock is about 1408 million years old.

These layers formed before the magma cut through, so they must be older than 1408 million years.

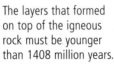

The layers that formed on top of the igneous rock must be younger than 1408 million years.

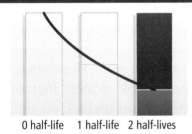

0 half-life 1 half-life 2 half-lives

After 1408 million years, or 2 half-lives, only one-fourth of the uranium 235 in the igneous rock remains.

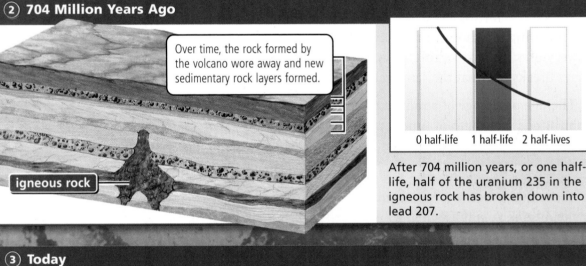

READING VISUALS How do the relative amounts of uranium 235 and lead 207 in the igneous rock change over time?

Radioactive dating works best with igneous rocks. Sedimentary rocks are formed from material that came from other rocks. For this reason, any measurements would show when the original rocks were formed, not when the sedimentary rock itself formed.

Just as uranium 235 can be used to date igneous rocks, carbon 14 can be used to find the ages of the remains of some things that were once alive. Carbon 14 is an unstable form of carbon, an element found in all living things. Carbon 14 has a half-life of 5730 years. It is useful for dating objects between about 100 and 70,000 years old, such as the wood from an ancient tool or the remains of an animal from the Ice Age.

RESOURCE CENTER
CLASSZONE.COM

Find out more about how scientists date rocks.

Using Absolute and Relative Age

Scientists must piece together information from all methods of determining age to figure out the story of Earth's past.

- Radioactive dating of igneous rocks reveals their absolute age.
- Interpreting layers of sedimentary rock shows the relative order of events.
- Fossils help to sort out the sedimentary record.

You have read that it is not possible to date sedimentary rocks with radioactivity directly. Geologists, however, can date any igneous rock that might have cut through or formed a layer between sedimentary layers. Then, using the absolute age of the igneous rock, geologists can estimate the ages of nearby sedimentary layers.

CHECK YOUR READING How might the absolute age of an igneous rock layer help scientists to determine the ages of nearby sedimentary rock layers?

4.2 Review

KEY CONCEPTS

1. What can you tell from undisturbed rock layers? Discuss the concept of relative age in your answer.

2. How can index fossils help scientists determine the ages of rock layers?

3. What property of radioactive elements makes them useful for determining absolute age?

CRITICAL THINKING

4. **Provide Examples** What are some things in your life for which you know only their relative ages?

5. **Apply** In your daily life are there index events (like index fossils) that tell you approximate times even when you can't see a clock? What are they?

⬤ CHALLENGE

6. **Apply** A rock contains a radioactive element with a half-life of 100 million years. Tests show that the element in the rock has gone through three half-lives. How old is the rock?

MATH TUTORIAL
CLASSZONE.COM
Click on Math Tutorial for more help with reading line graphs and multiplying whole numbers.

Mammoths were close relatives of today's elephants. Mammoths lived earlier in the Cenozoic era and are now extinct.

Dating Mammoth Bones

Imagine that scientists find an ancient lakebed with hundreds of well-preserved mammoth bones in it. They are able to measure the amount of carbon 14 that remains in the bones. Carbon 14 has a half-life of approximately 5700 years. How could you use the half-life of carbon 14 to determine how old the bones are?

Example

Mammoth bone A has $\frac{1}{4}$ of its original carbon 14. How old is mammoth bone A? Use the half-life of carbon 14 and the graph below.

(1) Find $\frac{1}{4}$ on the vertical axis and follow the line out to the red curved line.

(2) Then follow the line down to the horizontal axis to determine that the carbon 14 in the bone has been through 2 half-lives.

(3) 5700 × 2 = 11,400

   ↑   ↑
years per   number of
half-life   half-lives

ANSWER Bone A is 11,400 years old.

Half-Lives

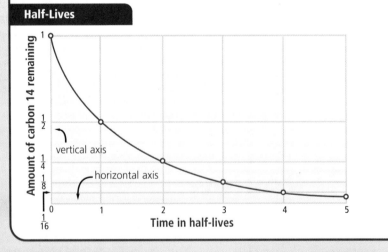

Answer the following questions.

1. Mammoth bone B has $\frac{1}{8}$ of its original carbon 14. How old is mammoth bone B?

2. Mammoth bone C has $\frac{1}{16}$ of its original carbon 14. How old is mammoth bone C?

CHALLENGE Mammoth bone D is 28,500 years old. What fraction of the original carbon 14 remains in bone D?

4.3 The geologic time scale shows Earth's past.

◀ **BEFORE, you learned**

- Rocks and fossils give clues about life on Earth
- Layers of sedimentary rocks show relative ages
- Radioactive dating of igneous rocks gives absolute ages

▶ **NOW, you will learn**

- That Earth is always changing and has always changed in the past
- How the geologic time scale describes Earth's history

VOCABULARY

uniformitarianism p. 128
geologic time scale p. 129

EXPLORE Time Scales

How do you make a time scale of your year?

PROCEDURE

1. Divide your paper into three columns.

2. In the last column, list six to ten events in the school year in the order they will happen. For example, you may include a particular soccer game or a play.

3. In the middle column, organize those events into larger time periods, such as soccer season, rehearsal week, or whatever you choose.

4. In the first column, organize those time periods into even larger ones.

MATERIALS

- pen
- sheet of paper

WHAT DO YOU THINK?

How does putting events into categories help you to see the relationship among events?

OUTLINE

Remember to start an outline in your notebook for this section.

I. Main idea
  A. Supporting idea
    1. Detail
    2. Detail
  B. Supporting idea

Earth is constantly changing.

In the late 1700s a Scottish geologist named James Hutton began to question some of the ideas that were then common about Earth and how Earth changes. He found fossils and saw them as evidence of life forms that no longer existed. He also noticed that different types of fossilized creatures were found in different layers of rocks. Based on his observations of rocks and other natural evidence, Hutton came up with a new theory to explain the story told in the rocks. He was the first to present a hypothesis about Earth's changing over time.

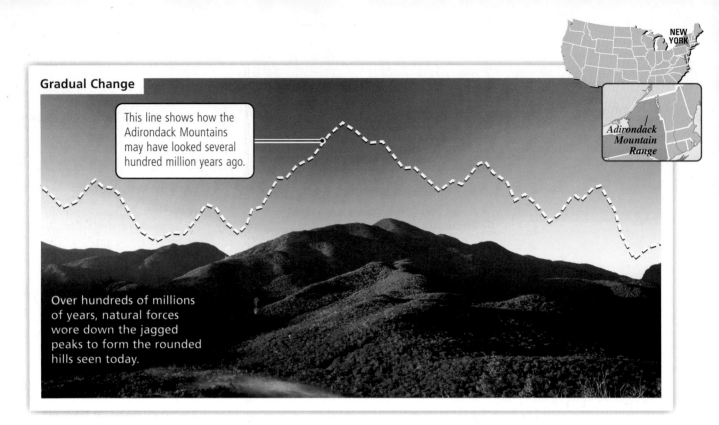

Gradual Change

This line shows how the Adirondack Mountains may have looked several hundred million years ago.

Adirondack Mountain Range

Over hundreds of millions of years, natural forces wore down the jagged peaks to form the rounded hills seen today.

Hutton recognized that Earth is a constantly changing place. Wind, water, heat, and cold break down rocks. Other processes, such as volcanic eruptions and the building up of sediment, continue to form new rock. Earth's interior is constantly churning with powerful forces that move, fold, raise, and swallow the surface of the planet.

The same processes that changed Earth in the past continue to occur today. A billion years ago a river would have carried particles of rock just as a river does today. Similarly, volcanoes in the past would have erupted just as volcanoes do today. Hutton's theory of **uniformitarianism** (YOO-nuh-fawr-mih-TAIR-ee-uh-nihz-uhm) is the idea that

READING TiP

To remember what *uniformitarianism* means, think of the word *uniform*, which means "same."

- Earth is an always-changing place
- the same forces of change at work today were at work in the past

Although this idea may seem simple, it is very important. The theory of uniformitarianism is the basis of modern geology.

Some changes on Earth are gradual. Mountains form and are worn down over many millions of years. Climate and the amount of ice on land can change over hundreds or thousands of years. Other changes are fast. A volcanic eruption, an earthquake, or a flood can cause huge changes over a period of minutes or days. Fast or slow, Earth is always changing.

CHECK YOUR READING What was the new idea that Hutton had about Earth? Describe the idea in your own words.

Fast Change

Mount St. Helens

WASHINGTON

COMPARE AND CONTRAST These photos show Mount St. Helens before and after it erupted in 1980. What rapid changes occurred during the eruption?

The geologic time scale divides Earth's history.

From a person's point of view, 4.6 billion years is a tremendous amount of time. To help make sense of it, scientists have organized Earth's history in a chart called the geologic time scale. The **geologic time scale** divides Earth's history into intervals of time defined by major events or changes on Earth.

Scientists use information from fossils and radioactive dating to figure out what happened over the 4.6 billion years of Earth's history. The oldest evidence of life is from about 3.8 billion years ago, but life may be even older. Organisms with more than one cell appeared around 1 billion years ago, and modern humans appeared only 100,000 years ago.

Imagine Earth's history compressed into one year. If Earth forms on January 1, the first life we have evidence for appears in the beginning of March. Life with more than one cell appears months later, in the middle of October. Humans do not show up until 11 minutes before midnight on the last day of the year, and they do not understand how old Earth is until about a second before midnight.

first humans

If Earth's history is compared to a calendar year, humans appear just before midnight on December 31.

READING TiP

As you read, find the eons, eras, and periods on the chart below.

Divisions of Geologic Time

The geologic time scale is divided into eons, eras, periods, and epochs (EHP-uhks). Unlike divisions of time such as days or minutes, the divisions of the geologic time scale have no fixed lengths. Instead, they are based on changes or events recorded in rocks and fossils.

Eon The largest unit of time is an eon. Earth's 4.6-billion-year history is divided into four eons.

Era Eons may be divided into eras. The most recent eon is divided into three eras: the Paleozoic, the Mesozoic, and the Cenozoic.

Period Each era is subdivided into a number of periods.

Epoch The periods of the Cenozoic, the most recent era, are further divided into epochs.

Geologic Time Scale

The geologic time scale divides Earth's history into eons, eras, periods, and epochs.

Hadean eon	Archean eon

Precambrian time – 4.6 bya to 544 mya

| 4.6 bya* | 4 bya | 3.5 bya | 3 bya | Carboniferous period |

*bya = billion years ago
†mya = million years ago

Paleozoic era				
Cambrian period	Ordovician period	Silurian period	Devonian period	

| 544 mya | 490 mya | 443 mya | 417 mya | 354 mya | 29 my |

Precambrian Time at 3.6 Billion Years Ago

For nearly 4 billion years, during most of Precambrian time, no plants or animals existed.

Paleozoic Era at 544 Million Years Ago

At the beginning of the Paleozoic era, all life lived in the oceans.

The Hadean, Archean, and Proterozoic eons together are called Precambrian time and make up almost 90 percent of Earth's history. The fossil record for Precambrian time consists mostly of tiny organisms that cannot be seen without a microscope. Other early forms of life had soft bodies that rarely formed into fossils.

The Phanerozoic eon stretches from the end of Precambrian time to the present. Because so many more changes are recorded in the fossil record of this eon, it is further divided into smaller units of time. The smaller time divisions relate to how long certain conditions and life forms on Earth lasted and how quickly they changed or became extinct.

CHECK YOUR READING What part of geologic time makes up most of Earth's history?

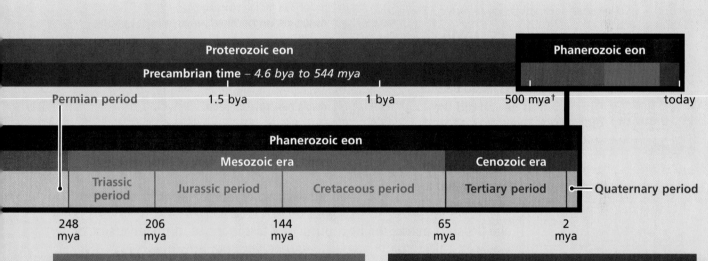

Proterozoic eon				Phanerozoic eon
Precambrian time – 4.6 bya to 544 mya				
Permian period	1.5 bya	1 bya	500 mya†	today

Phanerozoic eon

	Mesozoic era			Cenozoic era	
Triassic period	Jurassic period	Cretaceous period	Tertiary period	Quaternary period
248 mya	206 mya	144 mya	65 mya	2 mya

Mesozoic Era at 195 to 65 Million Years Ago

During the Mesozoic era, dinosaurs lived along with the first mammals, birds, and flowering plants.

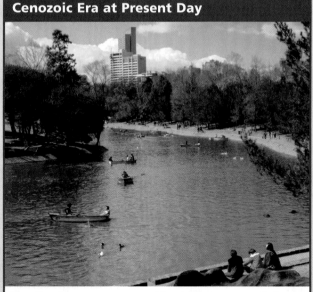

Cenozoic Era at Present Day

The first humans appeared in the later part of the Cenozoic era, which continues today.

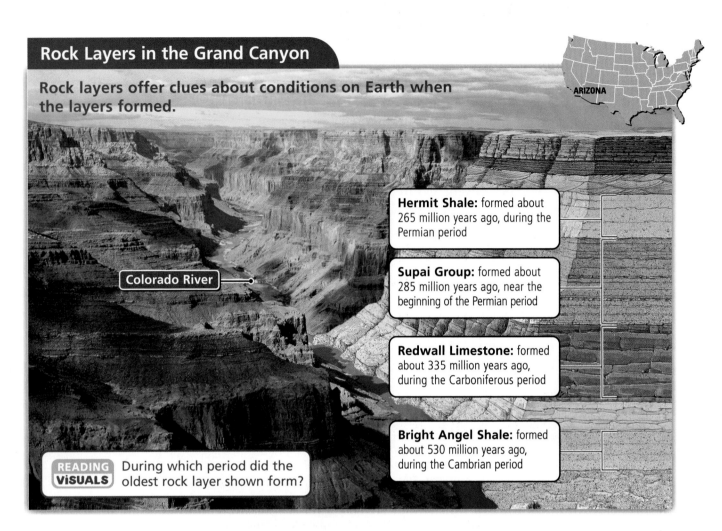

Rock Layers in the Grand Canyon

Rock layers offer clues about conditions on Earth when the layers formed.

ARIZONA

Colorado River

Hermit Shale: formed about 265 million years ago, during the Permian period

Supai Group: formed about 285 million years ago, near the beginning of the Permian period

Redwall Limestone: formed about 335 million years ago, during the Carboniferous period

Bright Angel Shale: formed about 530 million years ago, during the Cambrian period

READING VISUALS During which period did the oldest rock layer shown form?

Phanerozoic Eon

The most recent eon, the Phanerozoic, began around 544 million years ago. Its start marks the beginning of a fast increase in the diversity, or variety, of life. The Phanerozoic eon is divided into three eras:

- the Paleozoic, whose name means "ancient life"
- the Mesozoic, whose name means "middle life"
- the Cenozoic, whose name means "recent life"

The Paleozoic era is the first era of the Phanerozoic eon. At the start of the Paleozoic, all life lived in the ocean. Fish, the first animals with backbones, developed during this time. Toward the end of this era, life moved onto land. Reptiles, insects, and ferns were common. A mass extinction occurred at the end of the Paleozoic era, 248 million years ago. A mass extinction is when many different life forms all die out, or become extinct, at once. The cause of this extinction is not completely understood.

The Mesozoic era spans the next 183 million years and is best known for the dinosaurs that ruled Earth. Mammals, birds, and flowering plants also first appeared during the Mesozoic. For some of this time, parts of North America were covered by a vast sea. The end of the

READING TIP

As you read, find each era in the geologic time scale on pages 130–131.

Mesozoic marks the end of the dinosaurs and many other animals in another mass extinction. This extinction may have been caused by one or more giant asteroids that slammed into Earth, throwing huge amounts of dust into the air. The dust blocked the sunlight, causing plants to die and, along with them, many animals.

The Cenozoic era, the most recent era, began 65 million years ago and continues today. The Cenozoic is often called the Age of Mammals because it marks the time when mammals became a main category of life on Earth.

Around 22,000 years ago, early humans used mammoth bones as building materials. This reconstruction shows what a bone hut may have looked like.

The Cenozoic era is divided into two periods: the Tertiary and the Quaternary. The Quaternary period stretches from about 2 million years ago to the present. Most of the Quaternary has been a series of ice ages, with much of Europe, North America, and Asia covered in thick sheets of ice. Mammoths, saber-toothed cats, and other giant mammals were common during the first part of the Quaternary. Fossils of the first modern humans are also from this period; they are about 100,000 years old.

As the amount of ice on land shrank and grew, the ocean levels rose and fell. When the ocean levels fell, exposed land served as natural bridges that connected continents previously separated by water. The land bridges allowed humans and other animals to spread around the planet. It now seems that the end of Quaternary may be defined by the rise of human civilization.

CHECK YOUR READING
How did falling ocean levels lead to the spread of humans and other animals on Earth?

4.3 Review

KEY CONCEPTS

1. Describe the concept of uniformitarianism.
2. What does the geologic time scale measure?
3. What was life like on Earth for most of its history?

CRITICAL THINKING

4. **Apply** What period, era, and eon do you live in?
5. **Evaluate** Some cartoons have shown early humans keeping dinosaurs as pets. From what you know about Earth's history, is this possible? Why or why not?

CHALLENGE

6. **Infer** How might the geologic time scale be different if the event that caused the mass extinction 65 million years ago had never occurred?

CHAPTER INVESTIGATION

Geologic Time

OVERVIEW AND PURPOSE Geologists use information from rocks, fossils, and other natural evidence to piece together the history of Earth. The geologic time scale organizes Earth's history into intervals of time called eons, eras, periods, and epochs. In this investigation you will
- construct a model of the geologic time scale
- place fossil organisms and geologic events in the correct sequence on the timeline

▶ Procedure

1 Complete the geologic time scale conversion chart. Use the conversion 1 mm = 1 million years to change the number of years for each eon, era, period, and epoch on the chart into metric measurements (millimeters, centimeters, and meters).

2 Lay the adding-machine paper out in front of you. At the far right end of the strip write "TODAY" lengthwise along the edge.

3 Starting from the TODAY mark, measure back 4.6 meters, or 4600 million years. Label this point "AGE OF EARTH." Cut off excess paper.

step 4

4 Fold the paper in half lengthwise and then fold it in half lengthwise again. Unfold the paper. The creases should divide your paper into four rows.

5 At the far left end of the strip, label each of the four rows as shown.

step 5

6 Using the numbers from your chart, measure each eon. Start each measurement from the TODAY line and measure back in time. For example, the Archean eon started 3800 million years ago, so measure back 3.8 meters from today. Mark that distance and write "ARCHEAN EON." Do the same for the other eons.

step 6

ARCHEAN EON
3800 million years ago (3.8 meters)

AGE OF EARTH   TODAY

MATERIALS
- geologic time scale conversion chart
- adding-machine paper 5 meters long
- scissors
- colored markers, pens, or pencils
- metric tape measure or meter stick
- sticky notes

7 Repeat step 6 to measure and label the eras, periods, and epochs.

8 After all the eons, eras, periods, and epochs are measured and labeled, use the same measuring technique to add the fossils and events from the table below.

Table 1. Important Events in Earth's History

Fossils and Events	Time (millions of years ago)
First trilobite	554
First mammal	210
Greatest mass extinction	248
First green algae	1000
Early humans	2
Extinction of dinosaurs	65
First life forms	3800
Flowering plants	130

9 Draw pictures of the fossils and events or write the names of the fossils and events on the timeline. If you do not have space to write directly on the timeline, write on sticky notes and then place the sticky notes at the correct positions on the timeline.

▶ Observe and Analyze *Write It Up*

1. **COMPARE AND CONTRAST** The time from 4.6 billion years ago up until the beginning of the Phanerozoic eon is called Precambrian time. Find the part of your timeline that represents Precambrian time. How does Precambrian time compare in length with the rest of the geologic time scale?

2. **COMPARE AND CONTRAST** The Cenozoic era is the most recent era, and it includes the present. How does the Cenozoic era compare in length with the other eras?

3. **INTERPRET** Where on the timeline are the two major extinction events?

4. **INFER** What does the location of the two major extinction events suggest about how geologists divided the time scale into smaller units?

▶ Conclude *Write It Up*

1. **INTERPRET** Where are most of the life forms that you placed on your time line grouped?

2. **INFER** Judging by the locations of most of the life forms on your timeline, why do you think the shortest era on the timeline—the Cenozoic era—has been divided into so many smaller divisions?

3 **EVALUATE** What limitations or difficulties did you experience in constructing or interpreting this model of the geologic time scale?

4. **APPLY** Think about the relationships among fossils, rock layers, and the geologic time scale. Why do you think the geologists who first constructed the geologic time scale found it difficult to divide the first three eons into smaller time divisions?

▶ INVESTIGATE Further

CHALLENGE Choose several more events or life forms mentioned in the chapter. For each, find either an absolute date or a relative date that will allow you to place it in the correct position in the geologic sequence. Draw or label these new items on your timeline. What new patterns or connections did adding these events or life forms to the timeline reveal?

Geologic Time Scale Conversion Chart

Division of Geologic Time	Millions of Years Ago It Began	Measurement
Eons		4.6 meters
Hadean	4600	
Archean	3800	
Proterozoic	2500	
Phanerozoic	544	
Eras	544	

the **BIG** idea

Rocks, fossils, and other types of natural evidence tell Earth's story.

CONTENT REVIEW
CLASSZONE.COM

◀ KEY CONCEPTS SUMMARY

4.1 Earth's past is revealed in rocks and fossils.

Fossils are traces or remnants of past life. Many fossils are found in rock. Rocks, fossils, and other natural evidence provide information about how Earth and life on Earth have changed over time.

A cast fossil is formed when minerals take the shape of a decayed organism.

VOCABULARY
fossil p. 111
original remains p. 112
ice core p. 117

4.2 Rocks provide a timeline for Earth.

Sedimentary rock layers show the order in which rocks formed. The order of the layers is used to determine the **relative ages** of fossils found in the rock.

Radioactive dating can be used to determine the **absolute age** of igneous rock.

Scientists combine information about the relative and absolute ages of rocks and fossils to construct a timeline of Earth.

VOCABULARY
relative age p. 119
index fossil p. 121
absolute age p. 123
half-life p. 123

4.3 The geologic time scale shows Earth's past.

The **geologic time scale** divides Earth's history into eons, eras, periods, and epochs. The divisions are based on major changes or events that occurred in Earth's history.

EON
↓
ERA
↓
PERIOD
↓
EPOCH

VOCABULARY
uniformitarianism p. 128
geologic time scale p. 129

■ Phanerozoic eon   ■ Paleozoic era   ■ Mesozoic era   ■ Cenozoic era

Hadean eon	Archean eon	Proterozoic eon		
		Precambrian time		

| 4.6 bya* | 3 bya | 2 bya | 1 bya | 500 mya† | today |

*bya = billion years ago   †mya = million years ago

Vocabulary

Make a concept definition map for each of the vocabulary terms listed below. Write the term in the center box. Fill in the other boxes by answering the questions. A sample is shown below.

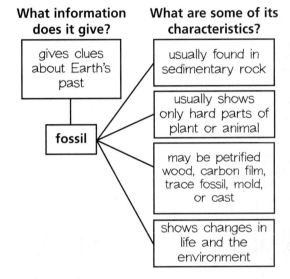

What information does it give?

gives clues about Earth's past

fossil

What are some of its characteristics?

usually found in sedimentary rock

usually shows only hard parts of plant or animal

may be petrified wood, carbon film, trace fossil, mold, or cast

shows changes in life and the environment

1. index fossil

2. ice core

3. original remains

Reviewing Key Concepts

Multiple Choice *Choose the letter of the best answer.*

4. Which of the following might show evidence of a year with low rainfall?
- **a.** tree rings
- **c.** original remains
- **b.** index fossils
- **d.** sedimentary rock

5. In which time span did dinosaurs live?
- **a.** Cenozoic era
- **c.** Paleozoic era
- **b.** Mesozoic era
- **d.** Precambrian time

6. Half-life is a measurement of
- **a.** fossil age
- **b.** radioactive breakdown
- **c.** cold climates
- **d.** relative age

7. What is the age of Earth?
- **a.** 570 million years
- **c.** 4.6 billion years
- **b.** 1.1 billion years
- **d.** 9.5 billion years

8. What was the earliest form of life?
- **a.** a fish
- **c.** a one-celled organism
- **b.** a fern
- **d.** a reptile

9. Which statement best describes the theory of uniformitarianism?
- **a.** Earth continues to change as it always has.
- **b.** Earth is changing, but not as quickly as it used to.
- **c.** Earth is changing, but faster than it used to.
- **d.** Earth is no longer changing.

10. How does petrified wood form?
- **a.** A log falls into water that freezes.
- **b.** Sedimentary rock forms over a log.
- **c.** Igneous rock covers a log and heats it.
- **d.** Water seeps through a log, replacing its cells with minerals.

11. A cast fossil is formed from
- **a.** igneous rock
- **c.** amber
- **b.** a mold
- **d.** wood

12. Which of these substances best preserves soft parts of an organism?
- **a.** sedimentary rock
- **c.** amber
- **b.** igneous rock
- **d.** air

13. Which part of an ancient reptile would you expect to see in a rock fossil?
- **a.** eye
- **c.** heart
- **b.** bone
- **d.** muscle

14. Which type of fossil would be most likely to show the complete outline of a leaf?
- **a.** petrified wood
- **c.** cast fossil
- **b.** carbon film
- **d.** trace fossil

Short Answer *Write a few sentences to answer each question.*

15. Why are no fossils found in igneous rocks?

16. Why is radioactive dating not useful for determining the ages of sedimentary rocks?

Thinking Critically

APPLY *Refer to the illustration below to answer the next four questions.*

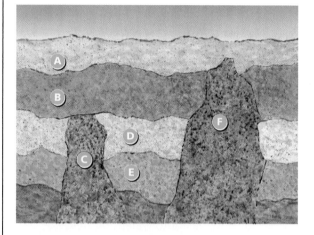

The illustration above is a side view of formations of sedimentary and igneous rock. *C* and *F* are igneous rock.

17. For which of the labeled rock formations could the absolute age be determined? Why?

18. Which of the labeled rock formations is the youngest? How do you know?

19. Which rock is younger, *C* or *D*? Why?

20. Which of the labeled rock layers is the oldest? Why?

21. INFER Why do you think the Hadean, Archean, and Proterozoic eons are not divided into eras, periods, or epochs?

22. COMPARE AND CONTRAST How is the geologic time scale like a calendar? How is it different?

23. CONNECT Copy the concept map below. Use the geologic time scale on pages 130–131 to complete the map.

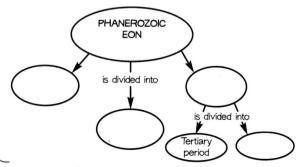

24. APPLY AND GRAPH Copy the graph below on your paper. Plot a point on the graph above each of the half-life numbers to show what percentage of the original unstable element remains. Note that the first point has been placed on the graph to show that all of the original element remains at the beginning, when no half-lives have passed.

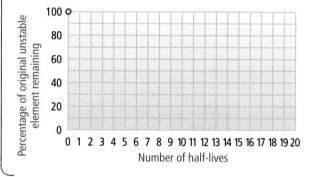

---

the BIG idea

25. SYNTHESIZE Look at the geologic time scale and think about the major events in the history of Earth and the changes in life forms that it shows. How do rocks, fossils, and other natural evidence tell Earth's story?

26. PREDICT What do you think will remain as evidence of today's world 100,000 years from now? How will the types of evidence differ from those that remain from 100,000 years ago?

UNIT PROJECTS

If you need to create graphs or other visuals for your project, be sure you have grid paper, poster board, markers, or other supplies.

Analyzing a Diagram

This diagram shows a cross section of rock layers. All of the layers are sedimentary, except for the area marked as igneous. Use the diagram to answer the questions below.

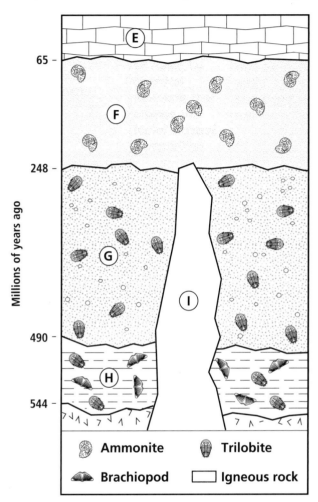

Millions of years ago

65 –
248 –
490 –
544 –

🐚 **Ammonite**   🪨 **Trilobite**

🐚 **Brachiopod**   ▢ **Igneous rock**

1. What is the approximate age of the oldest ammonite fossil shown in the diagram?
   - **a.** 65 million years
   - **b.** 248 million years
   - **c.** 480 million years
   - **d.** 540 million years

2. When did trilobites live on Earth?
   - **a.** within the last 65 million years
   - **b.** between 65 million years ago and 248 million years ago
   - **c.** between 248 million years ago and 544 million years ago
   - **d.** more than 544 million years ago

3. Which fossils are most common in the rock that is 500 million years old?
   - **a.** brachiopods
   - **b.** trilobites
   - **c.** ammonites
   - **d.** theropods

4. What is the best estimate of the age of rock I?
   - **a.** less than 300 million years old
   - **b.** 300 million years old
   - **c.** more than 300 million years old
   - **d.** more than 544 million years old

5. Which point shows where a fossil that is 500 million years old would most likely be found?
   - **a.** E
   - **b.** F
   - **c.** G
   - **d.** H

Extended Response

*Answer the two questions below in detail.
Include some of the terms shown in the word box.
In your answers, underline each term you use.*

index fossils	original remains	igneous rock
layers	folded	bent
ice core	tree ring	trilobite

6. Azeem is part of a team of scientists studying the natural history of a region. What types of natural evidence might he and his team look for? Why?

7. In studying fossils found in her community, Yvette noticed a pattern in their ages. People found older fossils close to the surface and younger fossils at greater depths. Explain how that might be.

TIMELINES in Science

THE STORY OF FOSSILS

Fossils are an important source of information about the history of life on Earth. The first observer to suggest that fossils provided clues to the past was Xenophanes. He lived in Greece around 500 B.C. Today, knowledge about fossils helps people find deposits of oil and understand changes in weather patterns. Above all, fossils reveal information about plants and animals that lived in the past.

The timeline shows a few events in the history of the study of fossils. Tools, such as radar and CT scanners that were invented for other purposes have helped scientists learn more from fossils. The boxes below the timeline highlight the role of technology, along with applications of knowledge about fossils.

1669

Scientist Notes Importance of Rock Layers

Danish-born scientist Nicolaus Steno recognizes that sediments form new layers of rock on top of old layers. Therefore, digging down provides a way to move back in time. Scientists plan to build on Steno's discovery to determine the ages of fossils found in rock layers.

EVENTS

| 1640 | 1660 | 1680 | 1700 |

APPLICATIONS AND TECHNOLOGY

This sandstone formation in Utah displays layers of sediment that were laid down one on top of another.

1799

Siberian Discovers Frozen Mammoth

While hunting for ivory tusks in Siberia, a man discovers a 37,000-year-old mammoth frozen in ice. Unfortunately, before scientists can study the five-ton animal, it thaws and wild animals eat most of it. However, the skeleton and bits of hair still provide clues to Earth's past.

1785

New Theory Suggests Naturalness of Change

James Hutton of Scotland revolutionizes geology with his theory of uniformitarianism. He argues that volcanoes, erosion, and other forces shaped Earth's landscape slowly over a very long period and continue to do so. Hutton's ideas challenge the belief that the landscape is the result of sudden changes and one-time events. His theory leads to a better understanding of the vast ages of Earth and fossils.

1824

Geologist Identifies Bones from Extinct Animal

English geologist William Buckland concludes that a fossilized jawbone comes from an enormous reptilelike animal that is extinct. He names the animal *Megalosaurus*. This is the first dinosaur to be given a scientific name.

1720	1740	1760	1780	1800	1820	1840

APPLICATION

Mapping Earth's Layers

In the late 1700s, the geologist William Smith helped survey land for canals throughout England and Wales. As workers dug deeper into the ground, Smith noticed that fossils always appeared in the same order. He used this information to create the first map showing the locations of rock layers under surface soil. It was published in 1815. As people began to understand the importance of rock layers, they collected more information from projects that required digging. Maps showing this type of information became more detailed and more useful. Today, geologists combine information collected in the field with data from satellite images to create precise maps of rock layers.

This map, hand-painted in 1815, was the first

1861

Workers Uncover Bird Fossil

Laborers digging up limestone rock in southern Germany find a fossil that looks like a lizard with wings. The fossil is about 150 million years old—the oldest known one of a bird.

1923

Dinosaur Eggs Show Link with Birds

Researchers in Mongolia find a nest of fossilized dinosaur eggs. The eggs are in a circle. This fact suggests that dinosaurs, like modern birds, moved their eggs and arranged their nests.

1965

Microfossils Cause Sensation

Two new scientific papers focus attention on Earth's earliest life forms. In these papers scientists describe rocks from Canada that contain microfossils of algae and fungi—traces of life vastly older than any others yet found. These findings trigger huge new efforts in scientific research on ancient life.

1860   1880   1900   1920   1940   1960   1980

TECHNOLOGY

Chemist Creates New Time Scale

In the 1890s, scientists studying radiation began to understand the idea of half-life. The chemist B. B. Boltwood used half-life data to identify the ages of various rocks and create a new geologic time scale. The ages he calculated were in the hundreds of millions or even billions of years—far greater than the ages many scientists had been using. The time scale continues to be modified as new technologies allow for ever more precise measurements.

The half-life of carbon 14 will be used to calculate the ages of the samples this researcher is preparing.

2000

Dinosaur Heart Surprises Many
North Carolina scientists use a medical device called a CT scanner to identify the first known fossilized dinosaur heart. The heart surprises those who thought all dinosaurs were cold-blooded. Its structure suggests that the dinosaur was warm-blooded.

2001

Researchers Find Earliest Mammal
Scientists in China find the oldest known mammal fossil. The 195-million-year-old skull is from an animal that weighed just 2 grams—less than the weight of a penny.

RESOURCE CENTER
CLASSZONE.COM
Learn more about fossils.

2000

When did life begin on Earth? Fossils have helped scientists answer this question. Many think that the oldest fossils date from 3.5 billion years ago. This date might be pushed back if new techniques identify even older fossils. Or the date might be pushed forward. Some scientists argue that the 3.5-billion-year-old traces in rocks are not really fossils at all. Rather, they argue, the traces are just signs of chemical reactions that did not involve any living organisms.

Research on fossils also helps people evaluate the impact of human activity on the environment. For example, the fossil record shows a pattern of warming and cooling in Earth's history. Human activity, such as burning of coal and oil, has helped cause Earth to get warmer over the past century. Further studies of fossils will help people understand how much of this warming is normal and how much is a result of human action.

ACTIVITIES

Reliving History

Get permission to dig a hole outside. Dig down two feet or more. Draw a sketch showing the layers of soil. Add notes to describe any variations that are not clear in the sketch. Try to explain the differences you notice in the layers.

Writing About Science

Suppose you are an archaeologist who has made one of the fossil discoveries on the timeline. Write a speech to your fellow scientists explaining the importance of your discovery.

TECHNOLOGY

CT Scans Show That *T. Rex* Could Smell
Computerized tomography (CT) scans are commonly used in medicine to search inside human bodies without surgery. A CT scan of the skull of a *Tyrannosaurus rex* known as Sue showed that it had a large area in its brain for smelling. Its sharp sense of smell, combined with its size and strength, made the tyrannosaur an effective hunter and scavenger.

This skull is part of Sue's skeleton—the largest and most complete *T. rex* yet found.

CHAPTER

5 Natural Resources

the **BIG** idea

Society depends on natural resources for energy and materials.

How do people obtain energy from Earth's resources?

Key Concepts

SECTION

5.1 **Natural resources support human activity.**
Learn about the costs and benefits of using natural resources to obtain energy and to make products.

SECTION

5.2 **Resources can be conserved and recycled.**
Learn about efforts to conserve and recycle natural resources.

SECTION

5.3 **Energy comes from other natural resources.**
Learn how nuclear power and renewable resources can provide energy to the world.

Internet Preview

CLASSZONE.COM

Chapter 5 online resources: Content Review, Simulation, Visualization, three Resource Centers, Math Tutorial, Test Practice

EXPLORE (the BIG idea)

Sunlight as an Energy Source

Tape black paper around two plastic cups. Half fill the cups with water. Fasten plastic wrap over each top with rubber bands. Place one cup in sunlight and one cup in shade. Wait half an hour. Remove the plastic wrap. Place a thermometer in each cup to measure the water temperature.

Observe and Think
What happened to the water temperature in each cup? How do you think people might use sunlight as a source of energy?

Saving Water as You Brush

Time how long it takes you to brush your teeth. Then set aside a bucket or large container and a measuring cup. Close the sink's drain; run the water for the same length of time you brushed your teeth. How many cups of water can you bail out of the sink?

Observe and Think
Estimate how much water you could save in a week by turning the water off as you brush.

Internet Activity: Resources

Go to **ClassZone.com** to learn more about natural resources and energy.

Observe and Think
What are the most important natural resources in your state?

NSTA scilinks.org SCiLINKS

Nonrenewable Resources Code: MDL056

Getting Ready to Learn

◀ CONCEPT REVIEW

- Fossils preserve the remains of living things from long ago.
- Fossils and half-lives of elements can be used to determine the age of Earth's rock layers.
- The same forces that have changed Earth in the past are still at work today.

◀ VOCABULARY REVIEW

fossil p. 111

half-life p. 123

See glossary for definitions.

geosphere, mineral

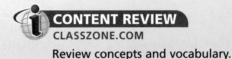
CONTENT REVIEW
CLASSZONE.COM
Review concepts and vocabulary.

▶ TAKING NOTES

CHOOSE YOUR OWN STRATEGY

As you read, take notes, using one or more of the strategies from earlier chapters—**main idea and detail notes, supporting main ideas, content frame,** or **outline.** Mix and match these strategies, or use an entirely different one.

VOCABULARY STRATEGY

Write each new vocabulary term in the center of a **four-square** diagram. Write notes in the squares around the term. Include a definition, some characteristics, and some examples. If possible, write some things that are not examples.

See the Note-Taking Handbook on pages R45–R51.

SCIENCE NOTEBOOK

Supporting Main Ideas

Content Frame

Main Idea and Detail Notes

Outline

I. Main Idea
   A. Supporting idea
      1. Detail
      2. Detail
   B. Supporting idea

Definition	Characteristics
a natural resource that can be replaced by nature in a fairly short time	
RENEWABLE RESOURCE	
Examples	Non-examples
wind, plant waste, wood	coal, natural gas, oil

5.1 Natural resources support human activity.

B

◀ **BEFORE, you learned**

- Earth's distant past is revealed in rocks and fossils
- Layers of sedimentary rock show relative ages
- Living things have inhabited Earth for over 3 billion years

▶ **NOW, you will learn**

- What makes a natural resource renewable or nonrenewable
- About benefits and costs of using fossil fuels
- How people use natural resources in modern life

VOCABULARY

natural resource p. 147
renewable resource p. 148
nonrenewable
  resource p. 148
fossil fuel p. 150

THINK ABOUT

What resources do you need the most?

Think about all the products you use at school and at home—clothing, books, video games, CDs, backpacks, and other items.

Which ones do you use the most often? What materials are these products made of? Plastic? Cloth? Metal? What would you lose if one of these materials, such as plastic, vanished from Earth overnight?

Natural resources provide materials and energy.

VOCABULARY
Use a four-square diagram for the term *natural resource* in your notebook.

For thousands of years, people have used natural resources to make tools, build cities, heat their homes, and in general make their lives more comfortable. A **natural resource** is any energy source, organism, or substance found in nature that people use.

The four parts of the Earth system—atmosphere, hydrosphere, biosphere, and geosphere—provide all the materials needed to sustain human life. The atmosphere, for instance, provides the air you breathe and the rain that helps living things grow. The hydrosphere contains all of Earth's waters in rivers, lakes, oceans, and underground. The biosphere and the geosphere are sources of food, fuel, clothing, and shelter.

However, people also know that there are costs as well as benefits in using natural resources. For example, burning coal produces heat but also releases smoke that pollutes the air. When forests are cut down, the soil beneath is exposed to the air. Wind and rain can strip away valuable topsoil, making it harder for new trees to grow. The soil can choke streams and rivers and kill fish and other animals living in the waters. As you can see, using resources from one part of Earth's system affects all the other parts.

People are also concerned about saving natural resources. Some resources, such as the water in a river or the wind used to turn a windmill, are constantly being replaced. But others, such as oil, take millions of years to form. If these resources are used faster than they are replaced, they will run out. Today people are more aware of which resources are renewable and which are nonrenewable.

CHECK YOUR READING Summarize the costs and benefits of using natural resources.

Renewable Resources

The charts on page 149 list some of the most common resources people use in modern life. As you might have guessed, sunlight, wind, water, and trees and other plants are renewable. A **renewable resource** is a natural resource that can be replaced in nature at about the same rate it is used.

For example, a lumber company might plant a new tree for each mature tree it cuts down. Over time, the forest will continue to have the same number of trees. However, if the trees are cut down faster than they can be replaced, even a renewable resource will run out.

Nonrenewable Resources

A **nonrenewable resource** is a natural resource that exists in a fixed amount or that is used up faster than it can be replaced in nature. This means the supply of any nonrenewable resource is limited. In general, all resources produced by geologic forces—coal, natural gas, oil, uranium—are nonrenewable. These resources form over millions of years.

Today people are using coal, oil, and natural gas much faster than they are forming in nature. As a result, these resources are becoming more scarce and expensive. Many countries realize that they must conserve their nonrenewable resources. Some, like the United States, are developing alternative energy sources, such as solar and wind energy.

CHECK YOUR READING Compare and contrast renewable and nonrenewable resources.

Natural Resources

Natural resources can be classified as renewable and nonrenewable resources.

Renewable Resources

Resource	Common Uses
Sunlight	power for solar cells and batteries, heating of homes and businesses, and generating electricity
Wind	power to move windmills that pump water, grind grain, and generate electricity
Water	power to generate electricity, transportation with boats and ships, drinking and washing
Trees and other plants	materials for furniture, clothing, fuel, dyes, medicines, paper, cardboard, and generating electricity
Animal waste	material for fuels

Nonrenewable Resources

Resource	Common Uses
Coal	fuel to generate electricity, chemicals for medicines and consumer products
Oil	fuel for cars, airplanes, and trucks; fuel for heating and generating electricity; chemicals for plastics, synthetic fabrics, medicines, grease, and wax
Natural gas	fuel for heating, cooking, and generating electricity
Uranium	fuel to generate electricity
Minerals and rocks	materials for coins, jewelry, building, computer chips, lasers, household products, paint, and dyes

READING VISUALS Read the common uses of each resource. Which of these resources are used to generate electricity?

Fossil fuels supply most of society's energy.

When you turn on the air conditioner, a computer, or a microwave oven, you may use energy from fossil fuels. Millions of people depend on these fuels—coal, oil, and natural gas—for electricity, heat, and fuel.

A **fossil fuel** is a nonrenewable energy source formed from ancient plants and animals buried in Earth's crust for millions of years. The energy in such a fuel represents a form of stored sunlight, since ancient organisms depended on the sun. The buried organisms form layers at the bottom of oceans, ponds, and swamps. Over a long time, this material is compressed and pushed deeper into Earth's crust. High heat and pressure change it chemically into coal, oil, and natural gas.

 CHECK YOUR READING Explain how fossil fuels are formed from ancient organisms.

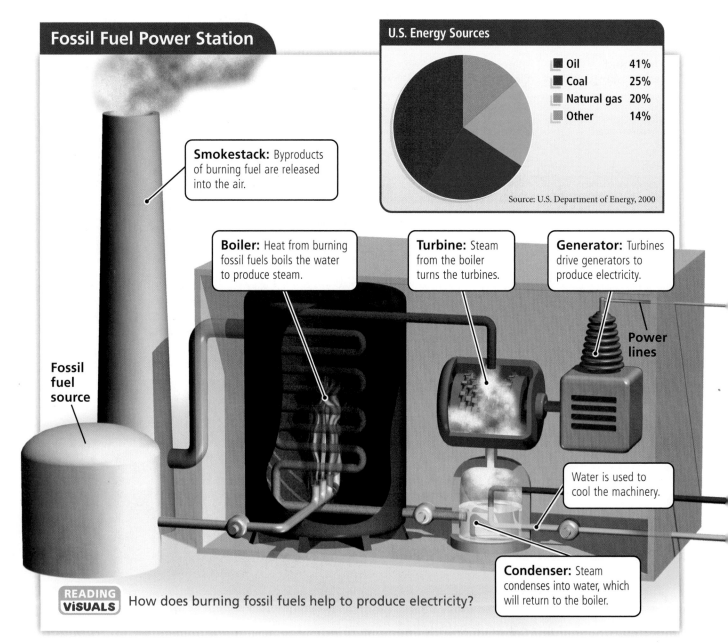

Fossil Fuel Power Station

Smokestack: Byproducts of burning fuel are released into the air.

U.S. Energy Sources

■ Oil	41%
■ Coal	25%
■ Natural gas	20%
■ Other	14%

Source: U.S. Department of Energy, 2000

Boiler: Heat from burning fossil fuels boils the water to produce steam.

Turbine: Steam from the boiler turns the turbines.

Generator: Turbines drive generators to produce electricity.

Power lines

Fossil fuel source

Water is used to cool the machinery.

Condenser: Steam condenses into water, which will return to the boiler.

READING VISUALS How does burning fossil fuels help to produce electricity?

Fossil fuels burn easily and produce a lot of heat. They are used to run most of the power plants that generate electricity. As shown in the diagram on page 150, heat from a burning fuel is used to change water into steam. The steam turns a turbine. The turbine drives a generator to produce electricity, which is carried through power lines to towns and cities. Electricity runs nearly everything in modern life, from giant factories to the smallest light in your home.

But these resources also harm the environment. Burning fossil fuels produces excess carbon dioxide, harmful acids, and other forms of pollution. Most of this pollution comes from power plants and fossil fuels burned by cars and other vehicles.

READING TiP

Turbine is based on the Latin *turbo,* which means "spinning top." *Generator* is based on the Latin *generāre,* which means "to produce."

Coal

Coal is a solid fossil fuel formed underground from buried and decayed plant material. As shown below, heat and pressure determine the type of coal formed. The hardest coal makes the best energy source. It burns hotter and much cleaner than softer coals. At one time, coal was the main source of energy in the United States.

1 Swamp plants decay and are compressed to form peat.

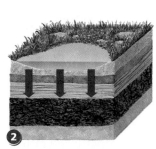

2 Sediments bury the peat, and rising pressure and heat change it into soft coal.

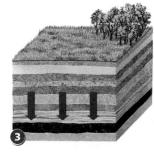

3 Over millions of years, increasing pressure and heat form harder coal.

4 It takes the longest time and the greatest heat and pressure to form the hardest coal.

The world's largest coal deposits are in the United States, Russia, and China. People use surface mining and deep mining to obtain coal. In surface mines, overlying rock is stripped away to expose the coal. In deep mines, miners must go underground to dig out the coal. Most of the world's coal is used to fuel power plants and to run factories that produce steel and cement.

When burned as a fuel, however, coal produces byproducts that pollute air and water. Also, surface mining can destroy entire landscapes. Coal dust in deep mines damages miners' lungs. Yet reducing pollution, restoring landscapes, and protecting miners cost millions of dollars. Society faces a difficult choice—keep the cost of energy low or raise the price to protect the environment and human health.

CHECK YOUR READING What is the main use of coal?

Oil and Natural Gas

READING TiP

Non- is a Latin prefix meaning "not." Porous rock is full of tiny cracks or holes. Therefore, *nonporous* rock is rock that does not have tiny cracks or holes.

Most oil and natural gas is trapped underground in porous rock. Heat and pressure can push the oil and natural gas upward until they reach a layer of nonporous rock, where they collect. As shown in the illustration below, wells can be drilled through the nonporous rock to bring the oil and natural gas to the surface. Major oil and natural gas deposits are found under the oceans as well as on land.

CHECK YOUR READING   How is oil removed from layers of rock?

Recovered oil is transported by ships, trucks, and pipelines from the wells to refineries. Refineries use heat to break down the oil into its different parts. Each part is used to make different products, from gasoline and jet fuel to cleaning supplies and plastics. Oil and natural gas burn at high temperatures, releasing energy. They are easily transported, which makes them ideal fuels to heat homes and to power vehicles.

There are costs in using oil. When ships that transport oil are damaged, they can spill millions of gallons into the environment. These spills pollute coastlines and waterways, killing many plants and animals. Cleaning up these spills costs governments millions of dollars each year. Even after the cleanup, some of the oil will remain in the environment for years.

Air pollution is another problem. Waste products from the burning of gasoline, jet fuels, and diesel fuels react with sunlight to produce smog—a foglike layer of air pollution. Some countries have passed clean air laws to reduce this pollution. Yet smog continues to be a problem in most large cities.

CHECK YOUR READING   What are the benefits and costs of using oil?

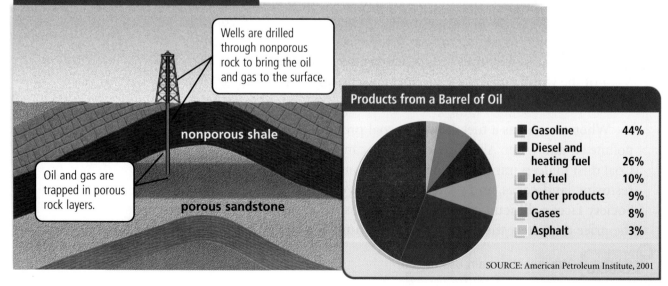

Oil and Natural Gas Wells

Wells are drilled through nonporous rock to bring the oil and gas to the surface.

nonporous shale

Oil and gas are trapped in porous rock layers.

porous sandstone

Products from a Barrel of Oil

■ Gasoline	44%
■ Diesel and heating fuel	26%
■ Jet fuel	10%
■ Other products	9%
■ Gases	8%
■ Asphalt	3%

SOURCE: American Petroleum Institute, 2001

INVESTIGATE Fossil Fuels

Why does an oil spill do so much harm?

SKILL FOCUS
Modeling

PROCEDURE

(1) Fill the pan about halfway with water. Using an eyedropper, carefully add 10 drops of oil in the middle of the pan. Rock the pan gently.

(2) Observe what happens to the drops of oil over the next 2 min. Record your observations in your **Science Notebook.**

(3) Place the plastic-foam ball in the oil slick, wait a few seconds, then carefully lift the ball out again. Examine it and record your observations.

WHAT DO YOU THINK?

• What happened when the drops of oil came in contact with the water?

• What might happen to an animal that swims through spilled oil?

CHALLENGE Think of a way to clean up the oil slick on the water. Discuss your ideas with your teacher before you test your cleaning method.

MATERIALS
• water
• vegetable oil
• large pan (at least 22 cm)
• plastic-foam ball (about 5 cm)
• eyedropper

TIME
20 minutes

Fossil fuels, minerals, and plants supply materials for modern products.

Many of the products you use come from fossil fuels. For example, oil is broken down into different chemicals used to make plastics. Plastic materials can be easily shaped, colored, and formed. They are used in electronic and computer equipment, in packaging, in cars and airplanes, and in such personal items as your shoes, toothbrush, and comb.

Minerals are found in cars and airplanes, tools, wires, computer chips, and probably your chair. Minerals such as limestone, gypsum, sand, and salt are used to make building materials and cement. In the United States, it takes 9,720 kilograms (20,000 lbs) of minerals every year to make the products used by just one person.

Plants are used to make another large group of products. For centuries people have used wood to build homes and to make furniture, household utensils, and different types of paper. Plants are also rich sources of dyes, fibers, and medicines. The plant indigo, for example, has been used to dye fabrics since Roman times.

These products benefit people's lives in many important ways, but they also have drawbacks. Fossil fuels must be burned to generate power for the factories and businesses that produce these products.

Consumer Products

Thousands of everyday products are made from natural resources.

Fossil Fuels

Fossil fuels are used to make thousands of products from aspirin to zippers. For example, oil-based plastics are used to make this motocross rider's safety helmet, suit, gloves, and boots. Gasoline powers the motorbike.

Minerals and Rocks

The U.S. Treasury uses zinc, copper, and nickel to mint over 14 billion coins a year. Gold and silver are used in special coins.

Trees and Other Plants

Each year, the United States produces about 400 billion square feet of corrugated cardboard used to make boxes of all sizes.

Factory waste can pollute air, water, and soil. Even making computer chips can be a problem. So much water is needed to clean the chips during manufacture that local water supplies may be reduced.

To maintain modern life and to protect the planet, people must use natural resources wisely. In the next section you will read about ways for every person to conserve resources and reduce pollution.

5.1 Review

KEY CONCEPTS

1. Define *renewable resource* and *nonrenewable resource.* Give four examples of each type of resource.

2. List three advantages and three disadvantages of using fossil fuels.

3. In what ways are natural resources used to make people's lives more comfortable?

CRITICAL THINKING

4. **Infer** Why do you think people are willing to accept the costs as well as the benefits of using fossil fuels?

5. **Predict** If supplies of coal, oil, and natural gas ran out tomorrow, what are some of the ways your life would change?

◐ CHALLENGE

6. **Apply** Suppose you are lost in the woods, miles from any city or town. You have some dried food and matches but no other supplies. What natural resources might you use to survive until you are found?

Got Oil Spills? Call in the Microbes!

You have seen the photographs. A beautiful coastline is fouled by dark, sticky oil. The oil slick coats birds and other animals the same dark color. Hundreds of experts and volunteers appear with buckets, chemicals, shovels, and brooms to clean up the mess.

But did you know that seawater and the world's beaches contain their own natural cleanup crews? These crews consist of tiny microbes that digest oil and other waste products and turn them into gases such as carbon dioxide.

Nature's Disposal Units Do a Great Job . . .

Scientists learned how effective oil-digesting microbes are during the 1989 *Exxon Valdez* oil spill in Alaska. Since then, cleanup crews have been using bacteria and other microbes to help clean up oil spills around the world. Scientists find that areas treated with microbes recover faster than areas treated with chemicals.

. . . But It Is Not All That Simple

Cleaning up oil spills is not as simple as watching millions of microbes munch their way through the mess. Scientists have had to solve a few problems.

- **Problem:** Microbes cannot multiply fast enough to handle a large oil spill. **Solution:** Add nutrients to help them multiply faster.
- **Problem:** There are not enough of the right types of microbes to digest oil. **Solution:** Grow the desired microbes in a laboratory, and add them into the polluted area.
- **Problem:** There is not enough oxygen in the water for all the microbes. **Solution:** Pump in more oxygen to help them work.

Who would have imagined that a partnership between people and microbes would be the best way to clean up oil spills?

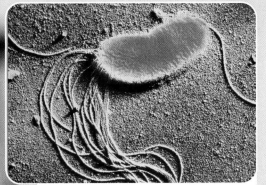

Above is the oil-eating microbe *Pseudomonas fluorescens*, magnified 17,300 times. Millions of microbes like this swim in the water layer that surrounds soil particles. They digest oil clinging to the particles.

This otter swam through a spill and was covered in black, sticky oil. Animals who try to clean their fur will swallow the oil, which is poisonous.

EXPLORE

1. **COLLECT DATA** Go to the EPA Web site to learn how the agency uses microbes to clean up different types of pollution. Look under the word *bioremediation,* which means "the correction of a problem through biological means."
2. **CHALLENGE** Do research on bioremediation and find out whether there are any drawbacks to using microbes to clean up pollution.

RESOURCE CENTER
CLASSZONE.COM
Read about microbes that eat pollutants for lunch.

5.2 Resources can be conserved and recycled.

<table>
<tr><td>◀ **BEFORE,** you learned</td><td>▶ **NOW,** you will learn</td></tr>
<tr><td>

- Natural resources are either renewable or nonrenewable
- Fossil fuels are used to supply most of society's energy and products, but at a cost to the environment

</td><td>

- How conservation can help people to reduce waste and reuse natural resources
- How recycling can help people to recover and extend natural resources

</td></tr>
</table>

VOCABULARY

conservation p. 157
recycling p. 158

EXPLORE Energy Use

What is your EQ (energy quotient)?

PROCEDURE

MATERIALS
- paper
- pen or pencil
- calculator

① Think about the electrical appliances you use every day at home (TV, computer, room lights, microwave, hair curler, hair dryer). Draw a usage chart like the one in the photo.

② Estimate the number of hours you use each item every day. Add up all the hours in each column.

③ Multiply the total of each column by 2.5 kilowatts. This is your energy quotient.

WHAT DO YOU THINK?
- Which item(s) do you use the most? How much of the use is necessary?
- What ways can you think of to conserve electricity each day?

Conservation involves reducing waste and reusing natural resources.

NOTE TAKING
You might want to take main idea and details notes as you read this section.

In the 1960s, each person in the United States produced 1.2 kilograms (2.7 lb) of trash a day. Today, that number has doubled. All together, the nation's households produce nearly 180 million tons of trash each year! Over half of this amount is buried in landfills.

Conservation programs can be used to extend natural resources, to protect human health, and to slow the growing mountain of trash. Read on to find out how much your efforts count.

Conservation means protecting, restoring, and managing natural resources so that they last as long as possible. Conserving resources can also reduce the amount of pollution released into the air, water, and soil. There are two ways every person can help: reducing and reusing.

VOCABULARY
Add a four-square diagram for the term *conservation* in your notebook.

Reduce You can reduce waste at the source, whether the source is a local retail store or your own home. Here are a few suggestions:

- When choosing between two similar products, choose the one with less packaging. Product packaging is a major source of paper and plastic waste.
- When brushing your teeth or washing your face, turn the water off until you are ready to rinse. You can save 8 to 23 liters (2 to 6 gal.) of water a day, or 2920 to 8395 liters (730 to 2190 gal.) per year.
- When eating in a restaurant or cafeteria, use only the napkins and ketchup and mustard packets that you really need. The less you throw away, the less garbage will be buried in a landfill.
- Where possible, use energy-efficient light bulbs in your home. Turn off lights and appliances when you are not using them.

Reuse Many products can be used more than once. Reusable products and containers conserve materials and resources. Here are some things that you can do:

- Refill plastic water bottles instead of buying new bottles.
- Donate old clothes and other items instead of throwing them away.
- Rinse and reuse plastic sandwich and storage bags.
- Cut the top off a half-gallon container to make a watering can.

Reducing Waste

You can reduce paper and plastic waste by choosing products with the least packaging.

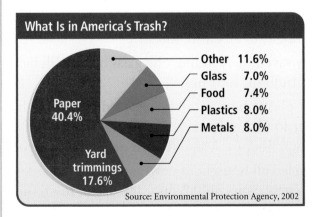

What Is in America's Trash?

Other 11.6%
Glass 7.0%
Food 7.4%
Plastics 8.0%
Metals 8.0%
Paper 40.4%
Yard trimmings 17.6%

Source: Environmental Protection Agency, 2002

This 1.9 liter (64 fl oz) carton has 1088 sq cm of packaging.

Eight travel-size containers provide 1.9 liters (64 fl oz) but have 2720 sq cm of packaging.

How can you tell which bulb wastes less energy?

The more heat a light bulb gives off, the more energy it wastes. Use what you know about how to measure the temperature of an object to design an experiment that confirms which type of light bulb wastes less energy.

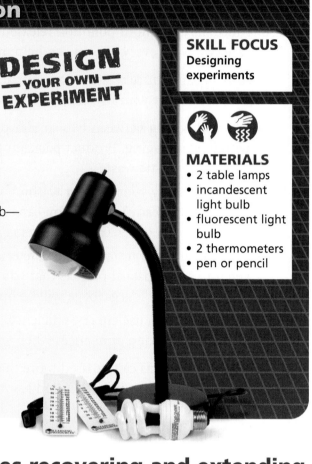

DESIGN
—YOUR OWN—
EXPERIMENT

SKILL FOCUS
Designing experiments

MATERIALS
• 2 table lamps
• incandescent light bulb
• fluorescent light bulb
• 2 thermometers
• pen or pencil

PROCEDURE

1. Figure out how you are going to test which light bulb—incandescent or fluorescent—wastes less energy.

2. Write up your procedure.

3. Conduct your experiment and record your results.

WHAT DO YOU THINK?

• What were the variables in your experiment?
• What were the results of your experiment?
• How does your experiment demonstrate which light bulb is less wasteful?

Recycling involves recovering and extending natural resources.

Did you know that recycling one aluminum can saves enough energy to run a television set for three hours? **Recycling** involves recovering materials that people usually throw away. Some common materials you can recycle are glass, aluminum cans, certain plastics, paper, scrap iron, and such metals as gold, copper, and silver. Here are a few statistics that might encourage you to recycle:

With every item you recycle, you help to recover and extend limited resources.

• Recycling 90 percent of the newspapers printed in the United States on just one Sunday would save 500,000 trees, equivalent to an entire forest.

• The energy saved by recycling one glass bottle will light a 100-watt bulb for four hours.

• Five 2-liter plastic bottles can be recycled into enough plastic fiber to fill a ski jacket. Thirty-six bottles will make enough fiber for a square yard of synthetic carpet.

• If you recycled all household newspapers, cardboard, glass, and metal, you could reduce the use of fossil fuels. It takes less energy to make products from recycled materials than to make new products.

Recycled: 500 kilograms (1,102 lb) of cans, glass, plastic, and paper

Buried in landfill: 2500 kilograms (5,512 lb) of garbage

The average family of four generates about 3,000 kilograms (6614 lb) of trash per year. Recycling is catching on, but there is still a long way to go.

It is important to remember that not every item can be recycled or reused. In the photograph above, for instance, only about one-fifth of the family's trash is being recycled. Even some types of plastic and glass items must be thrown away because they cannot be recovered. All the trash in the family's plastic bags will be buried in landfills. You can see why it is important to recycle the items you can and to avoid using items that cannot be recycled.

Recycling is only part of the solution to our resource problems. It takes time, energy, and money to collect waste materials, sort them, remove what can be used, and form new objects. Even with these limitations, however, recycling can help extend available resources and protect human health and the environment.

CHECK YOUR READING What are some of the benefits and drawbacks of recycling?

5.2 Review

KEY CONCEPTS

1. Give examples of ways people can reduce waste and conserve natural resources.

2. Explain how recycling can help people recover and extend natural resources.

3. What are some of the limitations of conservation and recycling programs?

CRITICAL THINKING

4. **Evaluate** How can conserving or recycling materials help protect the environment?

5. **Calculate** Your city pays $115 per ton to bury an average of 13 tons of garbage a month in a landfill. A recycling program could reduce that number to 8 tons a month. How much would the city save in landfill fees per month? per year?

CHALLENGE

6. **Synthesize** Work with a group of classmates to list some of the ways in which you could conserve and recycle resources in your home and at school. Create a graphic—such as a poster or advertisement—to present your ideas to the rest of the class.

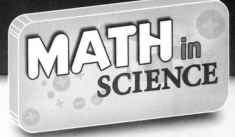

Gas Mileage

An automobile engineer ran tests on new cars to determine their gas mileage in miles per gallon. Her results were in decimals. You can compare two decimals by looking at their place values to determine which is greater.

Steps for comparing decimals

(1) Write the decimals in a column, lining up the decimal points.

(2) If necessary, write zeros to the right of one decimal so that both decimals have the same number of decimal places.

(3) Compare the place values from left to right.

MATH TUTORIAL

CLASSZONE.COM

Click on Math Tutorial for more help with comparing decimals.

Examples

Example A
For two mid-size sedans, she calculated the following mileages:

The tens digits are the same.

The ones digits are the same.

Car A: 28.450 mi/gal
Car B: 28.502 mi/gal

The tenths digits are different: 5 > 4.

ANSWER:
28.450 mi/gal < 28.502 mi/gal

Example B
For two sport utility vehicles (SUVs), she calculated the following mileages:

The tens digits are the same.

The ones digits are the same.

SUV A: 12.94 mi/gal
SUV B: 12.90 mi/gal

The tenths digits are the same.

The hundredths digits are different: 4 > 0.

ANSWER:
12.94 mi/gal > 12.90 mi/gal

Copy each statement and complete it with <, >, or =.

1. 34.75 mi/gal ___ 34.56 mi/gal

2. 50.5 mi/gal ___ 50.50 mi/gal

3. 52.309 mi/gal ___ 52.311 mi/gal

4. 26.115 mi/gal ___ 26.106 mi/gal

5. 41.75 mi/gal ___ 41.750 mi/gal

CHALLENGE Find a value of n that makes the following statement true:

38.0894 mi/gal > n > 38.08925 mi/gal

5.3 Energy comes from other natural resources.

BEFORE, you learned

- Conservation helps people reduce waste and reuse natural resources
- Recycling helps people recover and extend natural resources

NOW, you will learn

- About the benefits and costs of nuclear power
- How renewable resources are used to generate energy

VOCABULARY

nuclear fission p. 161
hydroelectric energy p. 164
solar cell p. 165
geothermal energy p. 166
biomass p. 168
hydrogen fuel cell p. 168

EXPLORE Nuclear Energy

How can you model splitting atoms?

PROCEDURE

1. Work in a small group for this activity. Draw a large circle on a piece of paper. Set the paper on the floor or on a countertop.

2. Put a handful of marbles in the circle (see the photograph). Imagine the circle is an atom and the marbles are particles in its nucleus.

3. Take turns shooting one marble into the others. Put the marbles back in the circle after each shot. Record your observations.

MATERIALS
- marbles
- large piece of paper
- pen or marker

WHAT DO YOU THINK?
- How many marbles were moved by each shot?
- What does this activity suggest will happen when the center of an atom is struck?

NOTE TAKING
As you read this section, pick a note-taking strategy that will help you list the benefits and limits of each type of energy source.

Nuclear power is used to produce electricity.

Fossil fuels are the most commonly used sources of energy, but they are not the only ones. The United States and many other countries use nuclear power to produce electricity. In the United States, nuclear power plants generate about 10 percent of the total energy used.

You learned that in fossil fuel power plants, water is boiled to make steam that turns a turbine, which drives a generator. In a nuclear power plant, the same process happens. However, the source of energy used to heat the water is nuclear fission. In the process of **nuclear fission,** the nucleus of a radioactive atom is split, forming lighter elements and releasing a huge amount of energy.

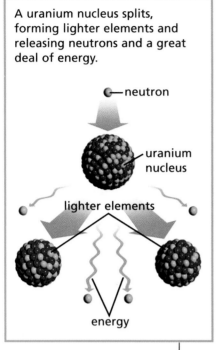

A uranium nucleus splits, forming lighter elements and releasing neutrons and a great deal of energy.

neutron

uranium nucleus

lighter elements

energy

Nuclear power plants use uranium atoms as fuel. When a uranium nucleus splits, it forms two smaller nuclei. It also releases two or three neutrons and a large amount of energy in the form of light and heat. The neutrons split other uranium nuclei in a process called a chain reaction. This process is similar to shooting one marble into a group of marbles. Every marble that is hit will strike others nearby.

The power-plant diagram below shows the reactor vessel where the chain reaction takes place. Control rods are used to limit the reaction to provide a safe amount of energy. The chain reaction creates enough heat to produce steam in the reactor vessel. The steam heats a coiled pipe, which is used to boil water in the heat exchanger.

Steam from the exchanger turns the turbines, which drive the generators that produce electricity. The steam condenses into water and is pumped back into the heat exchanger. Water from the cooling tower keeps the equipment from overheating. As you can see, nuclear power plants require an abundant water supply to produce steam and to stay cool.

Nuclear Power Plant

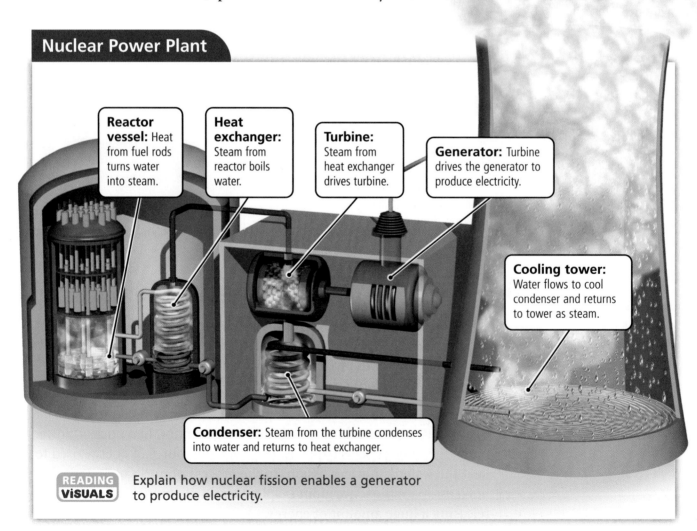

Reactor vessel: Heat from fuel rods turns water into steam.

Heat exchanger: Steam from reactor boils water.

Turbine: Steam from heat exchanger drives turbine.

Generator: Turbine drives the generator to produce electricity.

Cooling tower: Water flows to cool condenser and returns to tower as steam.

Condenser: Steam from the turbine condenses into water and returns to heat exchanger.

READING VISUALS Explain how nuclear fission enables a generator to produce electricity.

cooling towers

reactor buildings

turbine buildings

water source

Splitting just one atom of uranium releases 20 million times more energy than does burning one molecule of natural gas. However, nuclear fission also produces radioactive waste. Radioactivity is a form of energy that can cause death and disease if living things are exposed to it long enough. Nuclear waste from a power plant will remain radioactive for thousands of years. Countries that use nuclear energy face the challenge of storing this waste safely. The storage sites must keep any radioactivity from escaping until the waste material becomes harmless.

A nuclear power plant usually has three main sections: reactor buildings, turbine buildings, and cooling towers.

SIMULATION
CLASSZONE.COM

Explore how a nuclear power plant produces energy.

CHECK YOUR READING Explain how fission is used to generate energy.

Renewable resources are used to produce electricity and fuel.

Moving water, wind, Earth's internal heat, sunlight, living matter, and hydrogen are all sources of renewable energy. Unlike fossil fuels, many of these sources of energy are in unlimited supply. They usually produce electricity or fuel with little or no pollution. Using these clean energy sources helps preserve the environment and protect human health.

So far, however, these resources cannot produce enough energy to pay for the cost of developing them on a large scale. As a result, renewable resources provide only a small percentage of the energy used in the world. In the United States, only about 6 percent of the total energy used comes from these resources.

Scientists and engineers must improve the necessary technologies before renewable resources can supply clean energy to more of the world's people. Imagine if everyone's car ran on hydrogen and produced only water as a byproduct. Or think of solar panels generating enough electricity to light a major city. These visions could come true in your lifetime.

CHECK YOUR READING What makes renewable resources attractive as energy sources?

Hydroelectric Energy

Hydroelectric energy is electricity produced by moving water. If you have ever stood near a waterfall or even just turned on a faucet, you have felt the force of moving water. People can use flowing water to generate electricity.

In most cases, a dam is built across a large river, blocking the river's flow and creating an artificial lake, or reservoir. As the illustration below shows, water from the lake enters the dam through intake gates and flows down a tunnel. The fast flowing water turns turbines that drive generators, which produce electricity. Because hydroelectric power does not burn any fuel, it produces no pollution. Dams in the United States generate enough electricity to save 500 million barrels of oil a year.

However, building dams poses problems for the environment. By flooding land to create reservoirs, dams destroy wildlife habitats. In some rivers, such as the Snake and Columbia rivers in the United States, dams interfere with the annual migration of salmon and other fish. Also, areas near the end of the river may receive less water than before, making it harder to raise crops and livestock.

RESOURCE CENTER
CLASSZONE.COM

Learn more about the benefits and costs of renewable energy resources.

Areas with large rivers can use their power to produce electricity. The dam in the photo was built on the Yukon River in Alaska.

Hydroelectric Dam

Intake gate: Water from the reservoir enters intake gates.

reservoir

Tunnel: Water flows downhill, increasing in speed and force.

Generator: Turbines drive the generators to produce electricity.

Turbine: The moving water turns the turbines.

river

Outlet: Water flows out of the dam.

READING VISUALS What would happen if the level of the reservoir fell below the intake gate?

Solar Energy

Only a small fraction of the sun's energy falls on Earth. Yet even this amount is huge. Every day enough energy from the sun strikes the United States to supply all the nation's energy needs for one and a half years. The problem is how to use this abundant resource to produce electricity.

In an effort to solve the problem, scientists developed solar cells. A **solar cell** is a specially constructed sandwich of silicon and other materials that converts light energy to electricity. As shown in the diagram below, when sunlight strikes the cell, electrons move from the lower to the upper layer, producing an electric current. Individual solar cells can power small appliances, such as calculators and lights.

Solar cells can be wired together in solar panels, which provide heat and electricity for homes and businesses. Solar panels are also used to power some spacecraft and space stations once they are in orbit. To meet the energy needs of some cities, hundreds or even thousands of solar panels are built into large structures called arrays. Many western cities like Barstow, California, receive part of their electricity from solar arrays.

Sunlight is an unlimited source of clean energy. But current methods of collecting sunlight are expensive and somewhat inefficient. As solar technology improves, sunlight is likely to become an important energy source for the world.

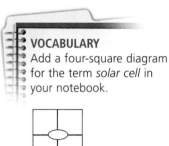

VOCABULARY
Add a four-square diagram for the term *solar cell* in your notebook.

READING TiP
Array refers to an arrangement of objects in rows and columns.

CHECK YOUR READING How can people use sunlight to produce electricity?

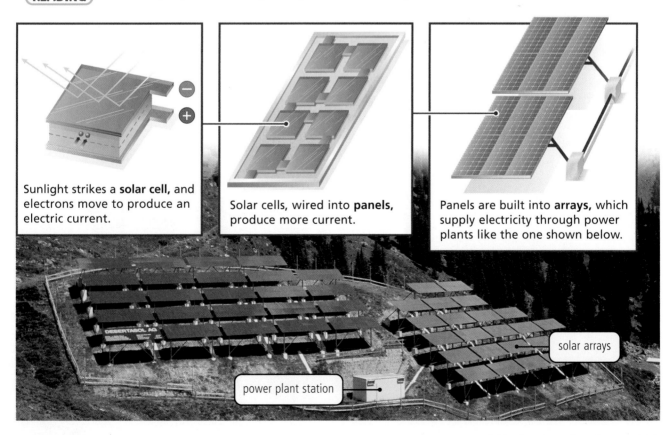

Sunlight strikes a **solar cell,** and electrons move to produce an electric current.

Solar cells, wired into **panels,** produce more current.

Panels are built into **arrays,** which supply electricity through power plants like the one shown below.

solar arrays

power plant station

Geothermal Energy

READING **TiP**

Geothermal combines the Greek prefix *geo-*, meaning "earth," and the Greek word *thermē*, meaning "heat."

Imagine tapping into Earth's heat to obtain electricity for your home. In some places, that is exactly what people do. They use **geothermal energy,** or energy produced by heat within Earth's crust.

Geothermal energy comes from underground water that is heated by hot rock. The illustration below shows how hot water is piped from a well into a power plant. This superheated water enters a flash tank and produces enough steam to run turbines, which power generators. Excess water is then pumped back into the ground. Some plants also pipe hot water into homes and businesses for heating.

In the United States, geothermal energy provides electricity for nearly 3.5 million homes. Other major geothermal power plants are in New Zealand and Iceland.

Geothermal energy is clean and renewable. So far, its use is limited to areas where hot water is fairly close to the surface. However, some companies are experimenting with pumping cold water into underground areas of hot rock found in all parts of Earth's crust. The rock heats the water, which is then pumped back to the surface and used

In Iceland, geothermal power plants like the one in the photograph supply nearly all of the country's electricity.

Geothermal Power Plant

Production well: Hot water is piped from the ground into the plant.

Flash tank: Water is changed into steam.

Turbine and generator: Steam turns turbines, which drive generators to produce electricity.

Cooling tower: Water from the tower cools steam in the condenser.

Condenser: Steam condenses into water.

Injection well: Excess water is pumped back into the ground.

READING **VISUALS** How is this plant similar to a nuclear power plant? How is it different?

to generate electricity. This new technique may allow more countries to make use of geothermal energy.

CHECK YOUR READING What is the source of geothermal energy?

Wind Energy

For thousands of years, people have captured the tremendous energy of wind to move ships, grind grain, and pump water from underground. Today, people also use wind energy—from the force of moving air—to generate electricity.

The modern windmill is made of metal and plastic and can stand as tall as a 40-story building. The blades act as a turbine, turning a set of gears that drives the generator. The amount of electricity a windmill produces depends on the speed and angle of the wind across its blades. The faster the blades turn, the more power the windmill produces.

> **REMINDER**
> The generator is the part that produces the electric current, whether it is driven by turbines or gears.

To supply electricity to an area, hundreds of windmills are built on a "wind farm." Wind farms, like the one in the photograph below, are already producing electricity in California, Hawaii, New Hampshire, and several other states. Other countries, such as Denmark and Germany, also use wind farms to supply electricity to some of their cities.

Although wind energy is clean and renewable, it has certain drawbacks. It depends on steady, strong winds blowing most of the time, which are found only in a few places. Wind farms take up a great deal of land, and the turning blades can be noisy. There is also a limit to how much power each windmill can produce. However, in the future, wind farms may become more productive and more widely used.

CHECK YOUR READING What factor determines how much electricity a windmill produces?

blade
gears
controller
generator

The blades turn the gears, which drive the generator to produce electricity. The controller points the windmill's head into the wind to keep the blades turning rapidly.

Biomass Energy

Biomass is organic matter, such as plant and animal waste, that can be used as fuel. The U.S. Department of Energy works with state and local groups to find ways of converting biomass materials into energy sources.

This wood-burning biomass plant sends electrical energy at a rate of 21 million watts to the San Francisco Bay area. Wood waste products are collected from farms and industries as fuel for the plant.

Each year biomass power stations in the United States burn about 60 million tons of wood and other plant material to generate 37 billion kilowatt hours of electricity. That is more electricity than the state of Colorado uses in an entire year. Small biomass stations are used in rural areas to supply power to farms and towns. Fast-growing trees, grasses, and other crops can be planted to supply a renewable energy source that is cheaper than fossil fuels.

Some plant and animal waste can be converted into liquid fuels. The sugar and starch in corn and potatoes, for example, are made into a liquid fuel called ethanol. Ethanol can be added to gasoline to form gasohol. This fuel can power small cars, farm machinery, and buses. A liquid fuel made from animal waste is used for heating and cooking in many rural areas around the world.

Although biomass is a renewable resource, certain problems limit its use. Burning wood and crops can release as much carbon dioxide into the air as burning fossil fuels does. Biomass crops take up land that could be used to raise food. Also, plant fuels such as ethanol are still too expensive to produce on a large scale. For now, biomass materials provide only a small part of the world's energy.

 CHECK YOUR READING What are the advantages and disadvantages of biomass fuels?

Hydrogen Fuel Cells

VISUALIZATION
CLASSZONE.COM

Watch a hydrogen fuel cell in action.

Scientists are also exploring the use of hydrogen gas as a renewable energy source. Hydrogen is the simplest atom, made up of one proton—the nucleus—and one electron. Scientists have found ways to separate hydrogen from water and from fossil fuels. It is a flammable gas and must be handled with care

Hydrogen is used in a **hydrogen fuel cell,** a device that produces electricity by separating hydrogen into protons and electrons. The diagram on page 169 shows hydrogen fuel entering on one side of the cell while oxygen from the air enters on the other side. Once in the cell, electrons flow out of the cell through wires, forming an electric current that powers the motor. The protons pass through a membrane and combine with oxygen to form water as a byproduct.

Hydrogen fuel cells are used to supply electrical energy on spacecraft and space stations. Fuel-cell buses are being tested in several countries.

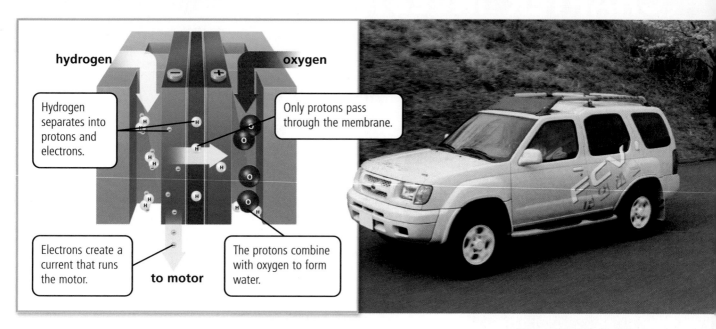

hydrogen   oxygen

Hydrogen separates into protons and electrons.

Only protons pass through the membrane.

Electrons create a current that runs the motor.

to motor

The protons combine with oxygen to form water.

A storage tank in the back of this SUV holds hydrogen fuel. Electrical energy from fuel cells powers the motor and a backup battery.

Also, some fuel-cell cars are now available to the public. Storage tanks in these vehicles carry hydrogen fuel for the cells.

Fuel-cell technology holds great promise for the future. Hydrogen is a clean source of energy, producing only water and heat as byproducts. If every vehicle in the world were powered by hydrogen, the level of air pollution would drop sharply.

However, hydrogen fuel cells are still too expensive to produce in large numbers. Separating hydrogen from water or from fossil fuels takes a great deal of energy, time, and money. Also, there are only a few fueling stations to supply cars and other vehicles that run on hydrogen. The U.S. Department of Energy is working with the automotive industry and other industries to solve these problems.

CHECK YOUR READING   Why is hydrogen considered a promising alternative energy source?

5.3 Review

KEY CONCEPTS

1. List the main advantages and disadvantages of nuclear energy as a power source.

2. Describe the advantages of using sunlight, water, and Earth's heat energy to produce electrical power.

3. What are some factors that limit the use of biomass, wind, and hydrogen as energy sources?

CRITICAL THINKING

4. **Evaluate** Do you think people would use a clean, renewable fuel that cost twice as much as gasoline? Explain.

5. **Calculate** One acre of corn yields 20 gallons of ethanol. A bus gets 20 miles per gallon and travels 9000 miles in one year. How many acres of corn are needed to fuel the bus for a year?

◆ CHALLENGE

6. **Synthesize** Review the energy sources discussed in this section. Then think of ways in which one or more of them could be used to supply electricity to a house in Florida and a house in Alaska. Which energy sources would be suitable in each environment? Describe your ideas in writing, or make sketches of the houses.

Wind Power

OVERVIEW AND PURPOSE Early windmills were used mainly to pump water and grind flour. In this lab, you will use what you have learned about renewable resources to

- build a model windmill and use it to lift a small weight
- improve its performance by increasing the strength of the wind source

▶ Problem

What effect will increasing the wind strength have on the lifting power of a model windmill?

▶ Hypothesize

After completing step 8 of the procedure, write a hypothesis to explain what you think will happen in the next two sets of trials. Your hypothesis should take the form of an "If . . . , then . . . , because . . ." statement.

▶ Procedure

MATERIALS
- half of a file folder
- metric ruler
- quarter
- scissors
- paper punch
- brass paper fastener
- drinking straw
- pushpin
- masking tape
- small paper clip
- pint carton
- 30 cm of string
- clock or stopwatch
- small desktop fan

1. Make a data table in your **Science Notebook,** like the one on page 171.

2. Cut a 15 cm square from a manila file folder. With a ruler, draw lines from the corners toward the center, forming an X. Where the lines cross, use a quarter to draw a circle. Cut inward along the lines from the four corners, stopping at the small circle. Punch a hole in each corner and in the center of the circle.

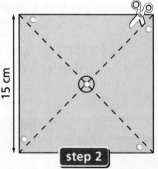

15 cm

step 2

3. Bend the cardboard to align the holes. Push a brass paper fastener through the holes toward the back of the pinwheel. Do not flatten the metal strips of the fastener.

4. Use a pushpin to poke a hole through a straw, about 4 cm from the end. Then push the metal strips through the hole and flatten them at right angles to the straw. Fold the tip of the straw over and tape it to the rest of the straw.

step 4

5 Cut the spout portion off the top of the pint carton. Punch two holes on opposite sides of the carton. Make sure the holes line up and are large enough for the straw to turn easily.

6 Slide the straw through the holes. Tape the string to the end of the straw. Tie a small paper clip (weight) to the other end of the string.

step 6

7 Test the model by blowing on the blades. Describe what happens to the weight.

8 Run three trials of the lifting power of the model windmill as you blow on the blades. Keep the amount of force you use constant. Have a classmate use a stopwatch or clock with a second hand to time the trials. Record the results in your data table. Average your results.

9 Vary the strength of the wind by using a desktop fan at different speeds to turn the windmill's blades. Remember to record your hypothesis explaining what you think will happen in the next two sets of trials.

▶ Observe and Analyze
Write It Up

1. **MODEL** Draw a picture of the completed windmill. What happens to the weight when the blades turn?

2. **IDENTIFY VARIABLES** What method did you use to increase the wind strength? Add a sketch of this method to your picture to illustrate the experimental procedure.

3. **RECORD OBSERVATIONS** Make sure your data table is completed.

4. **COMPARE** How did the average times it took to raise the weight at different wind strengths differ?

▶ Conclude
Write It Up

1. **INTERPRET** Answer the question posed under "problem" on page 170.

2. **ANALYZE** Did your results support your hypothesis?

3. **IDENTIFY LIMITS** What limitations or sources of error could have affected your experimental results?

4. **APPLY** Wind-powered turbines are used to generate electricity in some parts of the country. What might limit the usefulness of wind power as an energy source?

▶ INVESTIGATE Further

CHALLENGE How you can get your model windmill to do more work? You might try different weights, or you might build a larger windmill and compare it with your original. Create a new data table. Use a bar graph to compare different weights and wind strengths. How much wind power is needed to lift the additional weight?

Wind Power
Problem
Hypothesize
Observe and Analyze
Table 1. Time to Lift Weight

Wind Force Used	Trial Number	Time (sec)
Student powered	1	
	2	
	3	
	Average	
Fan on low speed	1	
	2	
	3	
	Average	
Fan on high speed	1	
	2	
	3	
	Average	

Conclude

the BIG idea

Society depends on natural resources for energy and materials.

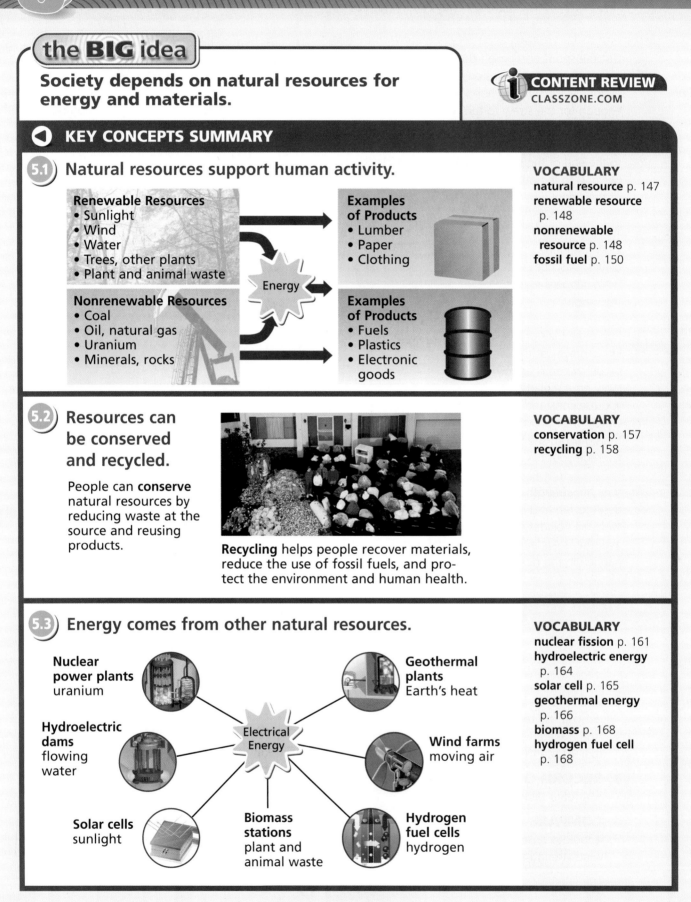

CONTENT REVIEW
CLASSZONE.COM

◀ KEY CONCEPTS SUMMARY

5.1 Natural resources support human activity.

Renewable Resources
- Sunlight
- Wind
- Water
- Trees, other plants
- Plant and animal waste

Energy

Examples of Products
- Lumber
- Paper
- Clothing

Nonrenewable Resources
- Coal
- Oil, natural gas
- Uranium
- Minerals, rocks

Examples of Products
- Fuels
- Plastics
- Electronic goods

VOCABULARY
natural resource p. 147
renewable resource p. 148
nonrenewable resource p. 148
fossil fuel p. 150

5.2 Resources can be conserved and recycled.

People can **conserve** natural resources by reducing waste at the source and reusing products.

Recycling helps people recover materials, reduce the use of fossil fuels, and protect the environment and human health.

VOCABULARY
conservation p. 157
recycling p. 158

5.3 Energy comes from other natural resources.

Nuclear power plants uranium

Hydroelectric dams flowing water

Solar cells sunlight

Biomass stations plant and animal waste

Electrical Energy

Geothermal plants Earth's heat

Wind farms moving air

Hydrogen fuel cells hydrogen

VOCABULARY
nuclear fission p. 161
hydroelectric energy p. 164
solar cell p. 165
geothermal energy p. 166
biomass p. 168
hydrogen fuel cell p. 168

Reviewing Vocabulary

Copy the chart below, and write each word's definition. Use the meaning of the underlined word part to help you.

Word	Meaning of Part	Definition
1. Natural <u>resource</u>	to rise again	
2. <u>Renew</u>able resource	to refresh	
3. <u>Non</u>renewable resource	not to refresh	
4. Fossil <u>fuel</u>	material that burns	
5. <u>Nuclear</u> energy	nut or kernel	
6. <u>Geo</u>thermal energy	heat	

Reviewing Key Concepts

Multiple Choice *Choose the letter of the best answer.*

7. What makes wind a renewable resource?

  a. no pollution   **c.** no waste products

  b. varied speeds   **d.** unlimited supply

8. Which of the following is a nonrenewable resource?

  a. trees   **c.** sunlight

  b. oil   **d.** geothermal energy

9. Fossil fuels provide most of the energy used in the United States because they

  a. are found everywhere in the world

  b. have no harmful byproducts

  c. are easy to transport and burn

  d. can be quickly replaced in nature

10. Which part of a power plant actually produces electricity?

  a. boiler   **c.** turbine

  b. generator   **d.** power lines

11. Which of the following is not a problem associated with the use of fossil fuels?

  a. air pollution   **c.** limited supply

  b. explosions   **d.** radiation

12. Which category of products is the most dependent on oil?

  a. pottery   **c.** plastics

  b. coins   **d.** paper

13. How do nuclear power plants generate the heat energy to turn water into steam?

  a. by drawing hot water from Earth's crust

  b. by producing an electric current

  c. by turning a turbine

  d. by splitting uranium atoms

14. Hydroelectric energy is produced by using the force of

  a. wind   **c.** moving water

  b. sunlight   **d.** living matter

15. Solar cells produce which of the following?

  a. heat energy   **c.** radiation

  b. steam   **d.** electricity

16. What limits the use of biomass liquid fuels?

  a. not enough plant material

  b. too expensive to mass-produce

  c. not enough energy generated

  d. too many harmful byproducts

17. Hydrogen fuel cells produce electricity when

  a. electrons from hydrogen leave the cell

  b. hydrogen is separated from fossil fuels

  c. protons from hydrogen combine with oxygen

  d. hydrogen fuel flows into the cell

Short Answer *Write a few sentences to answer each question.*

18. Why is it important to find renewable sources of energy?

19. Why is conservation of natural resources important?

20. How can recycling help reduce the use of fossil fuels?

Thinking Critically

Use the circle graphs below to answer the following questions.

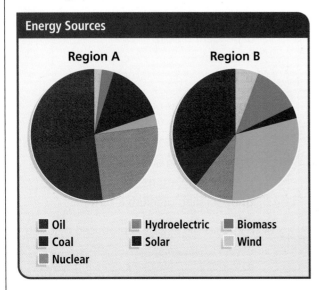

Energy Sources

Region A   Region B

■ Oil   ■ Hydroelectric   ■ Biomass
■ Coal   ■ Solar   ■ Wind
■ Nuclear

21. INTERPRET Which colors represent nonrenewable resources and which ones represent renewable resources?

22. CALCULATE Fossil fuels and nuclear energy together represent about what percentage of the total energy resources in region A? in region B?

23. PREDICT If the price of nonrenewable energy sources rises sharply, which region is likely to be affected more? Why?

24. DRAW CONCLUSIONS What might be one reason that region A uses a greater percentage of fossil fuels and nuclear energy than region B does?

25. INFER Look at the renewable energy sources used in each region. What can you infer about the climate in region A compared with the climate in region B?

26. IDENTIFY CAUSES Why might region B use so much more hydroelectric energy?

27. SYNTHESIZE Region C gets half of its electrical energy from fossil fuels. The region has only 100 days of clear sunlight a year but has abundant plant crops and strong, steady winds. Draw a circle graph for region C, showing the percentage of fossil fuels and the percentage of each renewable energy source the region might use. Explain your choices.

Charting Information

Copy and fill in this chart.

Type of Energy	Produces Energy From	Byproducts
28. uranium		radioactive waste
29. fossil fuel	burning oil, coal	
30.	moving air	none
31. river		
32. sunlight		
33.	burning wood	carbon dioxide
34. hydrogen		

the BIG idea

35. APPLY Look again at the photograph on pages 144–145. Reread the question on the photograph. Now that you have finished the chapter, what would you add to or change about your answer?

36. SYNTHESIZE Imagine that you are a scientist or engineer who is developing a new energy source. What characteristics would you want your energy source to have? List your choices in order of importance, with the most important first—for instance, nonpolluting, inexpensive to mass-produce, and so on.

37. APPLY If you were in charge of your town or city, what measures would you take to conserve natural resources?

UNIT PROJECTS

Evaluate all the data, results, and information in your project folder. Prepare to present your project.

Analyzing a Graph

This graph shows what happens to fuels consumed for energy in the United States. Some of this energy is used and some is lost as heat. Use the graph to answer the questions below.

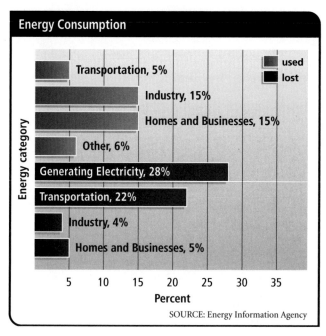

Energy Consumption

used
lost

Transportation, 5%
Industry, 15%
Homes and Businesses, 15%
Other, 6%
Generating Electricity, 28%
Transportation, 22%
Industry, 4%
Homes and Businesses, 5%

Energy category

Percent

5   10   15   20   25   30   35

SOURCE: Energy Information Agency

1. How much energy is used for transportation and industry?
   a. 15 percent   **c.** 30 percent
   b. 20 percent   **d.** 35 percent

2. What is the total amount of energy used and lost in industry?
   a. 4 percent   **c.** 19 percent
   b. 15 percent   **d.** 28 percent

3. What is the largest category of lost energy?
   a. transportation
   b. homes and businesses
   c. generating electricity
   d. industry

4. Which category would include energy used to heat a grocery store?
   a. used in homes and businesses
   b. used in industry
   c. used in transportation
   d. used in other ways

5. If cars burned fuel more efficiently, which category would probably be smaller?
   a. used in homes and businesses
   b. used in other ways
   c. lost in transportation
   d. lost in industry

6. Which statement is true about energy used and lost in transportation?
   a. The amount lost is greater than the amount used.
   b. The amount used is greater than the amount lost.
   c. The amounts used and lost are about the same.
   d. The amounts used and lost are very low in comparison to the other categories.

Extended Response

Answer the two questions below in detail.
Include some of the terms in the word box.
In your answers, underline each term you use.

reusing	recycling	conserve	extends
electricity	hot water	factories	

7. Explain the difference between reusing and recycling products. How does each activity help to reduce the use of natural resources?

8. Give three or more examples of ways in which people in the United States use or rely on energy resources every day.

Student Resource Handbooks

Scientific Thinking Handbook

Making Observations

An **observation** is an act of noting and recording an event, character-istic, behavior, or anything else detected with an instrument or with the senses.

Observations allow you to make informed hypotheses and to gather data for experiments. Careful observations often lead to ideas for new experiments. There are two categories of observations:

- **Quantitative observations** can be expressed in numbers and include records of time, temperature, mass, distance, and volume.

- **Qualitative observations** include descriptions of sights, sounds, smells, and textures.

EXAMPLE

A student dissolved 30 grams of Epsom salts in water, poured the solution into a dish, and let the dish sit out uncovered overnight. The next day, she made the following observations of the Epsom salt crystals that grew in the dish.

> To determine the mass, the student found the mass of the dish before and after growing the crystals and then used subtraction to find the difference.

> The student measured several crystals and calculated the mean length. (To learn how to calculate the mean of a data set, see page R36.)

Table 1. Observations of Epsom Salt Crystals

Quantitative Observations	Qualitative Observations
• mass = 30 g • mean crystal length = 0.5 cm • longest crystal length = 2 cm	• Crystals are clear. • Crystals are long, thin, and rectangular. • White crust has formed around edge of dish.

> Photographs or sketches are useful for recording qualitative observations.

Epsom salt crystals

MORE ABOUT OBSERVING

- Make quantitative observations whenever possible. That way, others will know exactly what you observed and be able to compare their results with yours.

- It is always a good idea to make qualitative observations too. You never know when you might observe something unexpected.

Predicting and Hypothesizing

A **prediction** is an expectation of what will be observed or what will happen. A **hypothesis** is a tentative explanation for an observation or scientific problem that can be tested by further investigation.

SCIENTIFIC THINKING
HANDBOOK

EXAMPLE

Suppose you have made two paper airplanes and you wonder why one of them tends to glide farther than the other one.

1. Start by asking a question.

2. Make an educated guess. After examination, you notice that the wings of the airplane that flies farther are slightly larger than the wings of the other airplane.

3. Write a prediction based upon your educated guess, in the form of an "If . . . , then . . ." statement. Write the independent variable after the word *if,* and the dependent variable after the word *then.*

4. To make a hypothesis, explain why you think what you predicted will occur. Write the explanation after the word *because.*

1. Why does one of the paper airplanes glide farther than the other?

2. The size of an airplane's wings may affect how far the airplane will glide.

3. Prediction: If I make a paper airplane with larger wings, then the airplane will glide farther.

> To read about independent and dependent variables, see page R30.

4. Hypothesis: If I make a paper airplane with larger wings, then the airplane will glide farther, because the additional surface area of the wing will produce more lift.

> Notice that the part of the hypothesis after *because* adds an explanation of why the airplane will glide farther.

MORE ABOUT HYPOTHESES

- The results of an experiment cannot prove that a hypothesis is correct. Rather, the results either support or do not support the hypothesis.

- Valuable information is gained even when your hypothesis is not supported by your results. For example, it would be an important discovery to find that wing size is not related to how far an airplane glides.

- In science, a hypothesis is supported only after many scientists have conducted many experiments and produced consistent results.

Inferring

An **inference** is a logical conclusion drawn from the available evidence and prior knowledge. Inferences are often made from observations.

EXAMPLE

A student observing a set of acorns noticed something unexpected about one of them. He noticed a white, soft-bodied insect eating its way out of the acorn.

> The student recorded these observations.

Observations

- There is a hole in the acorn, about 0.5 cm in diameter, where the insect crawled out.
- There is a second hole, which is about the size of a pinhole, on the other side of the acorn.
- The inside of the acorn is hollow.

> Here are some inferences that can be made on the basis of the observations.

Inferences

- The insect formed from the material inside the acorn, grew to its present size, and ate its way out of the acorn.
- The insect crawled through the smaller hole, ate the inside of the acorn, grew to its present size, and ate its way out of the acorn.
- An egg was laid in the acorn through the smaller hole. The egg hatched into a larva that ate the inside of the acorn, grew to its present size, and ate its way out of the acorn.

> When you make inferences, be sure to look at all of the evidence available and combine it with what you already know.

MORE ABOUT INFERENCES

Inferences depend both on observations and on the knowledge of the people making the inferences. Ancient people who did not know that organisms are produced only by similar organisms might have made an inference like the first one. A student today might look at the same observations and make the second inference. A third student might have knowledge about this particular insect and know that it is never small enough to fit through the smaller hole, leading her to the third inference.

Identifying Cause and Effect

In a **cause-and-effect relationship,** one event or characteristic is the result of another. Usually an effect follows its cause in time.

There are many examples of cause-and-effect relationships in everyday life.

Cause	Effect
Turn off a light.	Room gets dark.
Drop a glass.	Glass breaks.
Blow a whistle.	Sound is heard.

Scientists must be careful not to infer a cause-and-effect relationship just because one event happens after another event. When one event occurs after another, you cannot infer a cause-and-effect relationship on the basis of that information alone. You also cannot conclude that one event caused another if there are alternative ways to explain the second event. A scientist must demonstrate through experimentation or continued observation that an event was truly caused by another event.

EXAMPLE

Make an Observation

Suppose you have a few plants growing outside. When the weather starts getting colder, you bring one of the plants indoors. You notice that the plant you brought indoors is growing faster than the others are growing. You cannot conclude from your observation that the change in temperature was the cause of the increased plant growth, because there are alternative explanations for the observation. Some possible explanations are given below.

- The humidity indoors caused the plant to grow faster.

- The level of sunlight indoors caused the plant to grow faster.

- The indoor plant's being noticed more often and watered more often than the outdoor plants caused it to grow faster.

- The plant that was brought indoors was healthier than the other plants to begin with.

To determine which of these factors, if any, caused the indoor plant to grow faster than the outdoor plants, you would need to design and conduct an experiment.

See pages R28–R35 for information about designing experiments.

Recognizing Bias

Television, newspapers, and the Internet are full of experts claiming to have scientific evidence to back up their claims. How do you know whether the claims are really backed up by good science?

Bias is a slanted point of view, or personal prejudice. The goal of scientists is to be as objective as possible and to base their findings on facts instead of opinions. However, bias often affects the conclusions of researchers, and it is important to learn to recognize bias.

When scientific results are reported, you should consider the source of the information as well as the information itself. It is important to critically analyze the information that you see and read.

SOURCES OF BIAS

There are several ways in which a report of scientific information may be biased. Here are some questions that you can ask yourself:

1. **Who is sponsoring the research?**

   Sometimes, the results of an investigation are biased because an organization paying for the research is looking for a specific answer. This type of bias can affect how data are gathered and interpreted.

2. **Is the research sample large enough?**

   Sometimes research does not include enough data. The larger the sample size, the more likely that the results are accurate, assuming a truly random sample.

3. **In a survey, who is answering the questions?**

   The results of a survey or poll can be biased. The people taking part in the survey may have been specifically chosen because of how they would answer. They may have the same ideas or lifestyles. A survey or poll should make use of a random sample of people.

4. **Are the people who take part in a survey biased?**

   People who take part in surveys sometimes try to answer the questions the way they think the researcher wants them to answer. Also, in surveys or polls that ask for personal information, people may be unwilling to answer questions truthfully.

SCIENTIFIC BIAS

It is also important to realize that scientists have their own biases because of the types of research they do and because of their scientific viewpoints. Two scientists may look at the same set of data and come to completely different conclusions because of these biases. However, such disagreements are not necessarily bad. In fact, a critical analysis of disagreements is often responsible for moving science forward.

Identifying Faulty Reasoning

Faulty reasoning is wrong or incorrect thinking. It leads to mistakes and to wrong conclusions. Scientists are careful not to draw unreasonable conclusions from experimental data. Without such caution, the results of scientific investigations may be misleading.

EXAMPLE

Scientists try to make generalizations based on their data to explain as much about nature as possible. If only a small sample of data is looked at, however, a conclusion may be faulty. Suppose a scientist has studied the effects of the El Niño and La Niña weather patterns on flood damage in California from 1989 to 1995. The scientist organized the data in the bar graph below.

The scientist drew the following conclusions:

1. The La Niña weather pattern has no effect on flooding in California.

2. When neither weather pattern occurs, there is almost no flood damage.

3. A weak or moderate El Niño produces a small or moderate amount of flooding.

4. A strong El Niño produces a lot of flooding.

Flood and Storm Damage in California

Estimated damage (millions of dollars): 0, 500, 1000, 1500, 2000

Weak–moderate El Niño

Strong El Niño

Starting year of season (July 1–June 30): 1989, 1992, 1995

SOURCE: *Governor's Office of Emergency Services, California*

For the six-year period of the scientist's investigation, these conclusions may seem to be reasonable. However, a six-year study of weather patterns may be too small of a sample for the conclusions to be supported. Consider the following graph, which shows information that was gathered from 1949 to 1997.

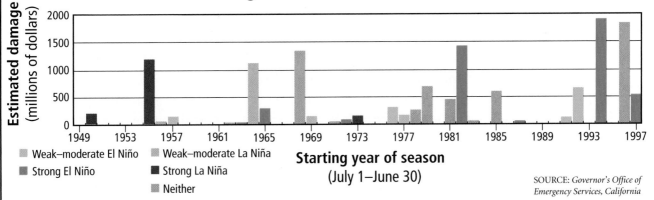

Flood and Storm Damage in California from 1949 to 1997

Estimated damage (millions of dollars): 0, 500, 1000, 1500, 2000

Starting year of season (July 1–June 30): 1949, 1953, 1957, 1961, 1965, 1969, 1973, 1977, 1981, 1985, 1989, 1993, 1997

Weak–moderate El Niño   Weak–moderate La Niña
Strong El Niño   Strong La Niña
Neither

SOURCE: *Governor's Office of Emergency Services, California*

The only one of the conclusions that all of this information supports is number 3: a weak or moderate El Niño produces a small or moderate amount of flooding. By collecting more data, scientists can be more certain of their conclusions and can avoid faulty reasoning.

Analyzing Statements

To **analyze** a statement is to examine its parts carefully. Scientific findings are often reported through media such as television or the Internet. A report that is made public often focuses on only a small part of research. As a result, it is important to question the sources of information.

Evaluate Media Claims

To **evaluate** a statement is to judge it on the basis of criteria you've established. Sometimes evaluating means deciding whether a statement is true.

Reports of scientific research and findings in the media may be misleading or incomplete. When you are exposed to this information, you should ask yourself some questions so that you can make informed judgments about the information.

1. **Does the information come from a credible source?**

   Suppose you learn about a new product and it is stated that scientific evidence proves that the product works. A report from a respected news source may be more believable than an advertisement paid for by the product's manufacturer.

2. **How much evidence supports the claim?**

   Often, it may seem that there is new evidence every day of something in the world that either causes or cures an illness. However, information that is the result of several years of work by several different scientists is more credible than an advertisement that does not even cite the subjects of the experiment.

3. **How much information is being presented?**

   Science cannot solve all questions, and scientific experiments often have flaws. A report that discusses problems in a scientific study may be more believable than a report that addresses only positive experimental findings.

4. **Is scientific evidence being presented by a specific source?**

   Sometimes scientific findings are reported by people who are called experts or leaders in a scientific field. But if their names are not given or their scientific credentials are not reported, their statements may be less credible than those of recognized experts.

Differentiate Between Fact and Opinion

Sometimes information is presented as a fact when it may be an opinion. When scientific conclusions are reported, it is important to recognize whether they are based on solid evidence. Again, you may find it helpful to ask yourself some questions.

1. **What is the difference between a fact and an opinion?**

   A **fact** is a piece of information that can be strictly defined and proved true. An **opinion** is a statement that expresses a belief, value, or feeling. An opinion cannot be proved true or false. For example, a person's age is a fact, but if someone is asked how old they feel, it is impossible to prove the person's answer to be true or false.

2. **Can opinions be measured?**

   Yes, opinions can be measured. In fact, surveys often ask for people's opinions on a topic. But there is no way to know whether or not an opinion is the truth.

HOW TO DIFFERENTIATE FACT FROM OPINION

Human Activities and the Environment

Unfortunately, human use of fossil fuels is one of the most significant developments of the past few centuries. Humans rely on fossil fuels, a non-renewable energy resource, for more than 90 percent of their energy needs.

This careless misuse of our planet's resources has resulted in pollution, global warming, and the destruction of fragile ecosystems. For example, oil pipelines carry more than one million barrels of oil each day across tundra regions. Transporting oil across such areas can only result in oil spills that poison the land for decades.

Opinions
Notice words or phrases that express beliefs or feelings. The words *unfortunately* and *careless* show that opinions are being expressed.

Opinion
Look for statements that speculate about events. These statements are opinions, because they cannot be proved.

Facts
Statements that contain statistics tend to be facts. Writers often use facts to support their opinions.

Lab Handbook

Safety Rules

Before you work in the laboratory, read these safety rules twice. Ask your teacher to explain any rules that you do not completely understand. Refer to these rules later on if you have questions about safety in the science classroom.

Directions

- Read all directions and make sure that you understand them before starting an investigation or lab activity. If you do not understand how to do a procedure or how to use a piece of equipment, ask your teacher.
- Do not begin any investigation or touch any equipment until your teacher has told you to start.
- Never experiment on your own. If you want to try a procedure that the directions do not call for, ask your teacher for permission first.
- If you are hurt or injured in any way, tell your teacher immediately.

Dress Code

goggles

apron

gloves

- Wear goggles when
  — using glassware, sharp objects, or chemicals
  — heating an object
  — working with anything that can easily fly up into the air and hurt someone's eye
- Tie back long hair or hair that hangs in front of your eyes.
- Remove any article of clothing—such as a loose sweater or a scarf—that hangs down and may touch a flame, chemical, or piece of equipment.
- Observe all safety icons calling for the wearing of eye protection, gloves, and aprons.

Heating and Fire Safety

fire
safety

heating
safety

- Keep your work area neat, clean, and free of extra materials.
- Never reach over a flame or heat source.
- Point objects being heated away from you and others.
- Never heat a substance or an object in a closed container.
- Never touch an object that has been heated. If you are unsure whether something is hot, treat it as though it is. Use oven mitts, clamps, tongs, or a test-tube holder.
- Know where the fire extinguisher and fire blanket are kept in your classroom.
- Do not throw hot substances into the trash. Wait for them to cool or use the container your teacher puts out for disposal.

Electrical Safety

electrical safety

- Never use lamps or other electrical equipment with frayed cords.
- Make sure no cord is lying on the floor where someone can trip over it.
- Do not let a cord hang over the side of a counter or table so that the equipment can easily be pulled or knocked to the floor.
- Never let cords hang into sinks or other places where water can be found.
- Never try to fix electrical problems. Inform your teacher of any problems immediately.
- Unplug an electrical cord by pulling on the plug, not the cord.

Chemical Safety

chemical safety

poison

fumes

- If you spill a chemical or get one on your skin or in your eyes, tell your teacher right away.
- Never touch, taste, or sniff any chemicals in the lab. If you need to determine odor, waft. Wafting consists of holding the chemical in its container 15 centimeters (6 in.) away from your nose, and using your fingers to bring fumes from the container to your nose.
- Keep lids on all chemicals you are not using.
- Never put unused chemicals back into the original containers. Throw away extra chemicals where your teacher tells you to.
- Pour chemicals over a sink or your work area, not over the floor.
- If you get a chemical in your eye, use the eyewash right away.
- Always wash your hands after handling chemicals, plants, or soil.

Wafting

LAB HANDBOOK

Glassware and Sharp-Object Safety

sharp objects

- If you break glassware, tell your teacher right away.
- Do not use broken or chipped glassware. Give these to your teacher.
- Use knives and other cutting instruments carefully. Always wear eye protection and cut away from you.

Animal Safety

- Never hurt an animal.
- Touch animals only when necessary. Follow your teacher's instructions for handling animals.
- Always wash your hands after working with animals.

Cleanup

disposal

- Follow your teacher's instructions for throwing away or putting away supplies.
- Clean your work area and pick up anything that has dropped to the floor.
- Wash your hands.

Using Lab Equipment

Different experiments require different types of equipment. But even though experiments differ, the ways in which the equipment is used are the same.

Beakers

- Use beakers for holding and pouring liquids.
- Do not use a beaker to measure the volume of a liquid. Use a graduated cylinder instead. (See page R16.)
- Use a beaker that holds about twice as much liquid as you need. For example, if you need 100 milliliters of water, you should use a 200- or 250-milliliter beaker.

Test Tubes

- Use test tubes to hold small amounts of substances.
- Do not use a test tube to measure the volume of a liquid.
- Use a test tube when heating a substance over a flame. Aim the mouth of the tube away from yourself and other people.
- Liquids easily spill or splash from test tubes, so it is important to use only small amounts of liquids.

Test-Tube Holder

- Use a test-tube holder when heating a substance in a test tube.
- Use a test-tube holder if the substance in a test tube is dangerous to touch.
- Make sure the test-tube holder tightly grips the test tube so that the test tube will not slide out of the holder.
- Make sure that the test-tube holder is above the surface of the substance in the test tube so that you can observe the substance.

Test-Tube Rack

- Use a test-tube rack to organize test tubes before, during, and after an experiment.

- Use a test-tube rack to keep test tubes upright so that they do not fall over and spill their contents.

- Use a test-tube rack that is the correct size for the test tubes that you are using. If the rack is too small, a test tube may become stuck. If the rack is too large, a test tube may lean over, and some of its contents may spill or splash.

Forceps

- Use forceps when you need to pick up or hold a very small object that should not be touched with your hands.

- Do not use forceps to hold anything over a flame, because forceps are not long enough to keep your hand safely away from the flame. Plastic forceps will melt, and metal forceps will conduct heat and burn your hand.

Hot Plate

- Use a hot plate when a substance needs to be kept warmer than room temperature for a long period of time.

- Use a hot plate instead of a Bunsen burner or a candle when you need to carefully control temperature.

- Do not use a hot plate when a substance needs to be burned in an experiment.

- Always use "hot hands" safety mitts or oven mitts when handling anything that has been heated on a hot plate.

Microscope

Scientists use microscopes to see very small objects that cannot easily be seen with the eye alone. A microscope magnifies the image of an object so that small details may be observed. A microscope that you may use can magnify an object 400 times—the object will appear 400 times larger than its actual size.

Body The body separates the lens in the eyepiece from the objective lenses below.

Nosepiece The nosepiece holds the objective lenses above the stage and rotates so that all lenses may be used.

High-Power Objective Lens This is the largest lens on the nosepiece. It magnifies an image approximately 40 times.

Stage The stage supports the object being viewed.

Diaphragm The diaphragm is used to adjust the amount of light passing through the slide and into an objective lens.

Mirror or Light Source Some microscopes use light that is reflected through the stage by a mirror. Other microscopes have their own light sources.

Eyepiece Objects are viewed through the eyepiece. The eyepiece contains a lens that commonly magnifies an image 10 times.

Coarse Adjustment This knob is used to focus the image of an object when it is viewed through the low-power lens.

Fine Adjustment This knob is used to focus the image of an object when it is viewed through the high-power lens.

Low-Power Objective Lens This is the smallest lens on the nosepiece. It magnifies an image approximately 10 times.

Arm The arm supports the body above the stage. Always carry a microscope by the arm and base.

Stage Clip The stage clip holds a slide in place on the stage.

Base The base supports the microscope.

VIEWING AN OBJECT

1. Use the coarse adjustment knob to raise the body tube.

2. Adjust the diaphragm so that you can see a bright circle of light through the eyepiece.

3. Place the object or slide on the stage. Be sure that it is centered over the hole in the stage.

4. Turn the nosepiece to click the low-power lens into place.

5. Using the coarse adjustment knob, slowly lower the lens and focus on the specimen being viewed. Be sure not to touch the slide or object with the lens.

6. When switching from the low-power lens to the high-power lens, first raise the body tube with the coarse adjustment knob so that the high-power lens will not hit the slide.

7. Turn the nosepiece to click the high-power lens into place.

8. Use the fine adjustment knob to focus on the specimen being viewed. Again, be sure not to touch the slide or object with the lens.

MAKING A SLIDE, OR WET MOUNT

① Place the specimen in the center of a clean slide.

② Place a drop of water on the specimen.

③ Place a cover slip on the slide. Put one edge of the cover slip into the drop of water and slowly lower it over the specimen.

④ Remove any air bubbles from under the cover slip by gently tapping the cover slip.

⑤ Dry any excess water before placing the slide on the microscope stage for viewing.

Spring Scale (Force Meter)

- Use a spring scale to measure a force pulling on the scale.

- Use a spring scale to measure the force of gravity exerted on an object by Earth.

- To measure a force accurately, a spring scale must be zeroed before it is used. The scale is zeroed when no weight is attached and the indicator is positioned at zero.

- Do not attach a weight that is either too heavy or too light to a spring scale. A weight that is too heavy could break the scale or exert too great a force for the scale to measure. A weight that is too light may not exert enough force to be measured accurately.

Graduated Cylinder

- Use a graduated cylinder to measure the volume of a liquid.

- Be sure that the graduated cylinder is on a flat surface so that your measurement will be accurate.

- When reading the scale on a graduated cylinder, be sure to have your eyes at the level of the surface of the liquid.

- The surface of the liquid will be curved in the graduated cylinder. Read the volume of the liquid at the bottom of the curve, or meniscus (muh-NIHS-kuhs).

- You can use a graduated cylinder to find the volume of a solid object by measuring the increase in a liquid's level after you add the object to the cylinder.

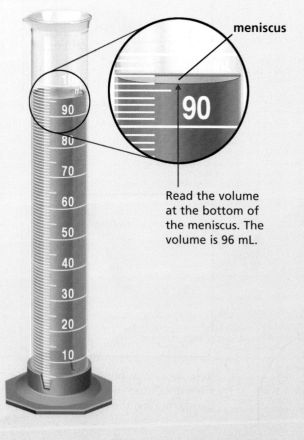

meniscus

Read the volume at the bottom of the meniscus. The volume is 96 mL.

Metric Rulers

- Use metric rulers or meter sticks to measure objects' lengths.

- Do not measure an object from the end of a metric ruler or meter stick, because the end is often imperfect. Instead, measure from the 1-centimeter mark, but remember to subtract a centimeter from the apparent measurement.

- Estimate any lengths that extend between marked units. For example, if a meter stick shows centimeters but not millimeters, you can estimate the length that an object extends between centimeter marks to measure it to the nearest millimeter.

- **Controlling Variables** If you are taking repeated measurements, always measure from the same point each time. For example, if you're measuring how high two different balls bounce when dropped from the same height, measure both bounces at the same point on the balls—either the top or the bottom. Do not measure at the top of one ball and the bottom of the other.

EXAMPLE

How to Measure a Leaf

1. Lay a ruler flat on top of the leaf so that the 1-centimeter mark lines up with one end. Make sure the ruler and the leaf do not move between the time you line them up and the time you take the measurement.

2. Look straight down on the ruler so that you can see exactly how the marks line up with the other end of the leaf.

3. Estimate the length by which the leaf extends beyond a marking. For example, the leaf below extends about halfway between the 4.2-centimeter and 4.3-centimeter marks, so the apparent measurement is about 4.25 centimeters.

4. Remember to subtract 1 centimeter from your apparent measurement, since you started at the 1-centimeter mark on the ruler and not at the end. The leaf is about 3.25 centimeters long (4.25 cm – 1 cm = 3.25 cm).

Triple-Beam Balance

This balance has a pan and three beams with sliding masses, called riders. At one end of the beams is a pointer that indicates whether the mass on the pan is equal to the masses shown on the beams.

1. Make sure the balance is zeroed before measuring the mass of an object. The balance is zeroed if the pointer is at zero when nothing is on the pan and the riders are at their zero points. Use the adjustment knob at the base of the balance to zero it.

2. Place the object to be measured on the pan.

3. Move the riders one notch at a time away from the pan. Begin with the largest rider. If moving the largest rider one notch brings the pointer below zero, begin measuring the mass of the object with the next smaller rider.

4. Change the positions of the riders until they balance the mass on the pan and the pointer is at zero. Then add the readings from the three beams to determine the mass of the object.

300 g	position of largest rider
90 g	position of middle rider
+ 3 g	position of smallest rider
393 g	mass of beaker

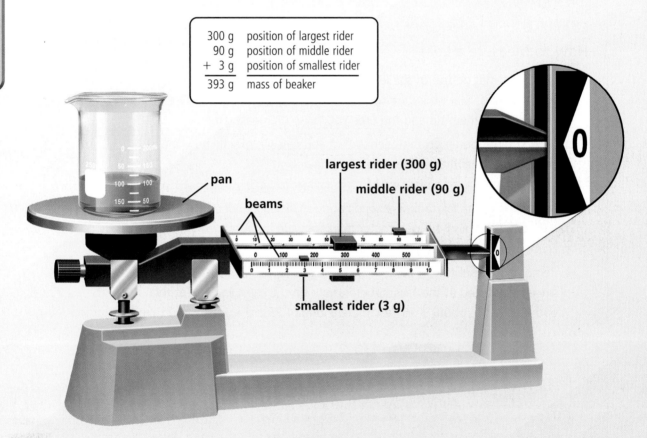

pan

beams

largest rider (300 g)

middle rider (90 g)

smallest rider (3 g)

Double-Pan Balance

This type of balance has two pans. Between the pans is a pointer that indicates whether the masses on the pans are equal.

1. Make sure the balance is zeroed before measuring the mass of an object. The balance is zeroed if the pointer is at zero when there is nothing on either of the pans. Many double-pan balances have sliding knobs that can be used to zero them.

2. Place the object to be measured on one of the pans.

3. Begin adding standard masses to the other pan. Begin with the largest standard mass. If this adds too much mass to the balance, begin measuring the mass of the object with the next smaller standard mass.

4. Add standard masses until the masses on both pans are balanced and the pointer is at zero. Then add the standard masses together to determine the mass of the object being measured.

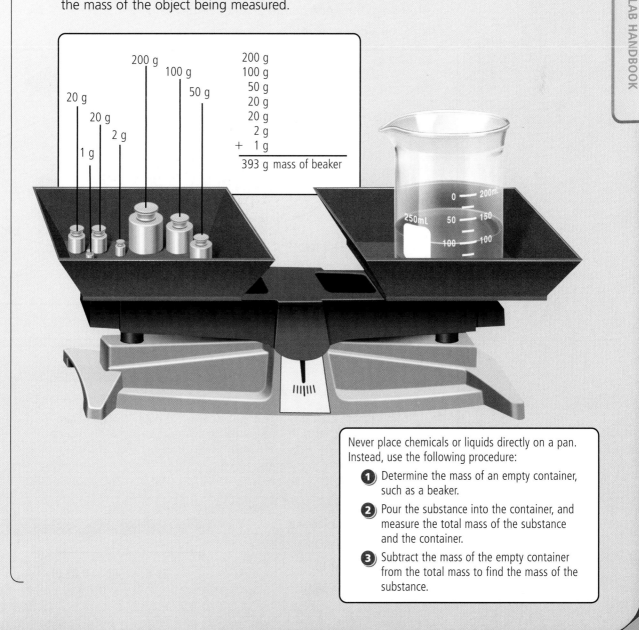

Never place chemicals or liquids directly on a pan. Instead, use the following procedure:

1. Determine the mass of an empty container, such as a beaker.

2. Pour the substance into the container, and measure the total mass of the substance and the container.

3. Subtract the mass of the empty container from the total mass to find the mass of the substance.

The Metric System and SI Units

Scientists use International System (SI) units for measurements of distance, volume, mass, and temperature. The International System is based on multiples of ten and the metric system of measurement.

Basic SI Units		
Property	**Name**	**Symbol**
length	meter	m
volume	liter	L
mass	kilogram	kg
temperature	kelvin	K

SI Prefixes		
Prefix	**Symbol**	**Multiple of 10**
kilo-	k	1000
hecto-	h	100
deca-	da	10
deci-	d	$0.1 \left(\frac{1}{10}\right)$
centi-	c	$0.01 \left(\frac{1}{100}\right)$
milli-	m	$0.001 \left(\frac{1}{1000}\right)$

Changing Metric Units

You can change from one unit to another in the metric system by multiplying or dividing by a power of 10.

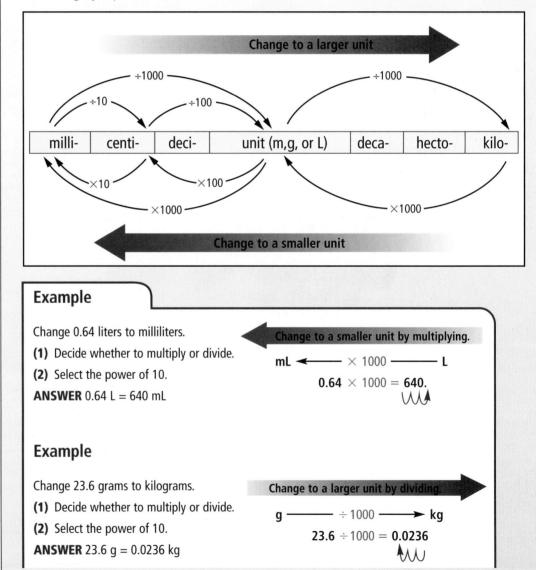

Example

Change 0.64 liters to milliliters.

(1) Decide whether to multiply or divide.

(2) Select the power of 10.

ANSWER 0.64 L = 640 mL

Change to a smaller unit by multiplying.

mL ◄——— × 1000 ——— L

0.64 × 1000 = 640.

Example

Change 23.6 grams to kilograms.

(1) Decide whether to multiply or divide.

(2) Select the power of 10.

ANSWER 23.6 g = 0.0236 kg

Change to a larger unit by dividing.

g ——— ÷ 1000 ——► kg

23.6 ÷ 1000 = 0.0236

Temperature Conversions

Even though the kelvin is the SI base unit of temperature, the degree Celsius will be the unit you use most often in your science studies. The formulas below show the relationships between temperatures in degrees Fahrenheit (°F), degrees Celsius (°C), and kelvins (K).

$$°C = \frac{5}{9}(°F - 32)$$

$$°F = \frac{9}{5}°C + 32$$

$$K = °C + 273$$

See page R42 for help with using formulas.

Examples of Temperature Conversions		
Condition	Degrees Celsius	Degrees Fahrenheit
Freezing point of water	0	32
Cool day	10	50
Mild day	20	68
Warm day	30	86
Normal body temperature	37	98.6
Very hot day	40	104
Boiling point of water	100	212

Converting Between SI and U.S. Customary Units

Use the chart below when you need to convert between SI units and U.S. customary units.

SI Unit	From SI to U.S. Customary			From U.S. Customary to SI		
Length	When you know	multiply by	to find	When you know	multiply by	to find
kilometer (km) = 1000 m	kilometers	0.62	miles	miles	1.61	kilometers
meter (m) = 100 cm	meters	3.28	feet	feet	0.3048	meters
centimeter (cm) = 10 mm	centimeters	0.39	inches	inches	2.54	centimeters
millimeter (mm) = 0.1 cm	millimeters	0.04	inches	inches	25.4	millimeters
Area	When you know	multiply by	to find	When you know	multiply by	to find
square kilometer (km²)	square kilometers	0.39	square miles	square miles	2.59	square kilometers
square meter (m²)	square meters	1.2	square yards	square yards	0.84	square meters
square centimeter (cm²)	square centimeters	0.155	square inches	square inches	6.45	square centimeters
Volume	When you know	multiply by	to find	When you know	multiply by	to find
liter (L) = 1000 mL	liters	1.06	quarts	quarts	0.95	liters
	liters	0.26	gallons	gallons	3.79	liters
	liters	4.23	cups	cups	0.24	liters
	liters	2.12	pints	pints	0.47	liters
milliliter (mL) = 0.001 L	milliliters	0.20	teaspoons	teaspoons	4.93	milliliters
	milliliters	0.07	tablespoons	tablespoons	14.79	milliliters
	milliliters	0.03	fluid ounces	fluid ounces	29.57	milliliters
Mass	When you know	multiply by	to find	When you know	multiply by	to find
kilogram (kg) = 1000 g	kilograms	2.2	pounds	pounds	0.45	kilograms
gram (g) = 1000 mg	grams	0.035	ounces	ounces	28.35	grams

Precision and Accuracy

When you do an experiment, it is important that your methods, observations, and data be both precise and accurate.

low precision

precision, but not accuracy

precision and accuracy

LAB HANDBOOK

Precision

In science, **precision** is the exactness and consistency of measurements. For example, measurements made with a ruler that has both centimeter and millimeter markings would be more precise than measurements made with a ruler that has only centimeter markings. Another indicator of precision is the care taken to make sure that methods and observations are as exact and consistent as possible. Every time a particular experiment is done, the same procedure should be used. Precision is necessary because experiments are repeated several times and if the procedure changes, the results will change.

EXAMPLE

Suppose you are measuring temperatures over a two-week period. Your precision will be greater if you measure each temperature at the same place, at the same time of day, and with the same thermometer than if you change any of these factors from one day to the next.

Accuracy

In science, it is possible to be precise but not accurate. **Accuracy** depends on the difference between a measurement and an actual value. The smaller the difference, the more accurate the measurement.

EXAMPLE

Suppose you look at a stream and estimate that it is about 1 meter wide at a particular place. You decide to check your estimate by measuring the stream with a meter stick, and you determine that the stream is 1.32 meters wide. However, because it is hard to measure the width of a stream with a meter stick, it turns out that you didn't do a very good job. The stream is actually 1.14 meters wide. Therefore, even though your estimate was less precise than your measurement, your estimate was actually more accurate.

Making Data Tables and Graphs

Data tables and graphs are useful tools for both recording and communicating scientific data.

Making Data Tables

You can use a **data table** to organize and record the measurements that you make. Some examples of information that might be recorded in data tables are frequencies, times, and amounts.

EXAMPLE

Suppose you are investigating photosynthesis in two elodea plants. One sits in direct sunlight, and the other sits in a dimly lit room. You measure the rate of photosynthesis by counting the number of bubbles in the jar every ten minutes.

1. Title and number your data table.
2. Decide how you will organize the table into columns and rows.
3. Any units, such as seconds or degrees, should be included in column headings, not in the individual cells.

Table 1. Number of Bubbles from Elodea

Time (min)	Sunlight	Dim Light
0	0	0
10	15	5
20	25	8
30	32	7
40	41	10
50	47	9
60	42	9

◄ Always number and title data tables.

The data in the table above could also be organized in a different way.

Table 1. Number of Bubbles from Elodea

Light Condition	Time (min)						
	0	10	20	30	40	50	60
Sunlight	0	15	25	32	41	47	42
Dim light	0	5	8	7	10	9	9

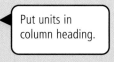

Put units in column heading.

Making Line Graphs

You can use a **line graph** to show a relationship between variables. Line graphs are particularly useful for showing changes in variables over time.

EXAMPLE

Suppose you are interested in graphing temperature data that you collected over the course of a day.

Table 1. Outside Temperature During the Day on March 7

	Time of Day						
	7:00 A.M.	9:00 A.M.	11:00 A.M.	1:00 P.M.	3:00 P.M.	5:00 P.M.	7:00 P.M.
Temp (°C)	8	9	11	14	12	10	6

1. Use the vertical axis of your line graph for the variable that you are measuring—temperature.

2. Choose scales for both the horizontal axis and the vertical axis of the graph. You should have two points more than you need on the vertical axis, and the horizontal axis should be long enough for all of the data points to fit.

3. Draw and label each axis.

4. Graph each value. First find the appropriate point on the scale of the horizontal axis. Imagine a line that rises vertically from that place on the scale. Then find the corresponding value on the vertical axis, and imagine a line that moves horizontally from that value. The point where these two imaginary lines intersect is where the value should be plotted.

5. Connect the points with straight lines.

Be sure to add a number and a title to your graph. ▶

vertical axis ▶

horizontal axis

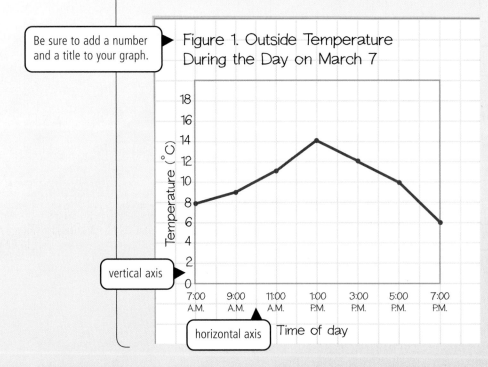

Figure 1. Outside Temperature During the Day on March 7

LAB HANDBOOK

Making Circle Graphs

You can use a **circle graph,** sometimes called a pie chart, to represent data as parts of a circle. Circle graphs are used only when the data can be expressed as percentages of a whole. The entire circle shown in a circle graph is equal to 100 percent of the data.

EXAMPLE

Suppose you identified the species of each mature tree growing in a small wooded area. You organized your data in a table, but you also want to show the data in a circle graph.

1. To begin, find the total number of mature trees.

   $56 + 34 + 22 + 10 + 28 = 150$

2. To find the degree measure for each sector of the circle, write a fraction comparing the number of each tree species with the total number of trees. Then multiply the fraction by 360°.

   Oak: $\frac{56}{150} \times 360° = 134.4°$

3. Draw a circle. Use a protractor to draw the angle for each sector of the graph.

4. Color and label each sector of the graph.

5. Give the graph a number and title.

Table 1. Tree Species in Wooded Area

Species	Number of Specimens
Oak	56
Maple	34
Birch	22
Willow	10
Pine	28

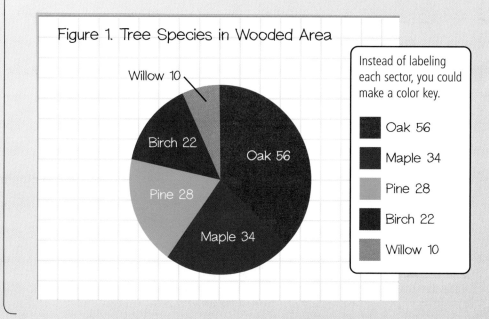

Figure 1. Tree Species in Wooded Area

Willow 10
Birch 22
Pine 28
Oak 56
Maple 34

Instead of labeling each sector, you could make a color key.

- Oak 56
- Maple 34
- Pine 28
- Birch 22
- Willow 10

Bar Graph

A **bar graph** is a type of graph in which the lengths of the bars are used to represent and compare data. A numerical scale is used to determine the lengths of the bars.

EXAMPLE

To determine the effect of water on seed sprouting, three cups were filled with sand, and ten seeds were planted in each. Different amounts of water were added to each cup over a three-day period.

Table 1. Effect of Water on Seed Sprouting

Daily Amount of Water (mL)	Number of Seeds That Sprouted After 3 Days in Sand
0	1
10	4
20	8

1. Choose a numerical scale. The greatest value is 8, so the end of the scale should have a value greater than 8, such as 10. Use equal increments along the scale, such as increments of 2.

2. Draw and label the axes. Mark intervals on the vertical axis according to the scale you chose.

3. Draw a bar for each data value. Use the scale to decide how long to make each bar.

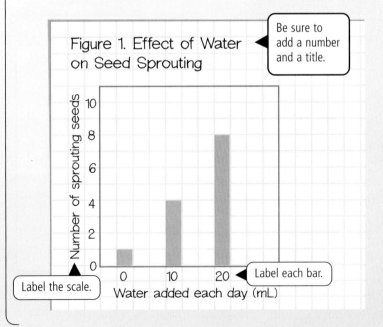

Figure 1. Effect of Water on Seed Sprouting

Be sure to add a number and a title.

Label the scale.

Label each bar.

Number of sprouting seeds

Water added each day (mL)

Double Bar Graph

A **double bar graph** is a bar graph that shows two sets of data. The two bars for each measurement are drawn next to each other.

EXAMPLE

The seed-sprouting experiment was done using both sand and potting soil. The data for sand and potting soil can be plotted on one graph.

1. Draw one set of bars, using the data for sand, as shown below.
2. Draw bars for the potting-soil data next to the bars for the sand data. Shade them a different color. Add a key.

Table 2. Effect of Water and Soil on Seed Sprouting

Daily Amount of Water (mL)	Number of Seeds That Sprouted After 3 Days in Sand	Number of Seeds That Sprouted After 3 Days in Potting Soil
0	1	2
10	4	5
20	8	9

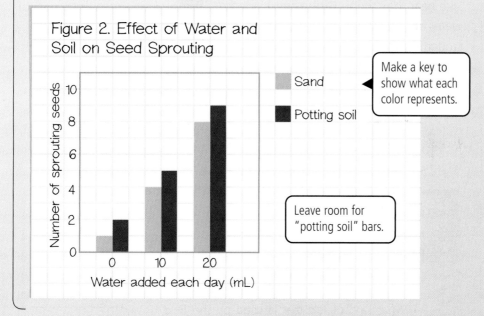

Figure 2. Effect of Water and Soil on Seed Sprouting

Make a key to show what each color represents.

Leave room for "potting soil" bars.

Designing an Experiment

Use this section when designing or conducting an experiment.

Determining a Purpose

You can find a purpose for an experiment by doing research, by examining the results of a previous experiment, or by observing the world around you. An **experiment** is an organized procedure to study something under controlled conditions.

1. Write the purpose of your experiment as a question or problem that you want to investigate.

2. Write down research questions and begin searching for information that will help you design an experiment. Consult the library, the Internet, and other people as you conduct your research.

> Don't forget to learn as much as possible about your topic before you begin.

EXAMPLE

Middle school students observed an odor near the lake by their school. They also noticed that the water on the side of the lake near the school was greener than the water on the other side of the lake. The students did some research to learn more about their observations. They discovered that the odor and green color in the lake

came from algae. They also discovered that a new fertilizer was being used on a field nearby. The students inferred that the use of the fertilizer might be related to the presence of the algae and designed a controlled experiment to find out whether they were right.

Problem

How does fertilizer affect the presence of algae in a lake?

Research Questions

- Have other experiments been done on this problem? If so, what did those experiments show?
- What kind of fertilizer is used on the field? How much?
- How do algae grow?
- How do people measure algae?
- Can fertilizer and algae be used safely in a lab? How?

> **Research**
> As you research, you may find a topic that is more interesting to you than your original topic, or learn that a procedure you wanted to use is not practical or safe. It is OK to change your purpose as you research.

Writing a Hypothesis

A **hypothesis** is a tentative explanation for an observation or scientific problem that can be tested by further investigation. You can write your hypothesis in the form of an "If . . . , then . . . , because . . ." statement.

Hypothesis

If the amount of fertilizer in lake water is increased, then the amount of algae will also increase, because fertilizers provide nutrients that algae need to grow.

Hypotheses
For help with hypotheses, refer to page R3.

Determining Materials

Make a list of all the materials you will need to do your experiment. Be specific, especially if someone else is helping you obtain the materials. Try to think of everything you will need.

Materials

- 1 large jar or container
- 4 identical smaller containers
- rubber gloves that also cover the arms
- sample of fertilizer-and-water solution
- eyedropper
- clear plastic wrap
- scissors
- masking tape
- marker
- ruler

Determining Variables and Constants

EXPERIMENTAL GROUP AND CONTROL GROUP

An experiment to determine how two factors are related always has two groups—a control group and an experimental group.

1. Design an experimental group. Include as many trials as possible in the experimental group in order to obtain reliable results.

2. Design a control group that is the same as the experimental group in every way possible, except for the factor you wish to test.

> **Experimental Group:** two containers of lake water with one drop of fertilizer solution added to each
>
> **Control Group:** two containers of lake water with no fertilizer solution added

> Go back to your materials list and make sure you have enough items listed to cover both your experimental group and your control group.

VARIABLES AND CONSTANTS

Identify the variables and constants in your experiment. In a controlled experiment, a **variable** is any factor that can change. **Constants** are all of the factors that are the same in both the experimental group and the control group.

1. Read your hypothesis. The **independent variable** is the factor that you wish to test and that is manipulated or changed so that it can be tested. The independent variable is expressed in your hypothesis after the word *if*. Identify the independent variable in your laboratory report.

2. The **dependent variable** is the factor that you measure to gather results. It is expressed in your hypothesis after the word *then*. Identify the dependent variable in your laboratory report.

> **Hypothesis**
> If the amount of fertilizer in lake water is increased, then the amount of algae will also increase, because fertilizers provide nutrients that algae need to grow.

Table 1. Variables and Constants in Algae Experiment

Independent Variable	Dependent Variable	Constants
Amount of fertilizer in lake water	Amount of algae that grow	• Where the lake water is obtained • Type of container used • Light and temperature conditions where water will be stored

> Set up your experiment so that you will test only one variable.

MEASURING THE DEPENDENT VARIABLE

Before starting your experiment, you need to define how you will measure the dependent variable. An **operational definition** is a description of the one particular way in which you will measure the dependent variable.

Your operational definition is important for several reasons. First, in any experiment there are several ways in which a dependent variable can be measured. Second, the procedure of the experiment depends on how you decide to measure the dependent variable. Third, your operational definition makes it possible for other people to evaluate and build on your experiment.

EXAMPLE 1

An operational definition of a dependent variable can be qualitative. That is, your measurement of the dependent variable can simply be an observation of whether a change occurs as a result of a change in the independent variable. This type of operational definition can be thought of as a "yes or no" measurement.

Table 2. Qualitative Operational Definition of Algae Growth

Independent Variable	Dependent Variable	Operational Definition
Amount of fertilizer in lake water	Amount of algae that grow	Algae grow in lake water

A qualitative measurement of a dependent variable is often easy to make and record. However, this type of information does not provide a great deal of detail in your experimental results.

EXAMPLE 2

An operational definition of a dependent variable can be quantitative. That is, your measurement of the dependent variable can be a number that shows how much change occurs as a result of a change in the independent variable.

Table 3. Quantitative Operational Definition of Algae Growth

Independent Variable	Dependent Variable	Operational Definition
Amount of fertilizer in lake water	Amount of algae that grow	Diameter of largest algal growth (in mm)

A quantitative measurement of a dependent variable can be more difficult to make and analyze than a qualitative measurement. However, this type of data provides much more information about your experiment and is often more useful.

Writing a Procedure

Write each step of your procedure. Start each step with a verb, or action word, and keep the steps short. Your procedure should be clear enough for someone else to use as instructions for repeating your experiment.

If necessary, go back to your materials list and add any materials that you left out.

Controlling Variables
The same amount of fertilizer solution must be added to two of the four containers.

Controlling Variables
All four containers must receive the same amount of light.

Procedure

1. Put on your gloves. Use the large container to obtain a sample of lake water.

2. Divide the sample of lake water equally among the four smaller containers.

3. Use the eyedropper to add one drop of fertilizer solution to two of the containers.

4. Use the masking tape and the marker to label the containers with your initials, the date, and the identifiers "Jar 1 with Fertilizer," "Jar 2 with Fertilizer," "Jar 1 without Fertilizer," and "Jar 2 without Fertilizer."

5. Cover the containers with clear plastic wrap. Use the scissors to punch ten holes in each of the covers.

6. Place all four containers on a window ledge. Make sure that they all receive the same amount of light.

7. Observe the containers every day for one week.

8. Use the ruler to measure the diameter of the largest clump of algae in each container, and record your measurements daily.

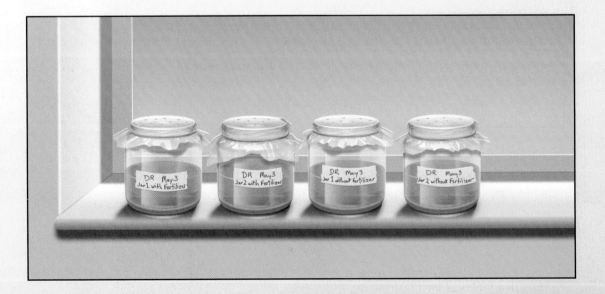

LAB HANDBOOK

Recording Observations

Once you have obtained all of your materials and your procedure has been approved, you can begin making experimental observations. Gather both quantitative and qualitative data. If something goes wrong during your procedure, make sure you record that too.

Observations
For help with making qualitative and quantitative observations, refer to page R2.

For more examples of data tables, see page R23.

Table 4. Fertilizer and Algae Growth

Date and Time	Experimental Group		Control Group		Observations
	Jar 1 with Fertilizer (diameter of algae in mm)	Jar 2 with Fertilizer (diameter of algae in mm)	Jar 1 without Fertilizer (diameter of algae in mm)	Jar 2 without Fertilizer (diameter of algae in mm)	
5/3 4:00 P.M.	0	0	0	0	condensation in all containers
5/4 4:00 P.M.	0	3	0	0	tiny green blobs in jar 2 with fertilizer
5/5 4:15 P.M.	4	5	0	3	green blobs in jars 1 and 2 with fertilizer and jar 2 without fertilizer
5/6 4:00 P.M.	5	6	0	4	water light green in jar 2 with fertilizer
5/7 4:00 P.M.	8	10	0	6	water light green in jars 1 and 2 with fertilizer and in jar 2 without fertilizer
5/8 3:30 P.M.	10	18	0	6	cover off jar 2 with fertilizer
5/9 3:30 P.M.	14	23	0	8	drew sketches of each container

Notice that on the sixth day, the observer found that the cover was off one of the containers. It is important to record observations of unintended factors because they might affect the results of the experiment.

Use technology, such as a microscope, to help you make observations when possible.

Drawings of Samples Viewed Under Microscope on 5/9 at 100x

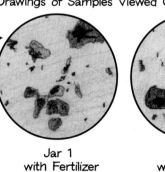
Jar 1 with Fertilizer

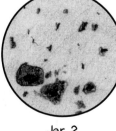
Jar 2 with Fertilizer

Jar 1 without Fertilizer

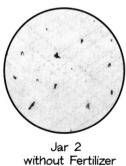
Jar 2 without Fertilizer

Summarizing Results

To summarize your data, look at all of your observations together. Look for meaningful ways to present your observations. For example, you might average your data or make a graph to look for patterns. When possible, use spreadsheet software to help you analyze and present your data. The two graphs below show the same data.

EXAMPLE 1

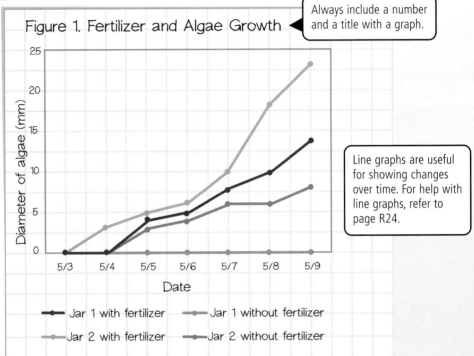

Always include a number and a title with a graph.

Line graphs are useful for showing changes over time. For help with line graphs, refer to page R24.

EXAMPLE 2

Bar graphs are useful for comparing different data sets. This bar graph has four bars for each day. Another way to present the data would be to calculate averages for the tests and the controls, and to show one test bar and one control bar for each day.

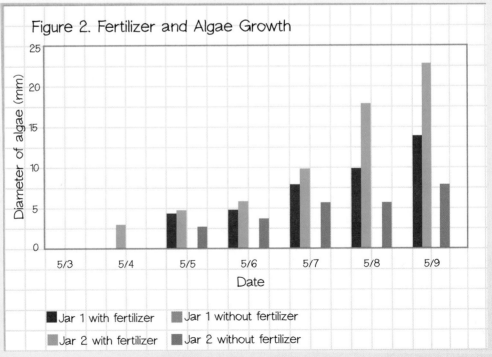

Drawing Conclusions

RESULTS AND INFERENCES

To draw conclusions from your experiment, first write your results. Then compare your results with your hypothesis. Do your results support your hypothesis? Be careful not to make inferences about factors that you did not test.

> For help with making inferences, see page R4.

Results and Inferences

The results of my experiment show that more algae grew in lake water to which fertilizer had been added than in lake water to which no fertilizer had been added. My hypothesis was supported. I infer that it is possible that the growth of algae in the lake was caused by the fertilizer used on the field.

> Notice that you cannot conclude from this experiment that the presence of algae in the lake was due only to the fertilizer.

QUESTIONS FOR FURTHER RESEARCH

Write a list of questions for further research and investigation. Your ideas may lead you to new experiments and discoveries.

Questions for Further Research

- What is the connection between the amount of fertilizer and algae growth?
- How do different brands of fertilizer affect algae growth?
- How would algae growth in the lake be affected if no fertilizer were used on the field?
- How do algae affect the lake and the other life in and around it?
- How does fertilizer affect the lake and the life in and around it?
- If fertilizer is getting into the lake, how is it getting there?

Math Handbook

Describing a Set of Data

Means, medians, modes, and ranges are important math tools for describing data sets such as the following widths of fossilized clamshells.

13 mm   25 mm   14 mm   21 mm   16 mm   23 mm   14 mm

Mean

The **mean** of a data set is the sum of the values divided by the number of values.

> **Example**
>
> To find the mean of the clamshell data, add the values and then divide the sum by the number of values.
>
> $$\frac{13 \text{ mm} + 25 \text{ mm} + 14 \text{ mm} + 21 \text{ mm} + 16 \text{ mm} + 23 \text{ mm} + 14 \text{ mm}}{7} = \frac{126 \text{ mm}}{7} = 18 \text{ mm}$$
>
> **ANSWER** The mean is 18 mm.

Median

The **median** of a data set is the middle value when the values are written in numerical order. If a data set has an even number of values, the median is the mean of the two middle values.

> **Example**
>
> To find the median of the clamshell data, arrange the values in order from least to greatest. The median is the middle value.
>
> 13 mm   14 mm   14 mm   16 mm   21 mm   23 mm   25 mm
>
> **ANSWER** The median is 16 mm.

Mode

The **mode** of a data set is the value that occurs most often.

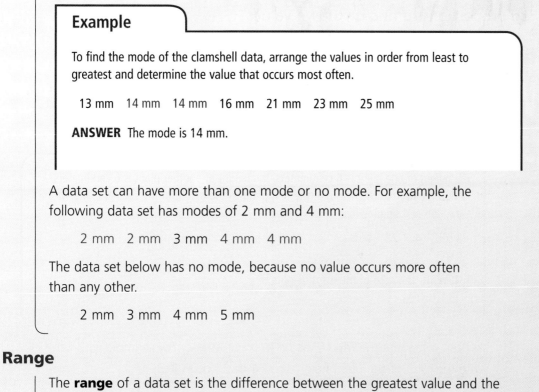

> ### Example
>
> To find the mode of the clamshell data, arrange the values in order from least to greatest and determine the value that occurs most often.
>
> 13 mm   14 mm   14 mm   16 mm   21 mm   23 mm   25 mm
>
> **ANSWER** The mode is 14 mm.

A data set can have more than one mode or no mode. For example, the following data set has modes of 2 mm and 4 mm:

2 mm   2 mm   3 mm   4 mm   4 mm

The data set below has no mode, because no value occurs more often than any other.

2 mm   3 mm   4 mm   5 mm

Range

The **range** of a data set is the difference between the greatest value and the least value.

> ### Example
>
> To find the range of the clamshell data, arrange the values in order from least to greatest.
>
> 13 mm   14 mm   14 mm   16 mm   21 mm   23 mm   25 mm
>
> Subtract the least value from the greatest value.
>
> 13 mm is the least value.
> 25 mm is the greatest value.
>
> 25 mm − 13 mm = 12 mm
>
> **ANSWER** The range is 12 mm.

Using Ratios, Rates, and Proportions

You can use ratios and rates to compare values in data sets. You can use proportions to find unknown values.

Ratios

A **ratio** uses division to compare two values. The ratio of a value a to a nonzero value b can be written as $\frac{a}{b}$.

Example

The height of one plant is 8 centimeters. The height of another plant is 6 centimeters. To find the ratio of the height of the first plant to the height of the second plant, write a fraction and simplify it.

$$\frac{8 \text{ cm}}{6 \text{ cm}} = \frac{4 \times \overset{1}{\cancel{2}}}{3 \times \underset{1}{\cancel{2}}} = \frac{4}{3}$$

ANSWER The ratio of the plant heights is $\frac{4}{3}$.

You can also write the ratio $\frac{a}{b}$ as "a to b" or as $a:b$. For example, you can write the ratio of the plant heights as "4 to 3" or as $4:3$.

Rates

A **rate** is a ratio of two values expressed in different units. A unit rate is a rate with a denominator of 1 unit.

Example

A plant grew 6 centimeters in 2 days. The plant's rate of growth was $\frac{6 \text{ cm}}{2 \text{ days}}$. To describe the plant's growth in centimeters per day, write a unit rate.

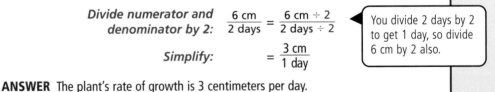

Divide numerator and denominator by 2: $\quad \frac{6 \text{ cm}}{2 \text{ days}} = \frac{6 \text{ cm} \div 2}{2 \text{ days} \div 2}$

Simplify: $\quad = \frac{3 \text{ cm}}{1 \text{ day}}$

You divide 2 days by 2 to get 1 day, so divide 6 cm by 2 also.

ANSWER The plant's rate of growth is 3 centimeters per day.

Proportions

A **proportion** is an equation stating that two ratios are equivalent. To solve for an unknown value in a proportion, you can use cross products.

> ### Example
>
> If a plant grew 6 centimeters in 2 days, how many centimeters would it grow in 3 days (if its rate of growth is constant)?
>
> | | |
> |---:|:---|
> | *Write a proportion:* | $\dfrac{6 \text{ cm}}{2 \text{ days}} = \dfrac{x}{3 \text{ days}}$ |
> | *Set cross products:* | $6 \text{ cm} \cdot 3 = 2x$ |
> | *Multiply 6 and 3:* | $18 \text{ cm} = 2x$ |
> | *Divide each side by 2:* | $\dfrac{18 \text{ cm}}{2} = \dfrac{2x}{2}$ |
> | *Simplify:* | $9 \text{ cm} = x$ |
>
> **ANSWER** The plant would grow 9 centimeters in 3 days.

Using Decimals, Fractions, and Percents

Decimals, fractions, and percentages are all ways of recording and representing data.

Decimals

A **decimal** is a number that is written in the base-ten place value system, in which a decimal point separates the ones and tenths digits. The values of each place is ten times that of the place to its right.

> ### Example
>
> A caterpillar traveled from point *A* to point *C* along the path shown.
>
>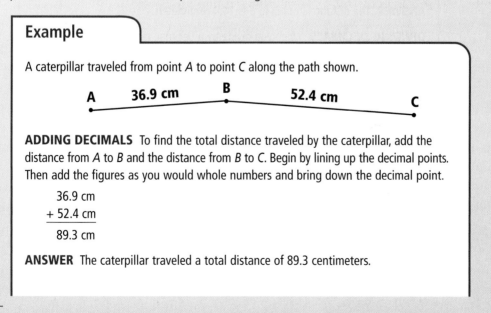
>
> **ADDING DECIMALS** To find the total distance traveled by the caterpillar, add the distance from *A* to *B* and the distance from *B* to *C*. Begin by lining up the decimal points. Then add the figures as you would whole numbers and bring down the decimal point.
>
> ```
>   36.9 cm
> + 52.4 cm
> ---------
>   89.3 cm
> ```
>
> **ANSWER** The caterpillar traveled a total distance of 89.3 centimeters.

Example *continued*

SUBTRACTING DECIMALS To find how much farther the caterpillar traveled on the second leg of the journey, subtract the distance from *A* to *B* from the distance from *B* to *C*.

$$
\begin{array}{r}
52.4 \text{ cm} \\
- \ 36.9 \text{ cm} \\
\hline
15.5 \text{ cm}
\end{array}
$$

ANSWER The caterpillar traveled 15.5 centimeters farther on the second leg of the journey.

Example

A caterpillar is traveling from point *D* to point *F* along the path shown. The caterpillar travels at a speed of 9.6 centimeters per minute.

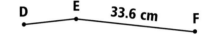
D   E   **33.6 cm**   F

MULTIPLYING DECIMALS You can multiply decimals as you would whole numbers. The number of decimal places in the product is equal to the sum of the number of decimal places in the factors.

For instance, suppose it takes the caterpillar 1.5 minutes to go from *D* to *E*. To find the distance from *D* to *E*, multiply the caterpillar's speed by the time it took.

Align as shown.

$$
\begin{array}{rl}
9.6 & \quad 1 \quad \text{decimal place} \\
\times \ 1.5 & \quad + \ 1 \quad \text{decimal place} \\
\hline
480 & \\
96 \quad & \\
\hline
14.40 & \quad 2 \quad \text{decimal places}
\end{array}
$$

ANSWER The distance from *D* to *E* is 14.4 centimeters.

DIVIDING DECIMALS When you divide by a decimal, move the decimal points the same number of places in the divisor and the dividend to make the divisor a whole number.

For instance, to find the time it will take the caterpillar to travel from *E* to *F*, divide the distance from *E* to *F* by the caterpillar's speed.

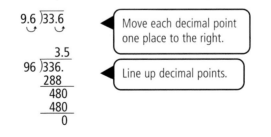

$$9.6 \overline{)33.6}$$ Move each decimal point one place to the right.

$$
\begin{array}{r}
3.5 \\
96 \overline{)336.} \\
\underline{288} \\
480 \\
\underline{480} \\
0
\end{array}
$$ Line up decimal points.

ANSWER The caterpillar will travel from *E* to *F* in 3.5 minutes.

Fractions

A **fraction** is a number in the form $\frac{a}{b}$, where b is not equal to 0. A fraction is in **simplest form** if its numerator and denominator have a greatest common factor (GCF) of 1. To simplify a fraction, divide its numerator and denominator by their GCF.

Example

A caterpillar is 40 millimeters long. The head of the caterpillar is 6 millimeters long. To compare the length of the caterpillar's head with the caterpillar's total length, you can write and simplify a fraction that expresses the ratio of the two lengths.

Write the ratio of the two lengths: $\dfrac{\text{Length of head}}{\text{Total length}} = \dfrac{6 \text{ mm}}{40 \text{ mm}}$

Write numerator and denominator as products of numbers and the GCF: $= \dfrac{3 \times 2}{20 \times 2}$

Divide numerator and denominator by the GCF: $= \dfrac{3 \times \overset{1}{\cancel{2}}}{20 \times \underset{1}{\cancel{2}}}$

Simplify: $= \dfrac{3}{20}$

ANSWER In simplest form, the ratio of the lengths is $\frac{3}{20}$.

Percents

A **percent** is a ratio that compares a number to 100. The word *percent* means "per hundred" or "out of 100." The symbol for *percent* is %.

For instance, suppose 43 out of 100 caterpillars are female. You can represent this ratio as a percent, a decimal, or a fraction.

Percent	Decimal	Fraction
43%	0.43	$\frac{43}{100}$

Example

In the preceding example, the ratio of the length of the caterpillar's head to the caterpillar's total length is $\frac{3}{20}$. To write this ratio as a percent, write an equivalent fraction that has a denominator of 100.

Multiply numerator and denominator by 5: $\dfrac{3}{20} = \dfrac{3 \times 5}{20 \times 5}$

$= \dfrac{15}{100}$

Write as a percent: $= 15\%$

ANSWER The caterpillar's head represents 15 percent of its total length.

Using Formulas

A **formula** is an equation that shows the general relationship between two or more quantities.

In science, a formula often has a word form and a symbolic form. The formula below expresses Ohm's law.

<table>
<tr><td>**Word Form**</td><td>**Symbolic Form**</td></tr>
<tr><td>Current = $\dfrac{\text{voltage}}{\text{resistance}}$</td><td>$I = \dfrac{V}{R}$</td></tr>
</table>

In this formula, I, V, and R are variables. A mathematical **variable** is a symbol or letter that is used to represent one or more numbers.

> The term *variable* is also used in science to refer to a factor that can change during an experiment.

Example

Suppose that you measure a voltage of 1.5 volts and a resistance of 15 ohms. You can use the formula for Ohm's law to find the current in amperes.

Write the formula for Ohm's law: $I = \dfrac{V}{R}$

Substitute 1.5 volts for V and 15 ohms for R: $I = \dfrac{1.5 \text{ volts}}{15 \text{ ohms}}$

Simplify: $I = 0.1$ amp

ANSWER The current is 0.1 ampere.

If you know the values of all variables but one in a formula, you can solve for the value of the unknown variable. For instance, Ohm's law can be used to find a voltage if you know the current and the resistance.

Example

Suppose that you know that a current is 0.2 amperes and the resistance is 18 ohms. Use the formula for Ohm's law to find the voltage in volts.

Write the formula for Ohm's law: $I = \dfrac{V}{R}$

Substitute 0.2 amp for I and 18 ohms for R: $0.2 \text{ amp} = \dfrac{V}{18 \text{ ohms}}$

Multiply both sides by 18 ohms: $0.2 \text{ amp} \cdot 18 \text{ ohms} = V$

Simplify: $3.6 \text{ volts} = V$

ANSWER The voltage is 3.6 volts.

Finding Areas

The area of a figure is the amount of surface the figure covers.

Area is measured in square units, such as square meters (m²) or square centimeters (cm²). Formulas for the areas of three common geometric figures are shown below.

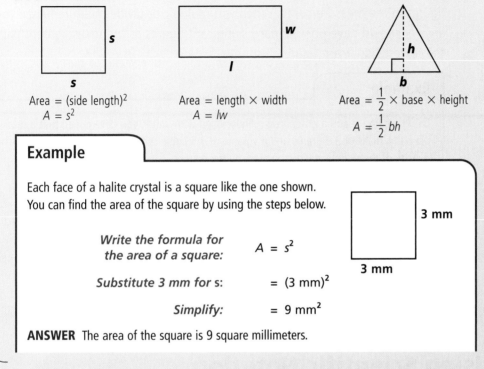

Area = (side length)²
$A = s^2$

Area = length × width
$A = lw$

Area = $\frac{1}{2}$ × base × height
$A = \frac{1}{2} bh$

Example

Each face of a halite crystal is a square like the one shown. You can find the area of the square by using the steps below.

3 mm

3 mm

Write the formula for the area of a square: $A = s^2$

Substitute 3 mm for s: $= (3 \text{ mm})^2$

Simplify: $= 9 \text{ mm}^2$

ANSWER The area of the square is 9 square millimeters.

Finding Volumes

The volume of a solid is the amount of space contained by the solid.

Volume is measured in cubic units, such as cubic meters (m³) or cubic centimeters (cm³). The volume of a rectangular prism is given by the formula shown below.

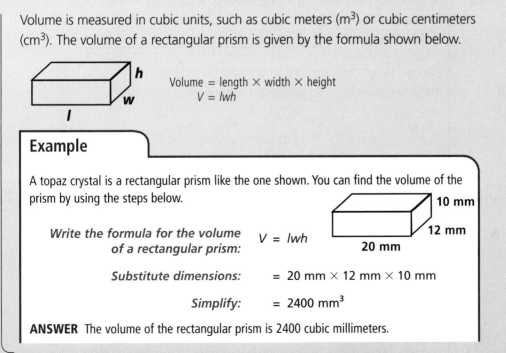

Volume = length × width × height
$V = lwh$

Example

A topaz crystal is a rectangular prism like the one shown. You can find the volume of the prism by using the steps below.

10 mm

12 mm

20 mm

Write the formula for the volume of a rectangular prism: $V = lwh$

Substitute dimensions: $= 20 \text{ mm} \times 12 \text{ mm} \times 10 \text{ mm}$

Simplify: $= 2400 \text{ mm}^3$

ANSWER The volume of the rectangular prism is 2400 cubic millimeters.

Using Significant Figures

The **significant figures** in a decimal are the digits that are warranted by the accuracy of a measuring device.

When you perform a calculation with measurements, the number of significant figures to include in the result depends in part on the number of significant figures in the measurements. When you multiply or divide measurements, your answer should have only as many significant figures as the measurement with the fewest significant figures.

Example

Using a balance and a graduated cylinder filled with water, you determined that a marble has a mass of 8.0 grams and a volume of 3.5 cubic centimeters. To calculate the density of the marble, divide the mass by the volume.

Write the formula for density: $\text{Density} = \dfrac{\text{mass}}{\text{Volume}}$

Substitute measurements: $= \dfrac{8.0 \text{ g}}{3.5 \text{ cm}^3}$

Use a calculator to divide: $\approx 2.285714286 \text{ g/cm}^3$

ANSWER Because the mass and the volume have two significant figures each, give the density to two significant figures. The marble has a density of 2.3 grams per cubic centimeter.

Using Scientific Notation

Scientific notation is a shorthand way to write very large or very small numbers. For example, 73,500,000,000,000,000,000,000 kg is the mass of the Moon. In scientific notation, it is 7.35×10^{22} kg.

Example

You can convert from standard form to scientific notation.

Standard Form	Scientific Notation
720,000	7.2×10^5
5 decimal places left	Exponent is 5.
0.000291	2.91×10^{-4}
4 decimal places right	Exponent is −4.

You can convert from scientific notation to standard form.

Scientific Notation	Standard Form
4.63×10^7	46,300,000
Exponent is 7.	7 decimal places right
1.08×10^{-6}	0.00000108
Exponent is −6.	6 decimal places left

Note-Taking Handbook

Note-Taking Strategies

Taking notes as you read helps you understand the information. The notes you take can also be used as a study guide for later review. This handbook presents several ways to organize your notes.

Content Frame

1. Make a chart in which each column represents a category.
2. Give each column a heading.
3. Write details under the headings.

NAME	GROUP	CHARACTERISTICS	DRAWING
snail	mollusks	mantle, shell	
ant	arthropods	six legs, exoskeleton	
earthworm	segmented worms	segmented body, circulatory and digestive systems	
heartworm	roundworms	digestive system	
sea star	echinoderms	spiny skin, tube feet	
jellyfish	cnidarians	stinging cells	

categories

details

Combination Notes

1. For each new idea or concept, write an informal outline of the information.
2. Make a sketch to illustrate the concept, and label it.

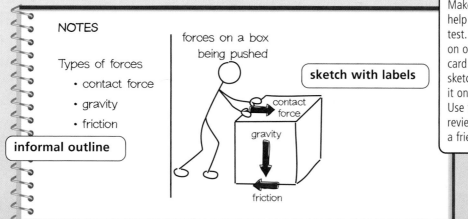

NOTES

Types of forces
- contact force
- gravity
- friction

informal outline

forces on a box being pushed

sketch with labels

contact force

gravity

friction

Make flash cards to help you study for a test. Write a concept on one side of each card and draw the sketch that goes with it on the other side. Use the cards to review concepts with a friend.

Main Idea and Detail Notes

1. In the left-hand column of a two-column chart, list main ideas. The blue headings express main ideas throughout this textbook.

2. In the right-hand column, write details that expand on each main idea.

You can shorten the headings in your chart. Be sure to use the most important words.

When studying for tests, cover up the detail notes column with a sheet of paper. Then use each main idea to form a question—such as "How does latitude affect climate?" Answer the question, and then uncover the detail notes column to check your answer.

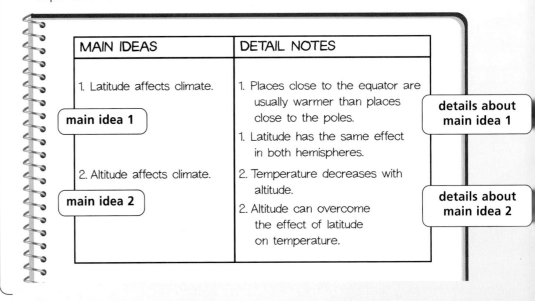

MAIN IDEAS	DETAIL NOTES
1. Latitude affects climate. main idea 1	1. Places close to the equator are usually warmer than places close to the poles. 1. Latitude has the same effect in both hemispheres. *details about main idea 1*
2. Altitude affects climate. main idea 2	2. Temperature decreases with altitude. 2. Altitude can overcome the effect of latitude on temperature. *details about main idea 2*

Main Idea Web

1. Write a main idea in a box.
2. Add boxes around it with related vocabulary terms and important details.

You can find definitions near highlighted terms.

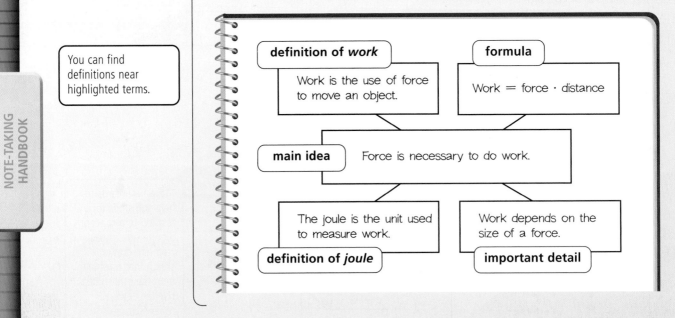

definition of *work*
Work is the use of force to move an object.

formula
Work = force · distance

main idea
Force is necessary to do work.

The joule is the unit used to measure work.
definition of *joule*

Work depends on the size of a force.
important detail

NOTE-TAKING HANDBOOK

Mind Map

1. Write a main idea in the center.
2. Add details that relate to one another and to the main idea.

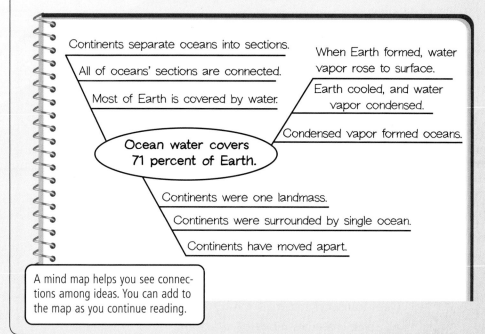

Continents separate oceans into sections.

All of oceans' sections are connected.

Most of Earth is covered by water.

When Earth formed, water vapor rose to surface.

Earth cooled, and water vapor condensed.

Condensed vapor formed oceans.

Ocean water covers 71 percent of Earth.

Continents were one landmass.

Continents were surrounded by single ocean.

Continents have moved apart.

A mind map helps you see connections among ideas. You can add to the map as you continue reading.

Supporting Main Ideas

1. Write a main idea in a box.
2. Add boxes underneath with information—such as reasons, explanations, and examples—that supports the main idea.

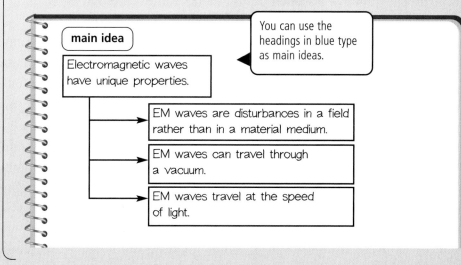

main idea

Electromagnetic waves have unique properties.

You can use the headings in blue type as main ideas.

EM waves are disturbances in a field rather than in a material medium.

EM waves can travel through a vacuum.

EM waves travel at the speed of light.

Outline

1. Copy the chapter title and headings from the book in the form of an outline.

2. Add notes that summarize in your own words what you read.

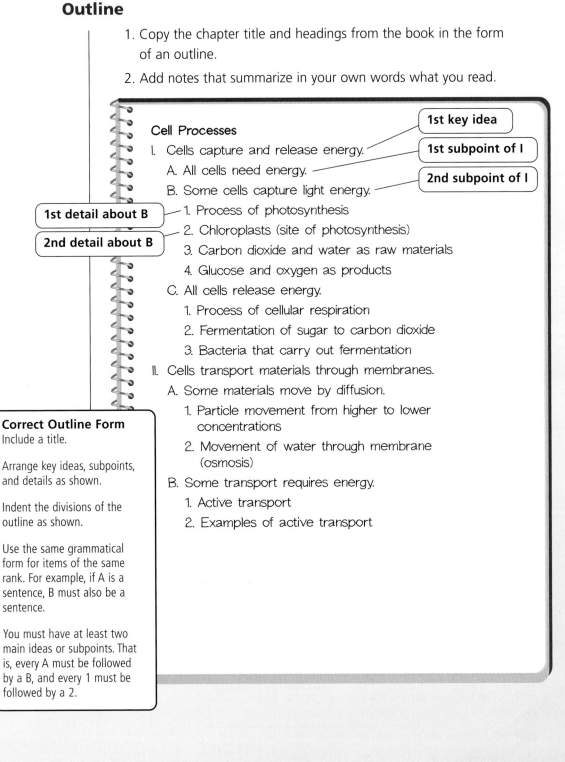

Cell Processes

I. Cells capture and release energy. — **1st key idea**
  A. All cells need energy. — **1st subpoint of I**
  B. Some cells capture light energy. — **2nd subpoint of I**
    1. Process of photosynthesis — **1st detail about B**
    2. Chloroplasts (site of photosynthesis) — **2nd detail about B**
    3. Carbon dioxide and water as raw materials
    4. Glucose and oxygen as products
  C. All cells release energy.
    1. Process of cellular respiration
    2. Fermentation of sugar to carbon dioxide
    3. Bacteria that carry out fermentation
II. Cells transport materials through membranes.
  A. Some materials move by diffusion.
    1. Particle movement from higher to lower concentrations
    2. Movement of water through membrane (osmosis)
  B. Some transport requires energy.
    1. Active transport
    2. Examples of active transport

Correct Outline Form
Include a title.

Arrange key ideas, subpoints, and details as shown.

Indent the divisions of the outline as shown.

Use the same grammatical form for items of the same rank. For example, if A is a sentence, B must also be a sentence.

You must have at least two main ideas or subpoints. That is, every A must be followed by a B, and every 1 must be followed by a 2.

Concept Map

1. Write an important concept in a large oval.

2. Add details related to the concept in smaller ovals.

3. Write linking words on arrows that connect the ovals.

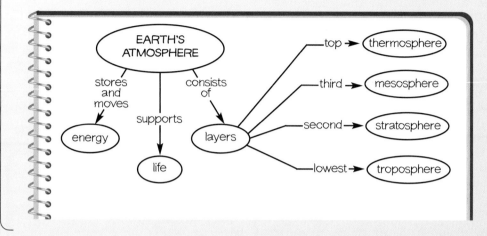

The main ideas or concepts can often be found in the blue headings. An example is "The atmosphere stores and moves energy." Use nouns from these concepts in the ovals, and use the verb or verbs on the lines.

Venn Diagram

1. Draw two overlapping circles, one for each item that you are comparing.

2. In the overlapping section, list the characteristics that are shared by both items.

3. In the outer sections, list the characteristics that are peculiar to each item.

4. Write a summary that describes the information in the Venn diagram.

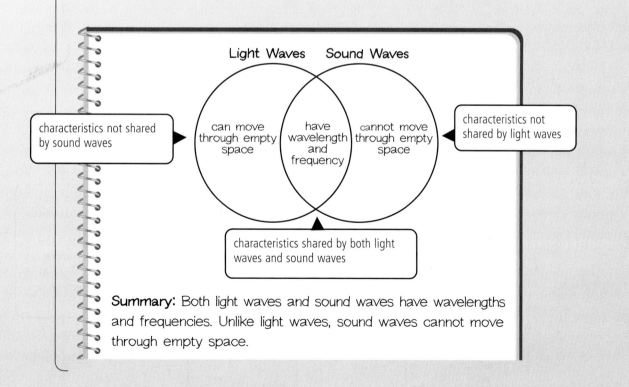

Summary: Both light waves and sound waves have wavelengths and frequencies. Unlike light waves, sound waves cannot move through empty space.

Vocabulary Strategies

Important terms are highlighted in this book. A definition of each term can be found in the sentence or paragraph where the term appears. You can also find definitions in the Glossary. Taking notes about vocabulary terms helps you understand and remember what you read.

Description Wheel

1. Write a term inside a circle.
2. Write words that describe the term on "spokes" attached to the circle.

When studying for a test with a friend, read the phrases on the spokes one at a time until your friend identifies the correct term.

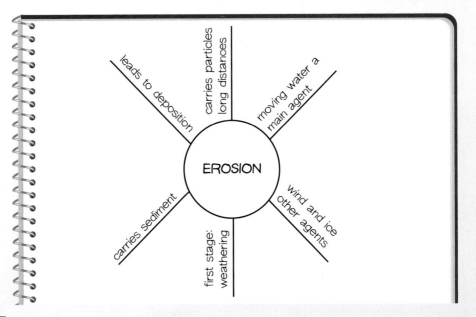

Four Square

1. Write a term in the center.
2. Write details in the four areas around the term.

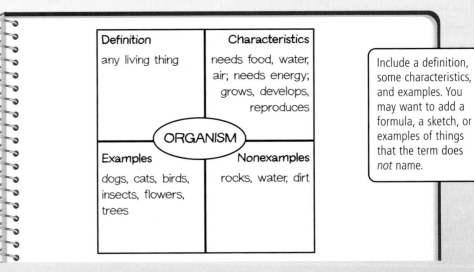

Include a definition, some characteristics, and examples. You may want to add a formula, a sketch, or examples of things that the term does *not* name.

Frame Game

1. Write a term in the center.

2. Frame the term with details.

Include examples, descriptions, sketches, or sentences that use the term in context. Change the frame to fit each new term.

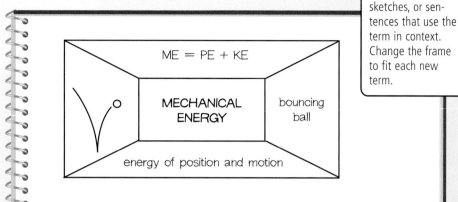

Magnet Word

1. Write a term on the magnet.

2. On the lines, add details related to the term.

You can also use phrases or sentences on the lines.

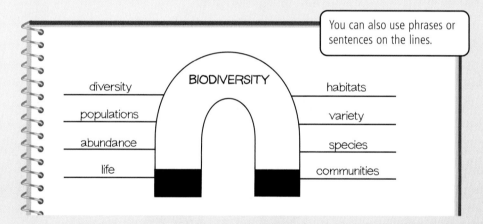

Word Triangle

1. Write a term and its definition in the bottom section.

2. In the middle section, write a sentence in which the term is used correctly.

3. In the top section, draw a small picture to illustrate the term.

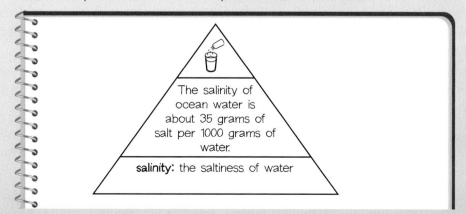

United States Physical Map

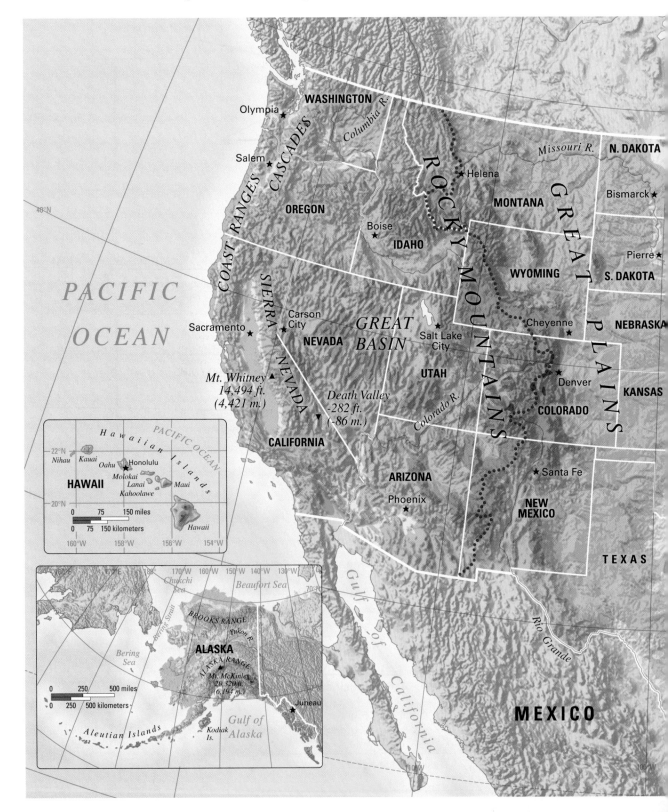

CANADA

MINNESOTA

L. Superior

MICHIGAN

L. Huron

L. Michigan

L. Ontario

L. Erie

St. Lawrence River

VERMONT

MAINE

Montpelier

★ Augusta

Concord

★ NEW HAMPSHIRE

NEW YORK

Boston

Albany ★

★ MASSACHUSETTS

Hudson R.

Providence

RHODE ISLAND

Hartford

CONNECTICUT

Trenton

NEW JERSEY

Dover

DELAWARE

Annapolis

MARYLAND

Washington, D.C.

St. Paul ★ WISCONSIN

Madison ★

Lansing ★

IOWA

Des Moines ★

PENNSYLVANIA

Harrisburg ★

ILLINOIS

INDIANA

OHIO

Columbus ★

incoln

Springfield ★

Indianapolis ★

W. VIRGINIA

Charleston ★

Richmond ★

MISSOURI

Ohio R.

Frankfort ★

VIRGINIA

Topeka ★

Jefferson City ★

KENTUCKY

Raleigh ★

KANSAS

Nashville ★

N. CAROLINA

KLAHOMA

TENNESSEE

S. CAROLINA

Columbia ★

klahoma y

ARKANSAS

Little Rock ★

Atlanta ★

Mississippi R.

ALABAMA

GEORGIA

TEXAS

MISSISSIPPI

Jackson ★

Montgomery ★

LOUISIANA

Tallahassee ★

GULF COASTAL PLAIN

ATLANTIC COASTAL PLAIN

APPALACHIAN MTS.

ATLANTIC

OCEAN

40°N

30°N

ustin

Baton Rouge ★

FLORIDA

Gulf of Mexico

0   125   250 miles
0   125   250 kilometers
Azimuthal Equal–Area Projection

90°W

80°W

Elevation

13,100 ft.	(4,000 m.)
6,600 ft.	(2,000 m.)
1,600 ft.	(500 m.)
650 ft.	(200 m.)
0 ft.	(0 m.)
Below sea level	

⊛ National capital
★ State capital
▲ Mountain peak
••• Continental Divide

APPENDIX

World Physical Map

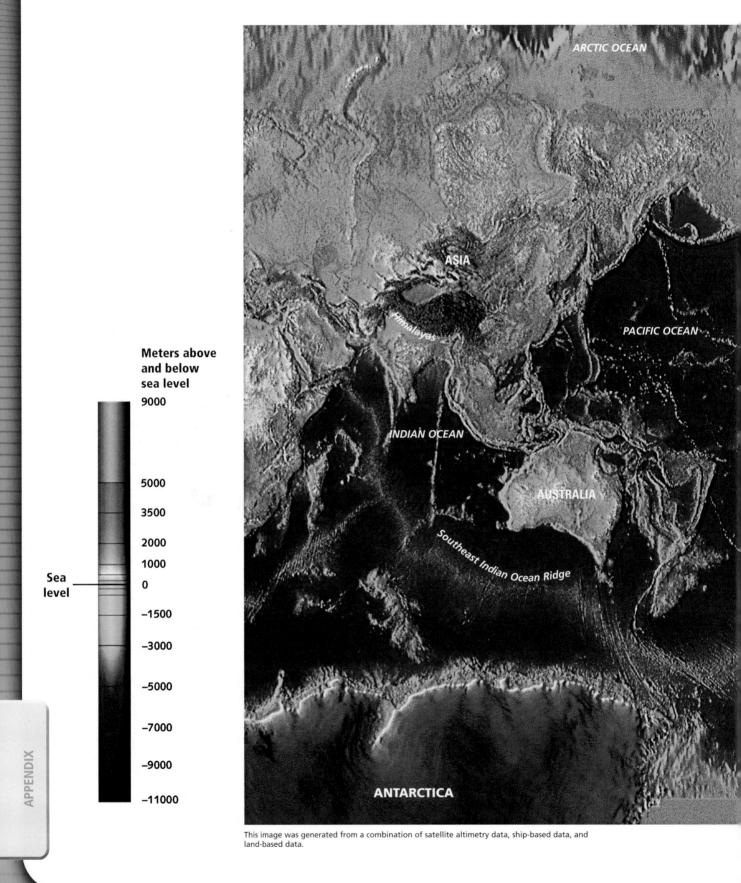

Meters above and below sea level

9000

5000

3500

2000

1000

Sea level — 0

−1500

−3000

−5000

−7000

−9000

−11000

ARCTIC OCEAN

ASIA

Himalayas

PACIFIC OCEAN

INDIAN OCEAN

AUSTRALIA

Southeast Indian Ocean Ridge

ANTARCTICA

This image was generated from a combination of satellite altimetry data, ship-based data, and land-based data.

GREENLAND

NORTH
AMERICA

EUROPE

Rocky Mountains

Appalachian Mts.

Alps

ATLANTIC OCEAN

Atlas Mts.

Mid-Atlantic Ridge

AFRICA

PACIFIC OCEAN

SOUTH
AMERICA

INDIAN OCEAN

East Pacific Rise

Andes

Southwest Indian Ocean Ridge

ANTARCTICA

ANTARCTICA

Tectonic Plates

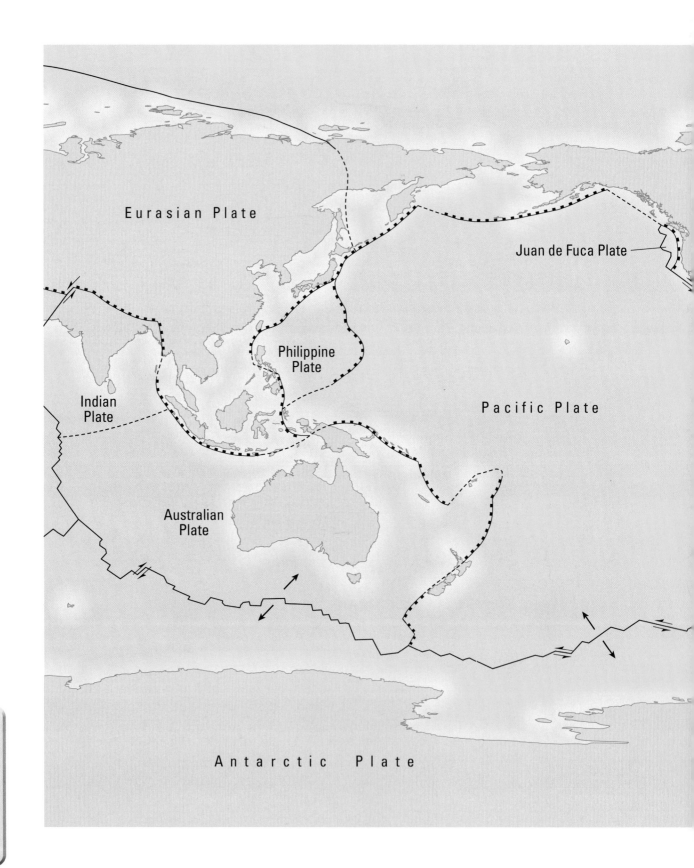

Eurasian Plate

Juan de Fuca Plate

Philippine Plate

Indian Plate

Pacific Plate

Australian Plate

Antarctic Plate

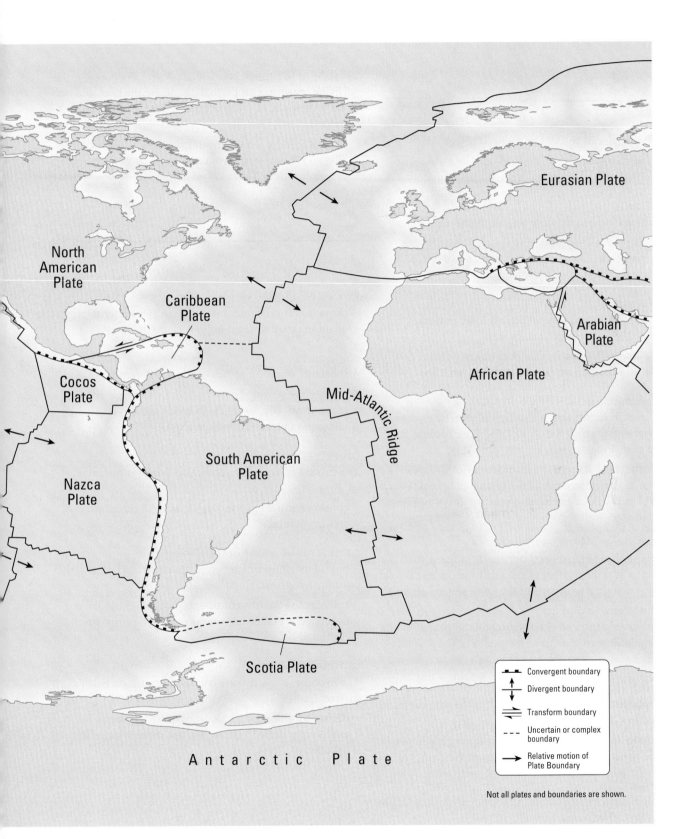

North American Plate

Eurasian Plate

Caribbean Plate

Arabian Plate

African Plate

Cocos Plate

Mid-Atlantic Ridge

Nazca Plate

South American Plate

Scotia Plate

Antarctic Plate

	Convergent boundary
	Divergent boundary
	Transform boundary
- - -	Uncertain or complex boundary
→	Relative motion of Plate Boundary

Not all plates and boundaries are shown.

Glossary

GLOSSARY

A, B

absolute age
The actual age in years of an event or object. (p. 123)

    edad absoluta La edad real en años de un evento u objeto.

acid rain
Rain that has become more acidic than normal due to pollution. (p. 100)

    lluvia ácida Lluvia que se ha vuelto más ácida de lo normal debido a la contaminación.

aftershock
A smaller earthquake that follows a more powerful earthquake in the same area. (p. 62)

    réplica Un terremoto más pequeño que ocurre después de uno más poderoso en la misma área.

asthenosphere (as-THEHN-uh-SFEER)
The layer in Earth's upper mantle and directly under the lithosphere in which rock is soft and weak because it is close to melting. (p. 11)

    astenosfera La capa del manto superior de la Tierra situada directamente bajo la litosfera en la cual la roca es blanda y débil por encontrarse próxima a su punto de fusión.

atmosphere (AT-muh-SFEER)
The outer layer of gases of a large body in space, such as a planet or star; the mixture of gases that surrounds the solid Earth; one of the four parts of the Earth system. (p. xix)

    atmósfera La capa externa de gases de un gran cuerpo que se encuentra en el espacio, como un planeta o una estrella; la mezcla de gases que rodea la Tierra sólida; una de las cuatro partes del sistema terrestre.

atom
The smallest particle of an element that has the chemical properties of that element. (p. xvii)

    átomo La partícula más pequeña de un elemento que tiene las propiedades químicas de ese elemento.

biomass
Organic matter that contains stored energy from sunlight and that can be burned as fuel. (p. 168)

    biomasa Materia orgánica que contiene energía almacenada proveniente de la luz del Sol y que puede ser usada como combustibl-

biosphere (BY-uh-SFEER)
All living organisms on Earth in the air, on the land, and in the waters; one of the four parts of the Earth system. (p. xix)

    biosfera Todos los organismos vivos de la Tierra, en el aire, en la tierra y en las aguas; una de las cuatro partes del sistema de la Tierra.

C

climate
The characteristic weather conditions in an area over a long period of time. (p. xxi)

    clima Las condiciones meteorológicas características de un lugar durante un largo período de tiempo.

compound
A substance made up of two or more different types of atoms bonded together.

    compuesto Una sustancia formada por dos o más diferentes tipos de átomos enlazados.

conservation
The process of saving or protecting a natural resource. (p. 157)

    conservación El proceso de salvar o proteger un recurso natural.

continental-continental collision
A boundary along which two plates carrying continental crust push together. (p. 31)

    colisión continente-continente Un límite a lo largo del cual dos placas de corteza continental empujan contra sí.

continental drift
The hypothesis that Earth's continents move on Earth's surface. (p. 14)

    deriva continental La hipótesis que postula que los continentes de la Tierra se mueven sobre la superficie del planeta.

convection

The transfer of energy from place to place by the motion of heated gas or liquid; in Earth's mantle, convection is thought to transfer energy by the motion of solid rock, which when under great heat and pressure can move like a liquid. (p. 17)

convección La transferencia de energía de un lugar a otro por el movimiento de un líquido o gas calentado; se piensa que en el manto terrestre la convección transfiere energía mediante el movimiento de roca sólida, la cual puede moverse como un líquido cuando está muy caliente y bajo alta presión.

convection current

A circulation pattern in which material is heated and rises in one area, then cools and sinks in another area, flowing in a continuous loop. (p. 17)

corriente de convección Un patrón de circulación en el cual el material se calienta y asciende en un área, luego se enfría y se hunde en otra área, fluyendo en un circuito continuo.

convergent boundary (kun-VUR-juhnt)

A boundary along which two tectonic plates push together, characterized either by subduction or a continental collision. (p. 22)

límite convergente Un límite a lo largo del cual dos placas tectónicas se empujan mutuamente; este límite se caracteriza por una zona de subducción o una colisión entre continentes.

crust

A thin outer layer of rock above a planet's mantle, including all dry land and ocean basins. Earth's continental crust is 40 kilometers thick on average and oceanic crust is 7 kilometers thick on average. (p. 11)

corteza Una delgada capa exterior de roca situada sobre el manto de un planeta que incluye toda la tierra seca y todas las cuencas oceánicas. La corteza continental de la Tierra tiene un grosor promedio de 40 kilómetros y la corteza oceánica tiene un grosor promedio de 7 kilómetros.

cycle

n. A series of events or actions that repeat themselves regularly; a physical and/or chemical process in which one material continually changes locations and/or forms. Examples include the water cycle, the carbon cycle, and the rock cycle.

v. To move through a repeating series of events or actions.

ciclo *s.* Una serie de eventos o acciones que se repiten regularmente; un proceso físico y/o químico en el cual un material cambia continuamente de lugar y/o forma. Ejemplos: el ciclo del agua, el ciclo del carbono y el ciclo de las rocas.

D

data

Information gathered by observation or experimentation that can be used in calculating or reasoning. *Data* is a plural word; the singular is *datum.*

datos Información reunida mediante observación o experimentación y que se puede usar para calcular o para razonar.

density

A property of matter representing the mass per unit volume.

densidad Una propiedad de la materia que representa la masa por unidad de volumen.

divergent boundary (dih-VUR-juhnt)

A boundary along which two tectonic plates move apart, characterized by either a mid-ocean ridge or a continental rift valley. (p. 22)

límite divergente Un límite a lo largo del cual dos placas tectónicas se separan; este límite se caracteriza por una dorsal oceánica o un valle de rift continental.

E

earthquake

A shaking of the ground caused by the sudden movement of large blocks of rocks along a fault. (p. 45)

terremoto Un temblor del suelo ocasionado por el movimiento repentino de grandes bloques de rocas a lo largo de una falla.

element

A substance that cannot be broken down into a simpler substance by ordinary chemical changes. An element consists of atoms of only one type.

elemento Una sustancia que no puede descomponerse en otra sustancia más simple por medio de cambios químicos normales. Un elemento consta de átomos de un solo tipo.

energy

The ability to do work or to cause a change. For example, the energy of a moving bowling ball knocks over pins; energy from food allows animals to move and to grow; and energy from the Sun heats Earth's surface and atmosphere, which causes air to move. (p. xv)

energía La capacidad para trabajar o causar un cambio. Por ejemplo, la energía de una bola de boliche en movimiento tumba los pinos; la energía proveniente de su alimento permite a los animales moverse y crecer; la energía del Sol calienta la superficie y la atmósfera de la Tierra, lo que ocasiona que el aire se mueva.

epicenter (EHP-ih-SEHN-tuhr)

The point on Earth's surface directly above the focus of an earthquake. (p. 52)

epicentro El punto en la superficie de la Tierra situado directamente sobre el foco sísmico.

evaporation

The process by which liquid changes into gas. (p. xv)

evaporación El proceso por el cual un líquido se transforma en gas.

experiment

An organized procedure to study something under controlled conditions. (p. xxiv)

experimento Un procedimiento organizado para estudiar algo bajo condiciones controladas.

F

fault

A fracture in Earth's lithosphere along which blocks of rock move past each other. (p. 45)

falla Una fractura en la litosfera de la Tierra a lo largo de la cual bloques de roca se mueven y pasan uno al lado de otro.

fault-block mountain

A mountain that forms as blocks of rock move up or down along normal faults in areas where the lithosphere is being pulled apart. (p. 82)

montaña de bloques de falla Una montaña que se forma cuando bloques de roca se mueven hacia arriba o hacia abajo a lo largo de fallas normales en las áreas donde la litosfera está siendo separada.

focus

In an earthquake, the point underground where the rocks first begin to move. (p. 52)

foco sísmico En un terremoto, el punto subterráneo donde comienza el movimiento de las rocas.

folded mountain

A mountain that forms as continental crust is compressed and rocks bend into large folds. (p. 80)

montaña plegada Una montaña que se forma cuando la corteza continental es comprimida y las rocas se doblan en grandes pliegues.

force

A push or a pull; something that changes the motion of an object. (p. xvii)

fuerza Un empuje o un jalón; algo que cambia el movimiento de un objeto.

fossil

A trace or the remains of a once-living thing from long ago. (p. 111)

fósil Un rastro o los restos de un organismo que vivió hace mucho tiempo.

fossil fuels

Fuels formed from the remains of prehistoric organisms that are burned for energy. (p. 150)

combustibles fósiles Combustibles formados a partir de los restos de organismos prehistóricos que son consumidos para obtener energía.

friction

A force that resists the motion between two surfaces in contact. (p. xxi)

fricción Una fuerza que resiste el movimiento entre dos superficies en contacto.

G

geologic time scale

The summary of Earth's history, divided into intervals of time defined by major events or changes on Earth. (p. 129)

escala de tiempo geológico El resumen de la historia de la Tierra, dividido en intervalos de tiempo definidos por los principales eventos o cambios en la Tierra.

geosphere (JEE-uh-SFEER)

All the features on Earth's surface—continents, islands, and seafloor—and everything below the surface—the inner and outer core and the mantle; one of the four parts of the Earth system. (p. xix)

geosfera Todas las características de la superficie de la Tierra, es decir, continentes, islas y el fondo marino, y de todo bajo la superficie, es decir, el núcleo externo e interno y el manto; una de las cuatro partes del sistema de la Tierra.

geothermal energy

Heat energy that originates from within Earth and drives the movement of Earth's tectonic plates. Geothermal energy can be used to generate electricity. (p. 166)

energía geotérmica Energía calorífica que se origina en el interior de la Tierra y que impulsa el movimiento de las placas tectónicas de planeta. La energía geotérmica puede usarse para generar electricidad.

geyser

A type of hot spring that shoots water into the air. (p. 100)

géiser Un tipo de fuente termal que dispara agua al aire.

gravity

The force that objects exert on each other because of their mass. (p. xvii)

gravedad La fuerza que los objetos ejercen entre sí debido a su masa.

H

half-life

The length of time it takes for half of the atoms in a sample of a radioactive element to change from an unstable form into another form. (p. 123)

vida media El tiempo que tardan la mitad de los átomos de una muestra de un elemento radioactivo en cambiar de una forma inestable a otra forma.

hot spot

An area where a column of hot material rises from deep within a planet's mantle and heats the lithosphere above it, often causing volcanic activity at the surface. (p. 27)

punto caliente Un área donde una columna de material caliente surge del interior del manto de un planeta y calienta la litosfera situada sobre él, con frecuencia ocasionando actividad volcánica en la superficie.

hydroelectric energy

Electricity that is generated by the conversion of the energy of moving water. (p. 164)

energía hidroeléctrica Electricidad que se genera por la conversión de la energía del agua en movimiento.

hydrogen fuel cell

A device that uses hydrogen and oxygen to produce electricity. The byproducts are heat and water. (p. 168)

celda de combustible de hidrógeno Un aparato que usa hidrógeno y oxígeno para producir electricidad. Los subproductos son calor y agua.

hydrosphere (HY-druh-SFEER)

All water on Earth—in the atmosphere and in the oceans, lakes, glaciers, rivers, streams, and underground reservoirs; one of the four parts of the Earth system. (p. xix)

hidrosfera Toda el agua de la Tierra: en la atmósfera y en los océanos, lagos, glaciares, ríos, arroyos y depósitos subterráneos; una de las cuatro partes del sistema de la Tierra.

hypothesis

A tentative explanation for an observation or phenomenon. A hypothesis is used to make testable predictions. (p. xxiv)

hipótesis Una explicación provisional de una observación o de un fenómeno. Una hipótesis se usa para hacer predicciones que se pueden probar.

I, J, K

ice core

A tubular sample that shows the layers of snow and ice that have built up over the years. (p. 117)

núcleo de hielo Una muestra tubular que presenta las capas de nieve y hielo que se han acumulado con los años.

index fossil

A fossil of an organism that was common, lived in many areas, and existed only during a certain span of time. Index fossils are used to help determine the age of rock layers. (p. 121)

fósil indicador Un fósil de un organismo que era común, vivió en muchas áreas y existió sólo durante cierto período de tiempo. Los fósiles indicadores se usan para ayudar a determinar la edad de las capas de roca.

inner core

A solid sphere of metal, mainly nickel and iron, at Earth's center. (p. 10)

núcleo interno Una esfera sólida de metal, principalmente níquel y hierro, que se encuentra en el centro de la Tierra.

L

lava

Molten rock that reaches a planet's surface through a volcano. (p. 87)

lava Roca fundida que llega a la superficie de un planeta a través de un volcán.

law
In science, a rule or principle describing a physical relationship that always works in the same way under the same conditions. The law of conservation of energy is an example.

    ley En las ciencias, una regla o un principio que describe una relación física que siempre funciona de la misma manera bajo las mismas condiciones. La ley de la conservación de la energía es un ejemplo.

liquefaction
A process in which the shaking of ground causes loose, wet soil to act like a liquid. (p. 62)

    licuación Un proceso en el cual el temblor del suelo ocasiona que la tierra húmeda y suelta actúe como un líquido.

lithosphere (LIHTH-uh-SFEER)
The layer of Earth made up of the crust and the rigid rock of the upper mantle, averaging about 40 kilometers thick and broken into tectonic plates. (p. 11)

    litosfera La capa de la Tierra compuesta por la corteza y la roca rígida del manto superior, con un promedio de 40 kilómetros de grosor y fracturada en placas tectónicas.

M

magnetic reversal
A switch in the direction of Earth's magnetic field so that the magnetic north pole becomes the magnetic south pole and the magnetic south pole becomes the magnetic north pole. (p. 24)

    inversión magnética Un cambio en la dirección del campo magnético de la Tierra, de modo que el polo norte magnético se convierte en el polo sur magnético y el polo sur magnético se convierte en el polo norte magnético.

mantle
The layer of rock between Earth's outer core and crust, in which most rock is hot enough to flow in convection currents; Earth's thickest layer. (p. 11)

    manto La capa de roca situada entre el núcleo externo y la corteza de la Tierra, en la cual la mayor parte de la roca es lo suficientemente caliente para fluir en corrientes de convección; la capa más gruesa de la Tierra.

mass
A measure of how much matter an object is made of.

    masa Una medida de la cantidad de materia de la que está compuesto un objeto.

matter
Anything that has mass and volume. Matter exists ordinarily as a solid, a liquid, or a gas. (p. xvii)

    materia Todo lo que tiene masa y volumen. Generalmente la materia existe como sólido, líquido o gas.

mid-ocean ridge
A long line of sea-floor mountains where new ocean crust is formed by volcanic activity along a divergent boundary. (p. 16)

    dorsal oceánica Una larga línea de montañas en el fondo marino donde se forma nueva corteza oceánica debido a la actividad volcánica a lo largo de un límite divergente.

mineral
A substance that forms in nature, is a solid, has a definite chemical makeup, and has a crystal structure.

    mineral Una sustancia sólida formada en la naturaleza, de composición química definida y estructura cristalina.

molecule
A group of atoms that are held together by covalent bonds so that they move as a single unit.

    molécula Un grupo de átomos que están unidos mediante enlaces covalentes de tal manera que se mueven como una sola unidad.

N

natural resource
Any type of matter or energy from Earth's environment that humans use to meet their needs. (p. 147)

    recurso natural Cualquier tipo de materia o energía del medio ambiente de la Tierra que usan los humanos para satisfacer sus necesidades.

nonrenewable resource
A resource that exists in a fixed amount or is used up more quickly than it can be replaced in nature. (p. 148)

    recurso no renovable Un recurso que existe en una cantidad fija o se consume más rápidamente de lo que puede reemplazarse en la naturaleza.

nuclear fission (FIHSH-uhn)
The process of splitting the nuclei of radioactive atoms, which releases huge amounts of energy mainly in the form of radiation and heat energy. (p. 161)

    fisión nuclear El proceso de rotura de los núcleos de átomos radioactivos, el cual libera inmensas cantidades de energía, principalmente en forma de radiación y energía calorífica.

O

oceanic-continental subduction
A boundary along which a plate carrying oceanic crust sinks beneath a plate with continental crust. (p. 33)

subducción océano-continente Un límite a lo largo del cual una placa de corteza oceánica se hunde bajo una placa de corteza continental.

oceanic-oceanic subduction
A boundary along which a plate carrying oceanic crust sinks beneath another plate with oceanic crust. (p. 32)

subducción océano-océano Un límite a lo largo del cual una placa de corteza oceánica se hunde bajo otra placa de corteza oceánica.

original remains
A fossil that is the actual body or body parts of an organism. (p. 112)

restos originales Un fósil que es en realidad el cuerpo o partes del cuerpo de un organismo.

outer core
A layer of molten metal, mainly nickel and iron, that surrounds Earth's inner core. (p. 10)

núcleo externo Una capa de metal fundido, principalmente níquel y hierro, que rodea al núcleo interno de la Tierra.

P, Q

Pangaea (pan-JEE-uh)
A hypothetical supercontinent that included all of the landmasses on Earth. It began breaking apart about 200 million years ago. (p. 16)

Pangea Un supercontinente hipotético que incluía todas las masas continentales de la Tierra. Empezó a fracturarse aproximadamente hace 200 millones de años.

pyroclastic flow (PY-roh-KLAS-tihk)
A dense cloud of superheated gases and rock fragments that moves quickly downhill from an erupting volcano. (p. 88)

corriente piroclástica Una nube densa de gases sobrecalentados y fragmentos de rocas que desciende rápidamente de un volcán en erupción.

R

radiation (ray-dee-AY-shuhn)
Energy that travels across distances as certain types of waves. (p. xv)

radiación Energía que viaja a través de las distancias en forma de ciertos tipos de ondas.

recycling
The reusing of materials that people would otherwise throw away, such as paper, glass, plastics, and certain metals. (p. 158)

reciclaje El reutilizar los materiales que la gente de otra forma desecharía, como el papel, el vidrio, los plásticos y ciertos metales.

relative age
The age of an event or object in relation to other events or objects. (p. 119)

edad relativa La edad de un evento u objeto en relación a otros eventos u objetos.

renewable resource
A natural resource that can be replaced in nature at about the same rate as it is used. (p. 148)

recurso renovable Un recurso natural que puede reemplazarse en la naturaleza casi al mismo ritmo al que es utilizado.

rift valley
A deep valley formed as tectonic plates move apart, such as along a mid-ocean ridge. (p. 23)

valle de rift Un valle profundo formado cuando las placas tectónicas se separan, como a lo largo de una dorsal oceánica.

rock
A naturally formed solid that is usually made up of one or more types of minerals.

roca Un sólido formado de manera natural y generalmente compuesto de uno o más tipos de minerales.

S

seismic wave (SYZ-mihk)
The vibrations caused by an earthquake. (p. 51)

onda sísmica Las vibraciones ocasionadas por un terremoto.

seismograph (SYZ-muh-GRAF)
An instrument that constantly records ground movements. (p. 56)

sismógrafo Un instrumento que registra constantemente los movimientos del suelo.

solar cell
A device that converts the energy of sunlight into electrical energy. (p. 165)

celda solar Un aparato que convierte la energía de la luz del Sol en energía eléctrica.

stress
The force applied by an object pressing on, pulling on, or pushing against another object. (p. 45)

tensión La fuerza aplicada por un objeto que presiona, jala o empuja contra otro objeto.

subduction
The process by which an oceanic tectonic plate sinks under another plate into Earth's mantle. (p. 30)

subducción El proceso mediante el cual una placa tectónica oceánica se hunde bajo otra placa y entra al manto de la Tierra.

system
A group of objects or phenomena that interact. A system can be as simple as a rope, a pulley, and a mass. It also can be as complex as the interaction of energy and matter in the four parts of the Earth system.

sistema Un grupo de objetos o fenómenos que interactúan. Un sistema puede ser algo tan sencillo como una cuerda, una polea y una masa. También puede ser algo tan complejo como la interacción de la energía y la materia en las cuatro partes del sistema de la Tierra.

T

technology
The use of scientific knowledge to solve problems or engineer new products, tools, or processes.

tecnología El uso de conocimientos científicos para resolver problemas o para diseñar nuevos productos, herramientas o procesos.

tectonic plate (tehk-TAHN-ihk)
One of the large, moving pieces into which Earth's lithosphere is broken and which commonly carries both oceanic and continental crust. (p. 12)

placa tectónica Una de las grandes piezas en movimiento en las que la litosfera de la Tierra se rompe y que comúnmente lleva corteza oceánica y continental.

theory
In science, a set of widely accepted explanations of observations and phenomena. A theory is a well-tested explanation that is consistent with all available evidence.

teoría En las ciencias, un conjunto de explicaciones de observaciones y fenómenos que es ampliamente aceptado. Una teoría es una explicación bien probada que es consecuente con la evidencia disponible.

theory of plate tectonics
A theory stating that Earth's lithosphere is broken into huge plates that move and change in size over time.

Teoría de la tectónica de placas Una teoría que establece que la litosfera de la Tierra está formada por enormes placas que se mueven y cambian de tamaño con el tiempo.

transform boundary
A boundary along which two tectonic plates scrape past each other, and crust is neither formed nor destroyed. (p. 22)

límite transcurrente Un límite a lo largo del cual dos placas tectónicas se rozan y no se forma corteza ni se destruye.

tsunami (tsu-NAH-mee)
A water wave caused by an earthquake, volcanic eruption, or landslide. (p. 62)

tsunami Una ola de agua ocasionada por un terremoto, erupción volcánica o derrumbe.

U

uniformitarianism
(YOO-nuh-fawr-mih-TAIR-ee-uh-nihz-uhm)
A theory stating that processes shaping Earth today, such as erosion and deposition, also shaped Earth in the past, and that these processes cause large changes over geologic time. (p. 128)

uniformismo Una teoría que afirma que los procesos que le dan forma a la Tierra hoy en día, como la erosión y la sedimentación, también le dieron forma a la Tierra en el pasado; además, afirma que estos procesos ocasionan grandes cambios en tiempo geológico.

V, W, X, Y, Z

variable

Any factor that can change in a controlled experiment, observation, or model. (p. R30)

> **variable** Cualquier factor que puede cambiar en un experimento controlado, en una observación o en un modelo.

volcano

An opening in the crust through which molten rock, rock fragments, and hot gases erupt; a mountain built up from erupted materials. (p. 86)

> **volcán** Una abertura en la corteza a través de la cual la roca fundida, fragmentos de roca y gases calientes hacen erupción; una montaña formada a partir de los materiales que surgen de una erupción.

volume

An amount of three-dimensional space, often used to describe the space that an object takes up.

> **volumen** Una cantidad de espacio tridimensional; a menudo se usa este término para describir el espacio que ocupa un objeto.

Index

Page numbers for definitions are printed in **boldface** type.
Page numbers for illustrations, maps, and charts are printed in *italics*.

INDEX

INDEX

INDEX

Q, R

Acknowledgments

Photography

Cover © Roger Ressmeyer/Corbis; **i** © Roger Ressmeyer/Corbis; **iii** *left (top to bottom)* Photograph of James Trefil by Evan Cantwell; Photograph of Rita Ann Calvo by Joseph Calvo; Photograph of Linda Carnine by Amilcar Cifuentes; Photograph of Sam Miller by Samuel Miller; *right (top to bottom)* Photograph of Kenneth Cutler by Kenneth A. Cutler; Photograph of Donald Steely by Marni Stamm; Photograph of Vicky Vachon by Redfern Photographics; **vi** © Robert Patrick/Corbis Sygma; **vii** © Douglas Peebles; **ix** Photographs by Sharon Hoogstraten; **xiv–xv** Doug Scott/age fotostock; **xvi–xvii** © Aflo Foto Agency; **xviii–ix** © Tim Fitzharris/Masterfile; **xx–xxi** AP/Wide World Photos; **xxii** © Vince Streano/Corbis; **xxiii** © Roger Ressmeyer/Corbis; **xxiv** *left* University of Florida Lightning Research Laboratory; *center* © Roger Ressmeyer/Corbis; **xxv** *center* © Mauro Fermariello/Science Researchers; *bottom* © Alfred Pasieka/Photo Researchers; **xxvi–xxvii** © Stocktrek/Corbis; *center* NOAA; **xxvii** *top* © Alan Schein Photography/Corbis; *right* Vaisala Oyj, Finland; **xxxii** © The Chedd-Angier Production Company; **2–3** © Stephen and Donna O'Meara/Photo Researchers; **3** *top* NASA/GSFC/METI/ERSDAC/JAROS, and U.S./Japan ASTER Science Team; **4** *top left* U.S. Geological Survey; *inset* Photograph by T. Miller/U.S. Geological Survey; *bottom* The Chedd-Angier Production Company; **5** NASA/GSFC/METI/ERSDAC/JAROS, and U.S./Japan ASTER Science Team; **6–7** Tony Waltham/Geophotos; **7, 9, 12, 14** Photographs by Sharon Hoogstraten; **15** © 1995–2002 Geoclassics. All rights reserved.; **20** Worldsat International/Photo Researchers; **22, 25** Photographs by Sharon Hoogstraten; **27** *top* © Christophe Ratier/NHPA/Photo Researchers; *bottom* © NASA/Photo Researchers; **29** *left* © Dr. John Brackenbury/Photo Researchers; *right* NASA; **30** Photograph by Sharon Hoogstraten; **31** © John Coletti/Stock Boston/PictureQuest; **33** Photograph by Sharon Hoogstraten; **34** © Lloyd Cluff/Corbis; **35** © Paul Chesley/Getty Images; **37** *left* © Albrecht G. Schaefer/Corbis; *right* © Mitch Diamond/Index Stock/PictureQuest; **42–43** © Robert Patrick/Corbis Sygma; **43, 45, 47** Photographs by Sharon Hoogstraten; **48** © Martin Miller/University of Oregon, Eugene, Oregon; **49** NOAA/National Geophysical Data Center; **50** *left* U.S. Geological Survey; *inset* © Bettmann/Corbis; **51, 53** Photograph by Sharon Hoogstraten; **59** AP/Wide World Photos; **60** Photograph by Sharon Hoogstraten; **61** © Mark Downey; **62** U.S. Geological Survey; **63** Commander Dennis J. Sigrist acting Director of the International Tsunami Information Center/NOAA; **66** © Roger Ressmeyer/Corbis; **68** *top* © Michael S. Yamashita/Corbis; *bottom left, bottom right* Photograph by Sharon Hoogstraten; **69** Photograph by Sharon Hoogstraten; **74–75** © Douglas Peebles; **75, 77** Photographs by Sharon Hoogstraten; **78** U.S. Department of the Interior; **79, 80** © Martin Miller/University of Oregon, Eugene, Oregon; **81** © Tim Hauf Photography/Visuals Unlimited; **82** Photograph by Sharon Hoogstraten; **83** © Martin Miller/University of Oregon, Eugene, Oregon; **84** © Phil Schermeister/Corbis; **85** © William Ervin/Photo Researchers; **86, 88** Photograph by Sharon Hoogstraten; **90** © G.R. Roberts Photo Library; **91** *left* © Tom Bean/Corbis; *right* © Krafft-Explorer/Photo Researchers; **92** © F. Gohier/Photo Researchers; **93** NASA/Carnegie Mellon University; **94** *top* © Krafft-Explorer/Photo Researchers; *bottom left, right* Photographs by Sharon Hoogstraten; **96** *top* © James A. Sugar/Corbis; *bottom* © Mark E. Gibson/Corbis; **97** *top* © Stephen and Donna O'Meara/Volcano Watch International/Photo Researchers; *bottom* © Sid Balatan/Black Star Publishing/PictureQuest; **98** U.S. Department of the Interior, U.S. Geological Survey, Reston, Virginia; **99** Photograph by Sharon Hoogstraten; **100** © The Image Bank/Getty Images; **101** © Simon Fraser/Photo Researchers; **102** © Peter Ryan/Photo Researchers; **103** *top right* © James Leynse/Corbis; *top left* © Raymond Gehman/Corbis; *center* Courtesy of the General Libraries, The University of Texas at Austin; *bottom* © Jeff Foott/Panoramic Images/National Geographic Image Collection; **104** *bottom left* © Sid Balatan/Black Star Publishing/PictureQuest; *bottom center* © The Image Bank/Getty Images; *bottom right* © Simon Fraser/Photo Researchers; **106** © Roger Ressmeyer/Corbis; **108–109** © Louis Psihoyos/psihoyos.com; **109** *top right* © Digital Vision; *center right* Photograph by Sharon Hoogstraten; *bottom right* © Chris Butler/Photo Researchers; **111** Photograph by Sharon Hoogstraten; **112** *top left* Latreille-Cerpolex; *center left* © Alfred Pasteka/Photo Researchers; *bottom left* © Dominique Braud/Animals Animals; **113** *bottom left, bottom right* Courtesy, American Museum of Natural History; **114** © 2001 Tom Bean; **115** *background* © Images Ideas, Inc./PictureQuest; *top left* © Dorling Kindersley; *top right* © John Elk III; *center right* © Kaj R. Svensson/Photo Researchers; *bottom right* © Francesc Muntada/Corbis; **116** © Doug Wilson/Corbis; **117** *top left* © B & C Alexander; *top right* © Maria Stenzel/National Geographic Image Collection; **118** © Chris Butler/Photo Researchers; *inset* © Robert Dowling/Corbis; **119** *left* Courtesy of The Bicycle Museum of America; *center* © Softride, Inc.; *right* © Photodisc/Getty Images; **120** *bottom left* © Tom Bean 1993; *bottom right* © Dr. Morley Read/Photo Researchers; **121** *top right* © Asa C. Thoresen/Photo Researchers; *bottom right* © Sinclair Stammers/Photo Researchers; **122** *bottom* Photograph by Sharon Hoogstraten; **124** *background* © G. Brad Lewis/Getty Images; **126** *left* © Jonathan Blair/Corbis; *inset* AP Wide World Photos; **127** Photograph by Sharon Hoogstraten; **128** © Sime s.a.s./eStock Photography/PictureQuest; **129** *left,right* © John

Marshall Photography; **130** *bottom left* Mural by Peter Sawyer © National Museum of Natural History, Smithsonian Institution, Washington, D.C.; *bottom right* Exhibit Museum of Natural History, The University of Michigan, Ann Arbor, Michigan; **131** *bottom left* © Ludek Pesek/Photo Researchers; *bottom right* © Steve Vidler/SuperStock; **132** © Tom Bean; **133** © Sisse Brimberg/National Geographic Image Collection; **134** *top* © Jonathan Blair/Corbis; *left, right* Photographs by Sharon Hoogstraten; **136** *center left* © Asa C. Thoresen/Photo Researchers; **140** *top* The Granger Collection; *bottom* © Tom Bean/Corbis; **141** *top* © Gianni Dagli Orti/Corbis; *center* The Natural History Museum, London; *bottom* Courtesy British Geological Survey; **142** *top left* © Sally A. Morgan/Ecoscene/Corbis; *top right* © Bettmann/Corbis; *bottom* © James King-Holmes/ Photo Researchers; **143** *top* © Mark A. Klinger/Carnegie Museum of Natural History; *bottom* © The Field Museum; **144–145** © Richard Folwell/Photo Researchers; **145** *top right, center right* Photographs by Sharon Hoogstraten; **147** © Corbis; **149** *top* © SuperStock; *bottom* © Gunter Marx Photography/Corbis; **153** Photograph by Sharon Hoogstraten; **154** *left* Diane Moore/Icon SMI; *top right* © Corbis; *bottom right* © Photodisc/Getty Images; **155** *left* © Photolink/Photodisc/PictureQuest; *inset* © Dr. Tony Braun/Photo Researchers; **156, 157** Photograph by Sharon Hoogstraten; **158** *top* Photograph by Sharon Hoogstraten; *bottom* © David Young-Wolff/PhotoEdit; **159** José Azel/Aurora; **160** *top* © Dick Luria/Index Stock/PictureQuest; *bottom* © Johnston Images/Picturesque/PictureQuest; **161** Photograph by Sharon Hoogstraten; **163** © Steve Allen/Brand X Pictures/PictureQuest; **164** © Beth Davidow/Visuals Unlimited; **165** © Martin Bond/Photo Researchers; **166** © James Stilling/Getty Images; **167** © Lynne Ledbetter/Visuals Unlimited; **168** Andrew Carlin/Tracy Operators; **169** © California Fuel Cell Partnership; **170** *top* © M.L. Sinibald/Corbis; *bottom left, right* Photograph by Sharon Hoogstraten; **171** Photograph by Sharon Hoogstraten; **172** *top left (1)* © SuperStock; *top left (2)* © Gunter Marx Photography/Corbis; *bottom* José Azel/Aurora.

Illustrations and Maps

Accurate Art Inc. **139**
Argosy **165, 167, 169**
Richard Bronson/Wildlife Art Ltd. **10–11, 38, 40, 72, 79, 81, 83, 87, 101, 104**
Peter Bull/Wildlife Art Ltd. **17, 40, 52, 58, 70, 122**
Stephen Durke **24, 65, 67, 70**
Chris Forsey **55**
Gary Hincks **23, 24, 26, 28, 31, 34, 35, 38, 90–91, 104, 132**
Mapquest.com, Inc. **13, 16, 19, 23, 27, 28, 31, 32, 34, 35, 36, 38, 46, 57, 63, 64, 65, 70, 78, 81, 89, 113, 128, 129, 132**
Janos Marffy **115, 124, 136, 151**
Precision Graphics **48, 49, 70, 92, 152**
SlimFilms **67, 70, 150, 162, 164, 166**
Dan Stuckenschneider **R11–R19, R22, R32**
Ron Wood/Wood Ronsaville Harlin **121, 138**